The Conscience of a Young Conservative

For Catherine L. Bollwark and Martha H. Bianchi

Of all tyrannies, a tyranny sincerely exercised for the good of its victims may be the most oppressive. It would be better to live under robber barons than under omnipotent moral busybodies. The robber baron's cruelty may sometimes sleep, his cupidity may at some point be satiated; but those who torment us for our own good will torment us without end for they do so with the approval of their own conscience. They may be more likely to go to Heaven yet are the same time likelier to make a Hell of earth. Their very kindness strings with intolerable insult.

- C.S. Lewis, The Humanitarian Theory of Punishment, 1953

Table of Contents

Chapter 1

Gun Politics

Mr. Chairman—A worthy member has asked, who are the militia, if they be not the people, of this country, and if we are not to be protected from the fate of the Germans, Prussians, &c. by our representation? I ask who are the militia? They consist now of the whole people, except a few public officers. But I cannot say who will be the militia of the future day. If that paper on the table gets no alteration, the militia of the future day may not consist of all classes, high and low, and rich and poor; but may be confined to the lower and middle classes of the people, granting exclusion to the higher classes of the people. If we should ever see that day, the most ignominious punishments and heavy fines may be expected. Under the present government all ranks of people are subject to militia duty.

- George Mason, Addresses to the Virginia Ratifying Convention, 1788.

Of all parts of the US Constitution, the twenty seven words comprising the second amendment are arguably the most frequently debated, if not the most controversial.

The first Supreme Court case regarding the Second Amendment took place in 1876,[1] but this case (the Cruikshank Case) only concerned whether the Second Amendment ensured a personal right to own a gun. Today, the Second Amendment debate has exploded into a wide variety of topics and arguments. While some modern critics of the Second Amendment argue that it does not grant a personal right to bear arms and only applies to a militia, most critics accept the premise that the Amendment offers this personal right, but that this right must be sacrificed to ensure the safety of others.[2]

Other critics of gun ownership argue that guns lead to an increase in crime, homicides and suicides, and put children at risk. Despite these criticisms, the writings of the Founding Fathers, in addition to early commentaries on the Constitution, demonstrate that the Second Amendment ensures a personal right to bear arms. Other research reveals that rather than increasing crime, allowing concealed firearms to be carried by law-abiding citizens can actually reduce crime. In addition, the number of guns per capita has no effect on the number of gun suicides, and the threat guns pose to children is on the decline.

Thanks to the mainstream media in America, the majority of the debate observed in the news favors an anti-gun stance. As an example, in the year 2001, the *New York Times* had printed over 50,000 words defending gun control, but only 163 on the positive effects of gun ownership by law abiding citizens. *USA Today* has done the same, but with a ratio of 5,660 words to none

---

[1] United States v. Cruikshank, 92 U.S. 542 (1876).

[2] Lacunes. "Americas Vigilante Values." *The Economist*. June 20, 1992.

from the other side. To the credit of *The Washington Post*, they have provided a public service in providing us the most balanced treatment seen in the major newspapers: with nearly 47,000 words discussing crimes committed with guns, and 950 words discussing the benefits of defensive usage of guns.[3] Television fares little better, with 4percent of stories favoring a pro-gun stance;[4] double that of *The Washington Post*, but hardly an improvement.

No issue of policy can be determined solely by hearing a position's pitfalls. To combat the bias, this chapter aims to combat the anti-gun case from all angles, whether it be from an historical, legislative, or criminological perspective.

---

[3] Lott Jr., John R. "Media Bias Against Guns." *Inprimus*, 25 May 2004. <http://www.hillsdale.edu/news/imprimis/archive/issue.asp?year=2004&month=09>.

[4] "Networks Use First Amendment Rights to Promote Opponents of Second Amendment Rights." *Media Watch*, July 1997. <http://hematite.com/dragon/mediawatch.html>.

Part 1: The Constitutional Case

Criticisms of an Individual Right to Bear Arms

The contention that the Second Amendment grants no individual right to bear arms is the oldest argument used in the debate over gun control. This argument dates back to 1876 when the Supreme Court weighed in on the issue. This argument is still popular today; Amitai Etzioni at the *Huffington Post* falsely claimed in 2008 that "until this year, whenever this issue reached the highest court of the land, in cases that span nearly 125 years, the court ruled that there is no constitutional barrier to limiting or removing guns owned by individuals."[5] This sort of argument seems purposefully vague. If the Supreme Court determined that criminals couldn't own guns it certainly fits the criteria for his argument, but in the larger scope of gun control, this is a fallacious claim.

Etzioni is at least not as desperate as others in trying to make a point. In attempting to frame historic Supreme Court cases as being against personal gun ownership, organizations like the ACLU have gone as far as misquoting the Supreme Court on the matter. One example of this mischaracterization comes from the 1876 Cruikshank Case ruling. According to the Massachusetts chapter of the ACLU, the case determined that the Second Amendment "is not a right granted by the Constitution."[6] Reading the entire ruling in context yields a much different

---

[5] Etzioni, Amitai. "No Right to Bear Arms." *Huffington Post*, 1 Aug. 2008. <http://www.huffingtonpost.com/amitai-etzioni/no-right-to-bear-arms_b_116437.html>.

[6] "The Myth of the Second Amendment." *Massachusetts American Civil Liberties Union*, 21 Dec. 2002. <http://www.freerepublic.com/focus/news/810561/posts>.

conclusion. To quote in full, the Cruikshank Case actually determined that:

> The right of the people peaceably to assemble for lawful purposes existed long before the adoption of the Constitution of the United States. In fact, it is, and always has been, one of the attributes of citizenship under a free government... It is found wherever civilization exists. It was not, therefore, a right granted to the people by the Constitution. The government of the United States when established found it in existence, with the obligation on the part of the States to afford it protection...
>
> ...The second and tenth counts are equally defective. The right there specified is that of "bearing arms for a lawful purpose." This is not a right granted by the Constitution. Neither is it in any manner dependent upon that instrument for its existence. The second amendment declares that it shall not be infringed; but this, as has been seen, means no more than that it shall not be infringed by Congress. This is one of the amendments that has no other effect than to restrict the powers of the national government, leaving the people to look for their protection against any violation by their fellow-citizens of the rights it recognizes, to what is called..."internal police."[7]

In other words, the right to bear arms is such an obvious right that we don't even need the Constitution to tell us we have that right. According to the ruling, the Constitution serves to protect that right, not to grant it. This is emphasized so heavily in the ruling that only an organization such as the ACLU could come to the opposite conclusion.

[7] United States v. Cruikshank, 92 U.S. 542 (1876)

The arguments presented by the Huffington Post and ACLU have been consistently contradicted by Supreme Court rulings both past and present. These rulings include that of Presser v. Illinois (1886), Miller v. Texas (1894), U.S. v. Miller (1939), Lewis v. U.S. (1980), U.S. v. Verdugo-Urquidez (1990), and Johnson v. Eisentrager (1950).[8] Two recent rulings that affirm gun ownership as an individual right are the cases of the District of Columbia. v. Heller (2008) and McDonald v. Chicago (2010).[9]

Personally, I find that the strongest confirmation of the right to bear arms comes not from court cases, but from the writings of the Founders themselves. After all, couldn't the Supreme Court just rule opposite to their previous rulings? The ACLU would be on much stronger ground if they directed their arguments away from Supreme Court cases and instead tried to deceive by misquoting the Founders.

Only Implied for a Militia?

At the crux of the argument that the Second Amendment grants no individual right to bear arms is a belief that it was implied only to protect the rights of the states to maintain a militia. This is unlikely to be the case because the Constitution already lays out the role of the States to provide arms to a militia in Article 1 Section 8 of the Constitution:

> To provide for the calling forth the Militia to execute the Laws of the Union, suppress Insurrections and repel Invasions. To provide for organizing, arming, and

[8] Presser v. Illinois, 116 U.S. 252 (1886). Miller v. Texas, 153 U.S. 535 (1894). U.S. v. Miller, 307 U.S. 174 (1939). Lewis v. U.S., 445 U.S. 55 (1980). United States v. Verdugo-Urquidez, 494 U.S. 259 (1990). Johnson v. Eisentrager, 339 U.S. 763, 784 (1950). Compiled from "Supreme Court Cases" <http://www.guncite.com/gc2ndsup.html>.

[9] Bernardo, Jack. "Fundamentals of the Us Federal Republic." (Kendall Hunt, 2012), p. 31

> disciplining, the Militia, and for governing such Part of them as may be employed in the Service of the United States, reserving to the States respectively, the Appointment of the Officers, and the Authority of training the Militia according to the discipline prescribed by Congress.[10]

Had the framers of the Second Amendment intended it only to apply to a militia, they would have used the word "state" instead of people; as the Bill of Rights always uses the word "people" when referring to individuals, and "state" when referring to the states.[11] Unless one employs the dubious analytical skills of the Massachusetts ACLU, why would the Second Amendment be an exception to this convention? The wording of "rights" being attributed to people is significant as well. As Justice Antonin Scalia points out in the case of District of Columbia v. Heller, "Nowhere else in the Constitution does a 'right' attributed to 'the people' refer to anything other than an individual right."[12]

James Madison's first draft of the Second Amendment is revealing in its intent. The draft reads: "The right of the people to keep and bear arms shall not be infringed; a well-armed and well-regulated militia being the best security of a free country."[13] In other words, Madison saw the people's right of owning guns as necessary *before* having a well-regulated militia. The term "well regulated" doesn't in anyway refer to a form of government

---

[10] Woods, Thomas E. "The Politically Incorrect Guide to American History." (Washington, D.C.: Regnery, 2004), pp. 22-23.

[11] Ibid., pp. 23-24.

[12] District of Columbia v. Heller 554 U. S. ____ - 07-290 (2008). <http://supreme.justia.com/us/554/07-290/opinion.html>.

[13] "Annals of Congress, House of Representatives, 1st Congress, 1st Session (June 8, 1789)." <http://memory.loc.gov/cgi-bin/ampage?collId=llac&fileName=001/llac001.db&recNum=227>.

regulation. In Federalist #29, Madison describes the meaning of the term as being "disciplined" and "trained."[14]

The Fourteenth Amendment, when analyzed in relationship to the Second, furthers the argument that the Second Amendment specifically applies to an individual right to bear arms. In the Dred Scott decision, which held that free blacks were not citizens and thus could not enjoy the same rights as white Americans, the right "to carry arms wherever they want"[15] was restricted from them. The Fourteenth Amendment restored these rights back to freed blacks. Senator Jacob Howard, who worked with the Joint Committee on Reconstruction in drafting the Fourteenth Amendment, described the purpose of the amendment as "protecting personal rights… including the right to keep and bear arms."[16]

The Founders and the Second Amendment

To uncover the intent of the Founding Fathers for the Second Amendment, the only reliable option is to investigate what they themselves said about the issue. In addition to the Founders writings, I also find early commentaries on the Constitution to be of great value. Although the views presented in early commentaries do not of course guarantee that the Second Amendment applied to "the people" and not "the state," it is likely that they were representative of the dominant view of their time.

Not a single one of the Founding Fathers denied that the Second Amendment gave the individual a right to bear arms, as long as that individual was not a criminal. Early commenters also concurred with the Founding Fathers on this premise.

---

[14] Hamilton, Alexander, James Madison, and John Jay. "The Federalist Papers." (LaVergne: Beacon Hill, 2009), p. 176.

[15] Dred Scott v. Sanford, 60 U.S. 393, 417 (1857).

[16] Cong. Globe, 29th Cong., 1st sess., 2764-65 (1866).

George Mason and James Madison are both considered to be the fathers of the Bill of Rights.[17] As such, the views of Mason and Madison should be regarded as the most significant of the Founders on this issue. Mason viewed guns as a means of preventing government tyranny, which he expressed when he said, "to disarm the people – that was the best and most effectual way to enslave them."[18] Madison's statement that "The right of the people to keep and bear arms shall not be infringed"[19] is nearly parallel to the wording of Second Amendment itself. Madison clearly intended for the Second Amendment to apply to people other than those serving in the militia, as Madison also stated; "Americans have the right and advantage of being armed – unlike the citizens of other countries whose governments are afraid to trust the people with arms."[20]

Supreme Court Justice Stephen Breyer, one of the Justices who voted against overturning the Washington D.C. handgun ban, argued that the only reason Madison wrote the Second Amendment was to appease the states in order that the Bill of Rights would be ratified.[21] Breyer's thesis is contradicted over two hundred years prior by Madison's own writings, specifically in Federalist #46 where Madison describes the role of men and arms in preventing the central government from overwhelming their sovereignty.[22]

---

[17] "The New United States of America Adopted the Bill of Rights: December 15, 1791." *The Library of Congress*. http://www.americaslibrary.gov/cgi-bin/page.cgi/jb/nation/bofright_1.

[18] Mason, George. "The Debates in the Several State Conventions On the Adoption of the Federal Constitution," (Charleston: Nabu Press, 2010), p. 380.

[19] Gales, Joseph, ed. "Annals of the Congress of the United States". (Charleston: Nabu, 2010), p. 434.

[20] Madison, "Federalist Papers," p. 184.

[21] Morrisey, Ed. "Breyer: Madison wrote 2nd Amendment to appease the states." *Hotair*, 13 Dec 2010. Http://www.hotair.com/archives/2010/12/13/breyer-madison-wrote-2nd-amendment-to-appease-the-states/

[22] Ibid. Can be found in: Madison, "Federalist Papers," pp. 180-185.

The rest of the Founding Fathers espoused the views of Mason and Madison. In his first annual message to Congress, George Washington stated that "a free people ought not only to be armed but disciplined."[23] Thomas Jefferson saw guns as the best protection against government tyranny,[24] while Thomas Paine had similar views, also seeing guns as important for protection against any kind of enemy. Paine has said, "guns, like laws, discourage and keep the invader and the plunderer in awe" and predicted that "horrid mischief would ensue were one half the world deprived the use of them"[25]

Perhaps the bluntest language comes from Samuel Adams when he said the Constitution would "never be construed to prevent the people of the United States who are peaceable citizens from keeping their own arms."[26]

Pro-gun positions can also be found in the writings of less well-known Founders including James Wilson,[27] Patrick Henry,[28] Zachariah Johnston[29] and Fisher Ames.[30]

So how is an opponent of individual gun ownership to deal with the words of the Founders? The *Huffington Post* blogger mentioned previously did talk about how some

---

[23] Washington, George. "First Annual Message to Congress." *TeachingAmericanHistory*, <http://www.teachingamericanhistory.org/library/index.asp?document=324>.

[24] Jefferson,Thomas. "Letter to William S. Smith in 1787," cited from Dahl, Robert A. "On Democracy" (Yale Nota Bene. New Haven: Yale University Press, 2000).

[25] Paine, Thomas. "XII.: Thoughts On Defensive War.1 - Thomas Paine, The Writings of Thomas Paine, Vol. I (1774-1779) [1774]." *The Online Library of Liberty*. <http://oll.libertyfund.org/?option=com_staticxt&staticfile=show.php%3Ftitle=343&chapter=17017&layout=html&Itemid=27>.

[26] Adams, Samuel. "Debates and Proceedings in the Convention of the Commonwealth of Massachusetts Held in the Year 1788 and Which Finally Ratified the Constitution of the United States" (Charleston: Nabu Press, 2010), pp. 86-87.

[27] Cited in: Barton, David. The Second Amendment: Preserving the Inalienable Right of Individual Self-protection. (Aledo, TX: WallBuilders, 2000), p. 11.

[28] Ibid., p. 25.

[29] Ibid., p. 26

[30] Ibid., p. 25

thoughtful critical readers emailed him with quotations from the Founders, to which he admits that his "response is that ours is a government by laws which cannot be trumped by quotations from even the most highly regarded patriotic icons."[31] He would be on much better ground arguing that quotations from our Founders do nothing to prove whether or not individual gun ownership is good for society, but this wasn't even what even his article was about. If, as this blogger would have us believe, even the framers of the Second Amendment didn't know what meaning they intended for it, what makes anyone think that a blogger for the *Huffington Post* is in a better position to know?

Early Commenters on the Constitution

In addition to the Founding Fathers, early legal scholars and commentaries on the Constitution provide much insight into how the Amendment is to be interpreted. These individuals include William Blackstone, Zephaniah Swift, William Rawle, Tench Coxe, and Albert Gallatin.

Blackstone's "Commentary on the Laws" was published while America was still a British colony, but would heavily influence American attorneys and judges during the early years of the Republic. Thomas Jefferson referred to lawyers using Blackstone's commentary with the same reverence that Muslims had for the Koran.[32] Although Blackstone's commentary was written before the ratification of the Bill of Rights, the Second Amendment guaranteed what Blackstone referred to as "The natural right of resistance and self-preservation."[33]

Swift wrote America's first legal text in 1792, which presents information in agreement with Blackstone's

---

[31] Etziono, "No Right To Bear Arms."
[32] Cited in Barton, p. 15.
[33] Ibid.

commentary, the only difference being that Swift wrote his text after the Bill of Rights was ratified. Swift writes that "self-defense, or self-preservation, is one of the first laws of nature, which no man ever resigned upon entering society."[34]

Rawle accepted the position of a U.S. Attorney from George Washington, and founded a legal society that later became a law academy. Rawle's book *Views on the Constitution* was one of the first lengthy commentaries on the Constitution. Regarding the Second Amendment, he says:

> No clause in the Constitution could by any rule of construction be conceived to give to Congress a power to disarm the people. Such a flagitious attempt could only be made under some general pretense by a state legislature. But if in any blind pursuit of inordinate power, either should attempt it, this amendment may be appealed to as a restraint on both.[35]

Tench Coxe served as a delegate for Pennsylvania in the Continental Congress, and commonly wrote anonymously under the name "A Pennsylvanian." In 1789, Coxe spoke of the Bill of Rights as asserting that the people are to be armed:

> As civil rulers, not having their duty to the people duly before them, may attempt to tyrannize, and as the military forces which must be occasionally raised to defend our country, might pervert their power to the injury of their fellow-citizens, the people are confirmed by the next article in their right to keep and bear their *private* arms.[36]

---

[34] Ibid., p. 16.

[35] Rawle, William. "CHAPTER X. Of the Restrictions On the Powers of Congress - and On the Executive and Judicial Authorities - Restrictions on the Powers of States and Security to the Rights of Individuals." <http://www.constitution.org/wr/rawle_10.htm>.

[36] Coxe, Tench. "Remarks on the First Part of the Amendments to the Federal Constitution," *Federal Gazette*, June 18, 1789.

Albert Gallatin of the New York Historical Society provided a similar conclusion to that of Coxe during the same year.[37] The modern constitutional scholar Stephen Halbrook observes regarding Coxe's writing that:

> A search of the literature of the time reveals that no writer disputed or contradicted Coxe's analysis that what became the Second Amendment protected the right of the people to keep and bear 'their private arms.' The only dispute was over whether a bill of rights was even necessary to protect such fundamental rights.[38]

In a rebuttal to Halbrook by Saul Cornell, a former director of research at the Second Amendment Research Center, he argued that Coxe's writings could not have been representative of the majority view at that time because only three of the eighty-four newspapers in America of the period published Coxe's paper.[39] Strangely enough, Cornell acknowledges that no one "bothered to refute Coxe." The real reason they may not have "bothered to refute Coxe" is because they either couldn't, or didn't need too since everyone held to his position. Even if we assume that Coxe's view didn't represent the view of the majority at that time (which doesn't seem to be the case), what the Founding Fathers thought of him is by far the most important. The writings of Madison confirm the validity of Coxe's arguments; in a letter to Coxe, Madison said he would be "indebted to the cooperation of your [Coxe's] pen."[40]

---

[37] Gallatin, Albert. "Quotes on the Second Amendment (October 7, 1789)." *New York Historical Society*, <http://www.madisonbrigade.com/a_gallatin.htm>.

[38] Halbrook, Stephen P. "The Right of the People or the Power of the State Bearing Arms, Arming Militias, and the Second Amendment." (Valparaiso Univ. Law Review, 1991), p. 133.

[39] Cornell, Saul. "The Second Amendment Under Fire: The Uses of History and the Politics of Gun Control." *History Matters: The U.S. Survey Course on the Web*. Jan. 2011. <http://historymatters.gmu.edu/d/5200>.

[40] Lund, Nelson Robert and Kopel, David B. "Unraveling Judicial Restraint: Guns, Abortion, and the Faux Conservatism of J. Harvie Wilkinson, III." (December 1, 2008).

The Evolution of Firearms

A humorous Twitter exchange between entrepreneur Carol Roth and CNN host Piers Morgan circulated the internet in late 2012. Morgan first tweeted "The 2nd Amendment was devised with muskets in mind, not high-powered handguns & assault rifles. Fact." Roth first replied "It was devised [for] people [to be] able [to] protect themselves with same type of weaponry used by those from whom they might need protection." Morgan than smugly asked "Where exactly does it say that in the Constitution - must have missed it?" to which Roth replied "right next to the word 'muskets'."

An amusing exchange for sure, but there is a deeper point, and that is that by Morgan's logic the Bill of Rights only applies to the world of 1791. But what are the other implications of this sort of "logic?" The First Amendment would be virtually meaningless. Freedom of speech couldn't be extended to the internet, freedom of the press couldn't be extended to television, freedom of religion couldn't extend to Mormonism, and the Eighth Amendment prohibiting cruel and unusual punishment wouldn't be applicable to any new forms of torture or punishment invented after 1791.

Part 2: The Case from Criminology

The case from criminology arguably makes the strongest case in favor of personal gun ownership. The form of gun

---

Journal of Law and Politics, Forthcoming; George Mason Law & Economics Research Paper No. 08-61.
< http://papers.ssrn.com/sol3/papers.cfm?abstract_id=1309714>.

ownership that much of my defense is based on is concealed carry. Since most crimes occur to the victim outside of their home,[41] concealed carry can be logically defended as an effective way to safeguard against those crimes.

More Guns, Less Crime

More Guns, Less Crime is the title of criminologist John Lott's controversial but groundbreaking book, which sets out to prove just what the title implies. Lott's argument is simply that guns are one of the best means of personal protection. Any time someone tries to write off this claim as merely a fringe idea, I recall a certain quote from Ghandi, that "Among the many misdeeds of the British rule in India, history will look upon the act of depriving a whole nation of arms as the blackest."[42]

The prison population in the US doesn't seem to have any objection to this claim. A 1982 survey in eleven state prisons found that 34 percent of prisoners had at least one experience where they had been scared off, wounded, or captured by an armed victim, while 40 percent decided not to commit a crime because they knew or believed that the victim was armed. In addition, 69 of these inmates knew other criminals who were scared off, wounded, or captured by an armed victim at least once.[43] An interview with prisoners conducted by John Stossel had similar findings.[44] "When you gonna rob somebody you don't know, it makes it harder because you don't know what to expect

---

[41] In 2002, approximately 1/3rd of violent crimes occurred near the residence of the victim. See: "Victims of Crime - When And Where Does Violent Crime Happen." *Library Index*, <http://www.libraryindex.com/pages/447/Victims-Crime-WHEN-WHERE-DOES-VIOLENT-CRIME-HAPPEN.html>.

[42] Ghandi, Mohandas. "Gandhi An Autobiography: The Story of My Experiments With Truth." (Trans. Mahadev Desai. Boston: Beacon, 1993), p. 446.

[43] Rossi, Peter H. and James Wright. "Armed and Considered Dangerous: A Survey of Felons and Their Firearms" (New York: Aldine Transaction, 1986), pp. 1, 32, and 155.

[44] Stossel, John. "Myths About Gun Control." *Rense*, 22 Oct. 2005. <http://www.rense.com/general68/myths.htm>.

out of them" said one of the prisoners. Comedians Penn and Teller even managed to interview a former L.A. gang member (anonymously) who said that "gang members like me like gun control laws because they're a joke.", adding, "gun laws don't affect me, the criminal, they restrict citizens."[45]

Around 8,600 murders were committed in the US in 2011 with guns – but there are reasons why this number is inflated. One reason is that the war on drugs has created a black market for drugs which has bred an enormous amount of violence. The Centers for Disease Control estimates that anywhere between 5 percent and 25 percent of US homicides are drug related.[46] A large portion of those murdered in high crime areas are criminals themselves. In Baltimore, 91 percent of those killed had criminal records. The figures were 75 percent for Philadelphia, 77 percent for Milwaukee, 64 percent for New Orleans, and 83 percent for Chicago.[47] An additional 390 of these deaths were justifiable homicides by police.[48] Justifiable homicides by citizens also inflates this number, though trying to calculate this number (and the difficulties therein) will be later discussed.

In the year 2000, guns were used in 533,470 violent crimes (4.5 percent of total crimes that year).[49] This is still a relatively small number when compared to the number of times guns are used for self-defense. Florida State University criminologist Gary Kleck's studies have put the number of times guns are used in self-defense annually at around 2.5 million[50]

---

[45] Penn & Teller: Bullshit! "Gun Control." Aired June 27th 2005.

[46] Smith, Noah. "The Single Best Anti-Gun-Death Policy? Ending the Drug War." *The Atlantic*, 21 Dec. 2012. <http://www.theatlantic.com/business/archive/2012/12/the-single-best-anti-gun-death-policy-ending-the-drug-war/266505/#>.

[47] Greenfield, Daniel. "America Doesn't Have a Gun Problem, It Has a Gang Problem." *Front Page Mag*, 31 Dec. 2012. <America Doesn't Have a Gun Problem, It Has a Gang Problem>.

[48] "Justifiable Homicide by Weapon, Law Enforcement, 2007–2011." *Federal Bureau of Investigation*. <http://www.fbi.gov/about-us/cjis/ucr/crime-in-the-u.s/2011/crime-in-the-u.s.-2011/tables/expanded-homicide-data-table-14>.

[49] "FBI — Uniform Crime Reports." <http://www.fbi.gov/about-us/cjis/ucr/ucr>.

[50] LaPierre, Wayne. "Guns, Crime and Freedom" (New York: Regnery Publishing Co, 1994), p. 23.

while the Department of Justice estimated this number at 1.5 million.[51] Thirteen other studies put this number anywhere between 800,000 and 2.5 million.[52] Kleck's studies were cited in the court case that later overturned the D.C. handgun ban, and continue to be commonly cited. Kleck himself pledges no allegiance to the political Right, as he's a lifelong Democrat and member of many left-leaning groups, including the ACLU.[53]

One critic of these studies, David McDowall, argues that the number of instances of gun usage in self-defense is actually much smaller. McDowall's studies contend that guns are used in self-defense only around 65,000 times per year.[54] Another study that placed self-defensive gun use low was the National Crime Victimization Survey, which was sponsored by the US Census Bureau for the US Bureau of Justice Statistics,[55] found 116,000 defensive uses each year. No other surveys are consistent with the NCVS however.[56] One significant difference between McDowall's and Kleck's study methodologies account for the discrepancy. If someone scares off a criminal without firing a shot, they are factored into Kleck's 2.5 million, but not into McDowall's sixty-five thousand. Criminals tend to retreat upon simply seeing the weapon without the intended victim having to fire it. Kleck's studies estimate that 75 percent of the time, simply showing the weapon without having to fire any shots is enough to ward off an attacker. Since the "75 percent" figure

---

[51] Cook, Philip J. and Jens Ludwig. "Guns in America: National Survey on Private Ownership and Use of Firearms." *National Institute of Justice*, May 1997. <http://www.ncjrs.gov/pdffiles/165476.pdf>.

[52] Kleck, Gary, and Mark Gerz. "Armed Resistance to Crime: The Prevalence and Nature of Self-Defense With a Gun." *Journal of Criminal Law and Criminology* Vol. 86, Issue 1, Fall 1995. Accessible online at: < http://www.saf.org/lawreviews/kleckandgertz1.htm>.

[53] "Who Is Gary Kleck?" *Gun Cite*. <http://www.guncite.com/gcwhoGK.html>

[54] Wellford, Charles F., John Pepper, and Carol Petrie. "Firearms and Violence: a Critical Review." (Washington, DC: National Academies, 2004), p. 103.

[55] Ibid., p. 104

[56] Ibid., p. 103.

doesn't account for warning shots, the percentage of cases where no non-fatal shots are required to remove an attacker is likely to be somewhat higher.

Either way, the lowest estimate of self-defensive gun use cited in various surveys by Kleck would still nearly quadruple McDowall's 65,000. Even Kleck's personal "2.5 million" figure can be further inflated. Earlier a study was cited showing that 40 percent of prisoners refrained from attacking a potential victim because they believed that the victim may have been armed, and it is impossible for someone to report deterring a crime if the criminal never in fact confronted them.

Another criticism of Kleck's studies is that his criteria for determining self-defensive use are too vague. The point being that this leniency would lead to a greater number of alleged self-defensive uses of guns. One author claimed that Kleck's surveys were so vague that even an event such as a person checking his basement after hearing a strange noise with his gun by his side would be included as an instance of defensive gun use. Had that author actually viewed Kleck's criteria, he would know this not to be the case. Kleck's criterion is simple: it excludes military use, police use, doesn't factor in defensive use against animals, and the defender had to actually see the person who was a threat.[57]

Granted, there is a margin of error due to people who exaggerate in responding to Kleck's survey, but as mentioned earlier, even Kleck's survey cannot account for criminals who decided not to commit a crime due to a belief that a victim had a firearm. Regardless, even I don't personally buy the "2.5 million figure," and would place a personal estimate less than half of

[57] Huemer, Michael. "Gun Control: Opposing Viewpoints." (Michigan: Greenhaven, 2007), p. 46.

Kleck's.[58] What really matters, however, is that the size of this number has to exceed the number of crimes committed per year with guns. Nearly 80 percent of Kleck's respondents could have fabricated their claims and this number would still exceed that of completed gun crimes.

The type of gun use that I mainly defend is concealed carry, where a law abiding citizen is allowed to conceal a firearm on themselves in public. As I mentioned earlier in the chapter, most crimes occur to the victim outside the home, so being able to use their firearm outside of the home is essential here. In "Right to Carry" states, anyone who completes the required training can carry a firearm in public. Today, forty-nine states today are Right to Carry states, but it was recently that so many states gained this status.. To give a brief overview on the differences in crime rates between RTC and non-RTC states in the not so distant past, Howard Nemerov summarizes the 2006 statistics on RTC vs. non-RTC states:

> The seven least violent states are all shall-issue right-to-carry (RTC). Of the seven most violent states, three are non-RTC (includes D.C.) Since about 75% of all states are RTC, 43% of the worst being non-RTC makes these states over-represented at the unpleasant end. The five states with the lowest murder rate are RTC, but two of the five worst are non-RTC. The eleven states with the lowest robbery rate are RTC, but of the eleven worst, 5 are non-RTC. Nine of 10 states with the lowest assault rates are RTC, while 3 of 10 with the highest rates are non-RTC. The only exception is in rates of rape, where three of the

[58] Of a population of 310 million, 2.5 million self-defensive gun uses per year would mean that 1 in every 124 Americans is using a gun in self-defense per year – and this is including all age groups. Additionally, the "1 in 124" figure would only become more implausible when we segregate out non-gun owners from the population sample.

> 10 lowest are non-RTC, while only one non-RTC state is in the 10 worst.[59]

What's true in the United States is also true worldwide. Despite common models for gun control such as that of Japan, which has very low crime and very few guns, countries like Switzerland, Israel, and New Zealand all have very relaxed gun laws and similar crime rates to the UK or Japan.[60] Switzerland goes to far as to issue all men assault rifles for militia service, which they keep in their homes afterwards.[61] Looking at the big picture, nations with high gun ownership average lower crime then their low gun counterparts. The seven nations with the most guns per capita have 1.2 murders per 100,000 people, while the nine nations with the fewest guns have 4.4 murders per 100,000.[62] I use overall murders here because I argue not that more guns equals less gun murders per se, but that more guns leads to a net decrease in all murders.[63]

There are very few instances of concealed carry being linked to higher murder rates. Even in these rare cases, guns are not the culprit. The State of Washington maintained a murder rate that increased and decreased in lockstep with the national average even after concealed carry was legalized in that state in 1961. The only period when Washington's murder rate rose relative to the

---

[59] Nemerov, Howard. "Gun Control: Examining the 2005 Fbi Crime Statistics," *NewsBusters*, 17 Nov. 2006. <http://newsbusters.org/node/9140>.
[60] Miron, Jeffrey A. "Violence, Gun, and Drugs: A Cross-Country Analysis," *Journal of Law and Economics*, Vol. 44, No.2, Part 2 (October 2001), p. 616.
[61] Halbrook, Steven P. "US vs. Switzerland Gun Laws." *The Wall Street Journal Europe*, 4 June 1999. <http://www.theblessingsofliberty.com/articles/article11.html>.
[62] Liptak, Adam. "Gun Laws and Crime: A Complex Relationship." *The New York Times*, 29 June 2008. <http://www.nytimes.com/2008/06/29/weekinreview/29liptak.html?_r=1&pagewanted=2>.
[63] A similar argument is made in: Lott, John R. "More Guns Less Crime." 1st ed. (University of Chicago: Chicago, 1998), p. 97.

national average was during the early 80's.[64] The "Green River Killer" in Washington was responsible for at least forty-eight murders of women from 1982-84. None of these murders were committed with a firearm, so his actions may have been deterred had the victims been carrying a gun. Unfortunately, they were not. The main point is that these murders would have occurred regardless of the gun policy at the time since the crime was not committed with a gun and the victims were not carrying a gun. In this instance the increase in crime can in no way be attributed to concealed carry.

Lott's *More Guns Less Crime* also details the effect that concealed carry has on crime overall. On average, when state concealed handgun laws went into effect murders fell by 7.7 percent, rapes fell 5.3 percent, aggravated assault fell 7.01 percent, robbery fell 2.2 percent, and violent crime as a whole fell 4.9 percent.[65] Some forms of crime did show increases however. Burglary increased by 0.5 percent, property crime by 2.7 percent, larceny by 3.3 percent, and auto theft by 7.7 percent after adjusting for other causes.[66] This still translates to a net reduction in crime. The increases in crime in certain categories are consistent with the logic of concealed carry. Crimes that involve interaction with the victim will be tend to be deterred when the intended victim is carrying a gun, and as a result, criminals will have to resort to other forms of crime. Most burglaries occur when no one is home, as is the same with property crime and larceny. The majority of car thefts also occur when the car owner is away from his vehicle.

Criticizing Lott

---

[64] Cramer, Clayton E., and David B. Kopel. "Shall Issue: The New Wave of Concealed Handgun Permit Laws." *Tennessee Law Review*, Spring 1995. <http://www.davekopel.com/2a/lawrev/shallissue.htm>.

[65] Lott "More Guns Less Crime," pp. 51-53.

[66] Ibid, p. 52.

The critical *More Guns More Crime* study published by Mark Duggan attempts to correlate the decline in crime with a decline in gun ownership. How does he measure this relationship? He acknowledges a 36 percent decline in gun homicides, and an 18 percent reduction in non-gun homicides during the 1993-1998 period, but also notes that 17 percent fewer households reported having at least one gun, according to national surveys. These statistics depend on what kind of surveys are used, as Gallup reported a smaller decline than Duggan does. Although Gallup does not have data for gun ownership in 1998, household gun ownership showed a decline of 12 percent between 1993-99.[67] The trend line follows a constant path downward from 48 percent to 36 percent so this is still in Duggan's favor. However, measuring gun ownership by household suffers from numerous flaws.

In the first place, the number of US households increased from 96.4 million in 1993 to 101 million in 1998.[68] An increased number of households makes it possible for there to be the same number households with guns in 1998 and 1993, with these households occupying a smaller percentage of the total number of households. Looking at the statistics in this way would account for around 5 percent of the decline. This is far from the most important factor, however. Underreporting is a very large factor in the margin of error. Considering how frequently guns are stigmatized in the media, underreporting of gun ownership is a very real possibility. While Gallup reported that 48 percent of households had a gun in the home in 1993, a Research Network poll found that only 31 percent of households had a gun that same

---

[67] Carlson, Darren K. "Americans and Guns: Danger or Defense?" *Gallup*, 4 Jan. 2005. <http://www.gallup.com/poll/14509/americans-guns-danger-defense.aspx>.

[68] "Household and Family Characteristics: March 1993 - U.S. Census Bureau." <www.census.gov/population/socdemo/hh-fam/p20-477/p20-477.pdf>. and "Projections of the Number of Households and Families in the United States: 1995 to 2010." <http://www.census.gov/prod/1/pop/p25-1129.pdf>.

year.[69] The only way to truly discover that percentage of households that underreport gun ownership would be to sample households that we know to have a gun in them. To this end, a few clever researchers surveyed subscribers to *Guns & Ammo* magazine through mail and found that 30 percent of subscribers denied owning a gun.[70]

Measuring gun ownership on a household basis tells us nothing about the number of individuals owning a gun. Hypothetically, let's say that in a society there are two households, each consisting of four individuals: a husband, a wife, and two children. When the husband in one of these homes purchases a gun, the household gun ownership rate climbs to 50 percent. But if the mother, and the two children in that same household all purchase firearms as well, the household gun ownership rate remains flat at 50 percent, even though individual gun ownership has quadrupled.

The greatest flaw in Duggan's study, however, is that he doesn't distinguish between overall gun ownership and concealed carry permits issued, and Lott's research is focused primarily on concealed carry. Even if there was a drop in overall gun ownership (which is unlikely), a decline in crime due to gun ownership would still be possible as long as the decline in ownership was offset by an increase in concealed carry permits. Since many states began allowing concealed carry permits just before or during the period Duggan measured, it is safe to assume an increase in permits during that period. Arizona began issuing concealed carry permits in 1992, Texas and Virginia in 1995, as did various other states during this period. Some states made it easier to obtain a permit, including Ohio in 1995.

---

[69] Gallant, Paul, Alan Chwick, and Joanne D. Eisen. "Declining U.S. Gun-Ownership – Reality or Wishful Thinking." *Ammoland*, 13 June 2011. <http://www.ammoland.com/2011/06/13/declining-us-gun-ownership/>.

[70] Ibid.

Other Arguments

There is no shortage of poor attempts to correlate gun control with lower crime. Many people will point to Britain as attesting to the success of gun control, because they have banned guns and have drastically lower gun crime than the US. It's seldom mentioned that Britain has always had lower gun crime than the US, and that gun crime actually increased after their gun ban. If anything, gun control in Britain and concealed carry in the US has helped close the gap – gun control increasing crime in Britain and concealed carry decreasing crime in the US. Just because there still exists a gap does not mean that the status quo is the cause of the gap. The consequences of the UK's gun ban will be examined more fully later.

The same analysis that I have presented above as applied to Britain could also be used to prove the "more guns less crime" thesis. Strong gun control laws have banned all handguns in Luxembourg, yet their murder rate is a multiple of Belgium, France, and Germany, where these strong restrictions do not apply.[71] Both Russia and Brazil have tougher gun control laws that the US but both have higher murder rates. [72] And while the US ranks #1 in gun ownership, it doesn't rank #1 in gun homicide. Actually, the US is down the list at #28.[73]

In the US, the town of Kennesaw is known as "Gun Town" because of a law passed in 1982 requiring all households to own a firearm. They've also enjoyed a murder rate of zero for over 25 years.[74] There was one firearm-related death fifteen years

---

[71] Sowell, Thomas. "Intellectuals and Society." (New York: Basic, 2009), p. 193
[72] Ibid.
[73] Swann, Ben. "Reality Check: Piers Morgan vs. Alex Jones, and the Truth about Gun Homicide Rates." *FOX 19*, 8 Jan. 2013. <http://www.fox19.com/story/20538164/piers-morgan-vs-alex-jones-and-gun-homicide-rates>.
[74] "25 Years Murder-Free in 'Gun Town USA': Crime Rate Plummeted after Law Requiring Firearms for Residents." *World Net Daily*, 19 Apr. 2007. <http://www.wnd.com/?pageId=41196>.

after the law was passed, but this involved two visitors in a motel room arguing over whether or not a .25 automatic could penetrate the chest of one of the men. [75] This was a dare, not a murder. Kennesaw's crime rate when the gun law was passed was 4,332 per 100,000 (compared to 3,899 for the national average), but stands at 2,027 in 2005.[76] More recently, Kennesaw was ranked as one of the "10 best towns for families" by *Family Circle* magazine.[77]

To get back to the argument that the US is saturated with both firearms and crime, it is important to understand why the US appears, at least on the surface, to be much more violent than other countries. The reason for this is because while the country is peaceful at large, our crime is concentrated in certain large metropolitan areas with populations exceeding 250,000. In a breakdown of crime by population group given by the FBI, it's shown that in 2011 metropolitan areas with populations exceeding 250,000 people had rates of murder and robbery more than double the national average.[78] Rates of violent crime in the metropolitan areas described are 754.5 per 100,000 people compared to 392.2 nationally, and aggravated assault is 414.8 per 100,000 compared to a national average of 243.5.[79] The US has

---

[75] Knox, Jeff. "Kennesaw Revisited." *Ohioans for Concealed Carry*, 10 Oct. 2008. <http://www.ohioccw.org/2008101040 81/kennesaw-revisited.html>.

[76] "25 Years Murder-Free in 'Gun Town USA'"

[77] Weiss, Michael J. "10 Best Towns for Families." *Family Circle*, Aug. 2007. <http://www.familycircle.com/family-fun/money/10-best-towns-for-families/?page=4>.

[78] Becker, Kyle. "Dropping the Hammer: Choose Your Own Crime Stats." *Independent Journal Review*, 4 Jan. 2013. <http://www.ijreview.com/2013/01/27890-choose-your-own-crime-stats/>.

[79] "Rate: Number of Crimes per 100,000 Inhabitants by Population Group, 2011 (Table 16)." *Federal Bureau of Investigation*, <http://www.fbi.gov/about-us/cjis/ucr/crime-in-the-u.s/2011/crime-in-the-u.s.-2011/tables/table_16_rate_number_of_crimes_per_100000_inhabitants_by_population_group_2011.xls>.

186 metropolitan statistical areas with populations exceeding 250,000,[80] while the UK has 32,[81] and Canada has 17.[82]

It is also worth noting that rates of gun ownership in these pockets of violence are lower than in the peaceful rural parts of the country.[83] In an appearance on the Rachel Maddow Show, Michael Moore attempted to make the case for gun control by pointing out that "the vast majority of these guns are owned by people who live in safe parts of town or mostly in suburbs and rural areas, places where there are very few murders." This leads to his question "So why do you have a gun then?" One writer *for Newsbusters* commented that Moore's faulty reasoning is no different than old newspaper headlines proclaiming, "Prison Populations Climbing Despite Falling Crime," as if there was a contradiction between the two.[84]

The Consequences of Gun Bans

Nearly every time a gun ban is implemented in any part of the world, crime rates increase. This section aims to focus on the increase in crime in the United Kingdom and Australia. The increase in the rates of crime after imposing gun control measures in the United Kingdom and Australia is especially significant.

One oft-cited explanation for the failure of gun control measures in certain states or cities is that the reason crime

---

[80] "List of Metropolitan Statistical Areas." *Wikipedia*, <http://en.wikipedia.org/wiki/List_of_Metropolitan_Statistical_Areas>.

[81] "List of metropolitan areas in the United Kingdom." *Wikipedia*, <http://en.wikipedia.org/wiki/List_of_metropolitan_areas_in_the_United_Kingdom>.

[82] "List of census metropolitan areas and agglomerations in Canada." *Wikipedia*, <http://en.wikipedia.org/wiki/List_of_census_metropolitan_areas_and_agglomerations_in_Canada> .

[83] Sowell, Thomas. "The Great Gun Control Fallacy." *The Guardian*, 18 Dec. 2012. <http://www.guardian.co.uk/commentisfree/2012/dec/18/great-gun-control-fallacy-thomas-sowell>.

[84] Coleman, Jack. "Michael Moore Flummoxed by Link Between More Guns, Less Crime." *Newsbusters*, 19 Jan. 2011. <http://newsbusters.org/blogs/jack-coleman/2011/01/19/michael-moore-flummoxed-link-between-more-guns-less-crime>.

increased is because guns were obtained in neighboring states or cities that do not have such gun control. Since both the UK and Australia are islands, it is more difficult for guns to be smuggled into these countries. As such, both England and Australia are ideal models for observing the effects gun control.

Measurements on the results of gun control in the UK will compare the averages of different crime measurements using a pre-ban period of 1990-1996 and a post ban period of 1997-2011. The only crime category where the gun ban in the UK didn't backfire is in the number of homicides committed per year with handguns, which averaged 61 in the pre-ban period, and 62 in the post-ban period.[85] There is a very small decline in homicides committed with a firearm per-capita by this measurement, but it's not like England and Wales ever had a gun violence problem in the first place.

The consequences of the ban can be measured in other categories. The average number of total homicides was 601 in the pre-ban period, and increased by 18 percent to 707 in the post-ban period.[86] The murder rate hasn't fallen below its pre-ban levels once in the 15 years after the ban was passed.[87] The number of firearm offences was also 31 percent higher in the post-ban period compared to the pre-ban period.[88] As murder rates fell in Canada, the United States, France, and Italy near the end of the twentieth century, Britain's continued to rise.[89] As of 2011, the UK's crime rate is the second highest in the European Union, and double that of the US.[90]

---

[85] Lott, John. "So Were Piers Morgan and Christiane Amanpour Dishonest about Crime Rates Last Night?" 20 Dec. 2012. <http://johnrlott.blogspot.com/2012/12/so-did-piers-morgan-and-christiane.html>.
[86] Ibid.
[87] Ibid.
[88] Ibid.
[89] Sowell, "Intellectuals and Society," pp. 193-194.
[90] I have seen a few people cite the following article claiming that the UK's violent crime rate is quadruple that of the US: Slack, James. "The Most Violent Country in

Australia had a low homicide rate before enacting gun control measures in 1996. Relative to the six years prior to enacting gun control, violent crime averaged 32 percent higher, armed robbery 74 percent higher, and aggravated assaults 32 percent higher.[91] During the 1997-1999 period, 90 percent of homicides committed with a firearm were committed with unregistered guns,[92] and this number rose to 93 percent by the 2007-2006 period.[93]

What has failed worldwide has also failed in America. Chicago banned guns in 1982. During the 19 years following the ban, there were only three years when the crime rate was as low as it was preceding the ban.[94] Additionally, the percentage of murders committed with a firearm increased after the ban, from roughly 40 percent at the time the ban was enacted to a peak of 96 percent in 2005.[95] After the removal of Chicago's gun ban in 2010 the crime trend reversed. During the first 6 months of 2011 there was 14 percent reduction in murders, which was a larger drop in murders than any year during the ban. The rates of robberies and assaults with guns dropped even faster than the rate

---

Europe: Britain Is Also Worse than South Africa and U.S." *The Daily Mail*, 3 July 2009. <http://www.dailymail.co.uk/news/article-1196941/The-violent-country-Europe-Britain-worse-South-Africa-U-S.html>.
I claim that the UK's violent crime rate is double the US's rather than quadruple because the UK defines violent crime differently than we do in the US. See: Reality Check with Ben Swann, FOX19, Aired January 17th 2013.

[91] Lott, John R., and Eli Lehrer. "More Gun Control Isn't the Answer." *The National Post*, 15 June 2004. <http://johnrlott.tripod.com/op-eds/NationalPost61504.html>.

[92] "Australian Crime: Facts and Figures 2000." *Australian Institute of Crimonology*. <http://www.aic.gov.au/documents/2/0/B/%7B20BA4DA2-BCE4-4A2F-8F79-D465384E7716%7Dfacts_and_figures_2000.pdf>.

[93] Dearden, Jack, and Warwick Jones. "Homicide in Australia : 2006-07 National Homicide Monitoring Program Annual Report." *Australian Institute of Criminology*, Jan. 2009. <http://www.aic.gov.au/publications/current%20series/mr/1-20/01.aspx>.

[94] Lott, John R. "Chicago Murder Rate Rises Despite Gun Ban." *NewsMax*, 6 May 2010. <http://www.newsmax.com/JohnLott/Lott-guns-Chicago-crime/2010/05/06/id/358060>.

[95] Agresi and Smith, "Gun Facts."

of robberies and assaults without guns.[96] Chicago still has very strict gun control laws and an enormous number of murders each year, but the point to be made here is that loosening up gun control laws even slightly was enough to cause a reduction in murders.

As the old saying goes, "when guns are outlawed, only outlaws will have guns."

Results: Police vs. The People

Not even the strongest gun control advocate should doubt that at the very least police should be able to carry firearms. This makes a comparison between police and an armed citizenry essential in demonstrating the effectiveness of concealed carry. Police have been killed while defending themselves, so how do ordinary citizens fare? Concealed carry holders have an advantage in defending others as well as themselves that the police typically don't have: namely, they are at the scene when the crime occurs. In most cases, police don't arrive until after the crime occurs. One study of newspaper reports in Missouri found that civilians are successful in scaring off, wounding, or capturing criminals 83 percent of the time, while police are only successful in doing so 68 percent of the time. Part of this difference is due to the time it takes an officer to arrive at the scene of the crime.[97] Being there as the crime is occurring is also instrumental in reducing deaths from mass shootings. Additionally, in only 2 percent of these interventions by armed citizens were innocent people injured (by the gun user), compared to 11 percent of cases where police intervened.[98]

---

[96] Lott, John R. "Chicago's Violent Crime Rates Plummet After SCOTUS Removes Handgun Ban." *Big Government*, 4 Oct. 2011. <http://biggovernment.com/jlott/2011/10/04/chicagos-violent-crime-rates-plummet-after-scotus-removes-handgun-ban/>.

[97] Clayton and Copel, "Can Citizens Use Guns Competently?"

[98] Ibid.

When a mass shooting is stopped by police, an average of 14.3 people are killed by the time the shooting is over, but only 2.3 are killed when the mass shooting is stopped by a civilian.[99] The 2.3 figure is worth noting, as a writer for *Mother Jones* was able to "prove" that a concealed carry holder has never stopped a mass shooting by defining a mass shooting as one where four or more people were killed.[100] Every mass public shooting that has occurred from 1950-2011 where more than three people have been killed (with the exception of Jared Loughner's attempted assassination of Rep. Gabby Giffords and one other shooting) has occurred in a gun-free zone.[101] In other words, *Mother Jones* was able to prove that a concealed carry gun holder has never prevented a mass shooting by only looking at mass public shootings where concealed carry permit holders couldn't exercise their rights.

As mentioned earlier, citizens kill innocent bystanders less frequently than the police do. One factor for why this is so is that a citizen confronting a criminal knows who to attack and has awareness of the situation, while a policeman arriving at the scene of a crime still occurring just jumped into a situation without the knowledge that the armed citizen has. Despite citizens killing fewer innocent bystanders, they do not fire less rounds than police do. One would think that this would result in an increased chance of hitting a bystander by accident, but this is

---

[99]Barker, Davi. "Auditing Shooting Rampage Statistics." *Daily Anarchist*, 31 July 2012. <http://dailyanarchist.com/2012/07/31/auditing-shooting-rampage-statistics/>.

[100] Follman, Mark. "More Guns, More Mass Shootings—Coincidence?" *Mother Jo*nes, 15 Dec. 2012. <http://www.motherjones.com/politics/2012/09/mass-shootings-investigation>.
Also see: Coulter, Ann. "Concealed-Carry Laws: The Best Way To Reduce Mass Shootings." *Investors Business Daily*, 20 Dec. 2012. <http://news.investors.com/ibd-editorials-on-the-right/122012-637844-mass-killers-deterred-by-gun-owners.htm?p=full>.

[101] Bennett, William J. "The Case for Gun Rights Is Stronger than You Think." *CNN*, 19 Dec. 2012. <http://www.cnn.com/2012/12/19/opinion/bennett-gun-rights/index.html>. Also See: Lott, John R. "Mayors Against Illegal Guns Gets Supposed List of Shootings Where Guns Were Allowed All Wrong." 2 Feb. 2012. <http://johnrlott.blogspot.com/2013/02/mayors-against-illegal-guns-supposed.html>.

not the case.. In addition to killing fewer innocent people, citizens kill more than twice the number of criminals than police do annually.[102]

Using FBI Supplementary Homicide reports, Gary Kleck places the number of defensible or justifiable homicides around 1,400 to 3,200 for civilians per year,[103] while the Department of Justice shows that this figure hovers around 500 for police.[104] The figure for police is slightly higher than reported, since many state or law enforcement jurisdictions don't report justifiable homicide data to the FBI.[105] There are also those criminals who escape alive, but not unscathed. Around 8,700-16,600 criminals are non-fatally wounded in a manner that qualifies as self-defense by the citizen.[106]

Would Banning Guns Even Be Possible?

With the poor results of gun bans in other countries being realized, it seems even more unlikely that the results in the US would fare any better, where over 300 million guns are in private hands. Additionally, fears about gun control propel citizens to purchase even more guns. Two months prior to the 2012 presidential election, the *Wall Street Journal* ran the headline "Gun Sales Hinge on Obama Re-Election." One firearms dealer quoted in the article says that "If Mr. Obama wins a second term

---

[102] Kleck, Gary. 1991. "Point Blank: Guns and Violence in America." (Hawthorne, N.Y.:Aldine de Gruyter), pp. 111-116, and 148.

[103] Ibid., pp. 111-117. Kleck's figure on justifiable homicide is much higher than the FBI gives, but Kleck attributes this to underreporting, since not all states report justifiable homicide statistics to the FBI.

[104] Fox, James A. "Justifiable Homicides by Police on the Rise." *Boston.com*, 22 Aug. 2012. <http://boston.com/community/blogs/crime_punishment/2012/08/justifiable_homicides_by_polic.html>.

[105] Kleck, "Point Blank," pp. 111-17.

[106] Kleck, Gary. "Crime Control through the Private Use of Armed Force." *Social Problems*, Vol. 35, No. 1. February, 1988).

they are preparing for a surge in sales—the same as they saw after he was elected in 2008."[107] This was indeed a good business call – as there were an additional 1.5 million background checks (compared to the year before) after Obama was first elected in 2008.[108]

Another phenomenon is the seemingly paradoxical rise in gun sales after public shootings. As was the case with Obama's election and re-election, the political reaction to such public shootings also generates fear of gun control measures. Applications for gun permits increased after the public shootings in Aurora, Colorado, Tucson, Arizona, and Newton, Connecticut.[109]

Minor Gun Control/Restrictions

When most people think about gun control they don't think about banning guns outright, but rather making the process of obtaining a firearm more difficult. Some people will accept the premise that banning guns increases crime, but still argue that milder restrictions should be placed on firearms. I'm in this camp myself, depending on what kind of regulation is being proposed. Below is a sample of some common forms of gun control that I hear advocated for today.

Gun Registration

Registration seems to be one of the most basic forms of gun control, and fails for the most basic reasons. Even leaving

---

[107] Banjo, Shelly. "Gun Sales Hinge on Obama Re-Election." *The Wall Street Journal*, September 14th 2012. P. B1.

[108] Allen, Nick. "US Guns Sales Soar after Barack Obama's Re-election." *The Telegraph*, 11 Nov. 2012. <http://www.telegraph.co.uk/news/worldnews/northamerica/usa/9670585/US-guns-sales-soar-after-Barack-Obamas-re-election.html>.

[109] Thompson, Mary. "Why Gun Sales Often Rise After Mass Shootings." *CNBC*, 17 Dec. 2012. <http://www.cnbc.com/id/100321785>.

aside the fact that criminals do not register their guns, law-abiding citizens show resistance to this kind of regulation as well. In Canada, 20,000 gun owners have publically refused to register their guns, while an estimated 300,000 have avoided registration without voicing any public disapproval.[110] Germany showed a similar resistance to gun registration. In 1972, Germany attempted to have all guns registered and only around 3 million out of 20 million total guns were registered.[111] New Zealand tried this as well but then realized it to be pointless and did away with gun registration.[112]

Gun registration costs money to enforce while producing no real results. For example, in Canada, the murder rate remained constant at 1.8 per 100,000 during the 10 years following their gun registration law;[113] yet enforcing the law proved costly, with the actual cost being 1,646 percent of the original predicted cost![114] States and cities such as Hawaii, Chicago, and Washington D.C. have demonstrated similar results. As John Lott observed in the year 2000, gun registration has "not been instrumental in identifying someone who committed a crime."[115] The same observation remains true today.

Gun registration yields a false sense of security, and at worst has the potential to lead to further gun control. Gun registration has led to gun confiscation in Canada, Germany, Australia, California, New York City, Bermuda, Cuba, Greece, Iceland, Jamaica, and Soviet Georgia.[116]

---

[110] Cited in: Smith, Guy. "Gun Facts." (Vol. 5.1, 2009), p. 14.
[111] Cited in Ibid., p. 15.
[112] Cited in Ibid., p. 14.
[113] Cited in Ibid., p. 16.
[114] Cited in Ibid., p. 14.
[115] Cited in Ibid., p. 57.
[116] Cited in Ibid., pp. 15-16.

Reducing Gun Clips

Following the attempted assassination of Congresswoman Gabrielle Giffords in Tucson by Jared Lee Loughner, a law was proposed by Rep. Carolyn McCarthy (D-NY) that would have banned ammunition clips holding more than 10 rounds. The logic behind this argument is that Loughner wasn't tackled until after he ran out of ammunition, which would have happened sooner if he had had a smaller clip.

Should we ignore the fact that during public shootings people are running for their lives, not counting how many shots their assailant has fired in hopes of later tackling them? The shooter will have time to reload; the Loughner case is the exception to the rule. Granted, for this specific case such a law would have had the potential to help, but why stop at 10 rounds? Why not two rounds? Or one? Anti-gun MSNBC host Lawrence O' Donnell supported these restrictive measures on his TV show shortly after the Tucson massacre, stating that "the first 10 shots are the criminal's fault and all other shots are the gun's fault."[117] The argument here makes little sense, especially in the light of the fact that on other occasions O'Donnell has expressed support for legislation that would "ban all guns."[118]

It should be obvious that just as criminals don't obey laws banning guns, they are not going to obey this law either. This gives them even more of an upper hand in an attack. For the sake of argument, let's grant that every clip size in the world was magically reduced. What then prevents a criminal from carrying multiple weapons? Of course, nothing prevents a criminal from doing so. However, almost no one carries multiple weapons for the purpose of self-defense, nor is it likely that they would do so to compensate for their limited ammunition.

---

[117] The Last Word with Lawrence O'Donnell, January 17th 2011.

[118] Aired on MSBNC"s "Morning Joe" on November 5th 2010.

As for the question of why any law abiding citizen would need more than ten rounds of ammunition, the answer is because most police need more than ten rounds of ammunition. From 1990-2000, the average NYPD member involved in a gunfight fired 10.3 shots per incident.[119] Studies differ as to whether or not armed civilians have better shooting accuracy than police, but regardless of the accuracy gap, limiting someone to ten rounds of ammunition ill prepares them to face two or more attackers.

Even if criminals did obey the law, the reasoning for this argument makes as much sense as would a law requiring a reduction in the size of cars' gas tanks to reduce the potential for harm caused by drunk drivers.

Background Checks

In March 2004, the Brady Law (named after Reagan's press secretary who was shot during Reagan's assassination attempt) became effective, requiring background checks before purchases of a firearm from a licensed firearms dealers or manufacturers. Whenever you hear Piers Morgan or some politician claim that 40 percent of guns require no background check, they're actually quoting a figure from before the Brady law went into effect.[120] Bill Clinton has credited the law with being the cause of declining gun crime,[121] but gun crime had already been on a decline since 2001; crime in fact fell at the

---

[119] Aveni, Thomas J. "Officer-Involved Shootings: What We Didn't Know Has Hurt Us." *The Police Policy Studies Council*, Aug. 2003. <http://www.theppsc.org/Staff_Views/Aveni/OIS.pdf>.

[120] Kessler, Glenn. "The Stale Claim That 40 Percent of Gun Sales Lack Background Checks." *The Washington Post*, 21 Jan. 2013. <http://www.washingtonpost.com/blogs/fact-checker/post/the-stale-claim-that-40-percent-of-gun-sales-lack-background-checks/2013/01/20/e42ec050-629a-11e2-b05a-605528f6b712_blog.html>.

[121] Butterfield, Fox. "Serious Crime Decreased for Fifth Year in a Row." *The New York Times*, 5 Jan. 1997. < http://www.nytimes.com/1997/01/05/us/serious-crime-decreased-for-fifth-year-in-a-row.html>.

same rate in the 18 states not affected by the Brady Law as the other 38 states that were affected by the law.[122]

The Brady Law had also been credited with preventing 100,000 criminals from obtaining firearms, though the General Accounting Office only reported 60,000 rejections. Of those 60,000, half were for paperwork being filed incorrectly, while only 3,000 were on grounds of the applicant's record of criminal violence.[123] By 1997, only four people had gone to jail as a result of the law. Despite these 60,000 rejections, there was no measurable effect on the average murder rate. The only decline in deaths that can be credited to the Brady Law was gun suicides in people aged 55 or older, but the average suicide rate for that age group remained constant because non-gun suicides rose.[124]

By June 2008, the Brady Law had prevented some 1.8 million people from obtaining firearms. The law's folly resides in the fact that it attempts to prevent crime without enforcing punishment. Of 3,352 prohibited persons who obtained firearms illegally, only 110 of them were prosecuted.[125] Given such inefficiency, it should come as no surprise that federal prosecutions of gun-related crimes dropped 44 percent during the Clinton administration And the Brady Law's inefficiency continued during the Bush years.[126]

The background check system is easily susceptible to fraud. Using fake driver's licenses, investigators had a 100 percent success rate in purchasing firearms in five states that met

[122] Cited in: Smith, "Gun Facts," p. 57.
[123] Lott, "More Guns, Less Crime," p. 161.
[124] Ludwig, Jens, and Philip J. Cook. "Homicide and Suicide Rates Associated With Implementation of the Brady Handgun Violence Prevention Act." *The Journal of American Medicine* 284.5 (2000): pp. 585-91
[125] Cited in: Smith, "Gun Facts," p. 58.
[126] Cited in Ibid., p. 57.

the minimum requirements of the federal government's background check system.[127]

While background checks aren't a foolproof system, this is one form of gun control that I do support myself to some extent. I think that the conversation regarding background checks should be over how we can strengthen our current system of checks, since they obviously do serve a purpose even though they are currently structured and enforced poorly.

Why Do These Measures Fail?

It should be obvious that the majority of criminals don't obtain their guns legally. A 1997 survey of federal inmates showed that the sources of illegal firearms were numerous: only 15 percent were obtained legally from a retail store, 2 percent were obtained from gun shows, 2 percent from a flea market, 4 percent from a pawnshop, 9 percent through the black market, 15 percent through drug dealers, 9 percent from theft, 3 percent were borrowed and 6 percent were classified as "other."[128] The National Annual Police Survey found that 94.9 percent of officers believe that through illegal means criminals are able to obtain any type of firearm,[129] and it looks like they have good reason to believe this to be the case.

It should then come as no surprise that most gun control measures don't affect criminals. In 2004, the National Academy of Sciences looked at eighty different gun control measures and

---

[127] Section titled "Firearms Purchased from Federal Firearms Licensees Using Bogus Identification." Sourced from: "Counterfeit Identification and Identification Fraud Raise Security Concerns. *Government Accountability Office*, September 9, 2003. <http://www.gao.gov/new.items/d031147t.pdf>.

[128] "Federal Firearm Offenders, 1992-98." *Bureau of Justice Statistics*. http://www.ojp.usdoj.gov/bjs/pub/pdf/ffo98.pdf.

[129] "17th Annual National Survey of Police Chiefs & Sheriffs, National Association of Chiefs of Police 2005." http://www.aphf.org/surveyresults.pdf.

failed to find evidence that any of them worked in preventing gun violence, suicide by gun, or gun accidents. Their analysis draws its information from 253 articles in journals, 99 books, and 43 government publications.[130]

Since most criminals obtain guns illegally, gun bans are not an adequate means of removing guns from the hands of criminals. One pro-gun control website argued that even though it would not rid society of the problem completely, it would reduce the amount of guns funneled into the black market.[131] Not exactly, as in 1986 1/5th of guns seized by the police were produced illegally or homemade.[132] This argument also ignores the fact that sources of firearms exist outside the States. Even if it were true that a gun ban would starve the black market of guns, it also reduces the number of times guns can be used in self-defense by potential victims by 100 percent.

None of this is to say that we should get rid of all forms of gun control, such as background checks, since they are at least working in the sense that they are deterring criminals enough to force them to use illegal guns. The only form of additional gun control that would succeed in reducing gun crime would be one that could prevent guns from entering the hands of criminals through secondary markets while drying up the current supply of illegal firearms. If anyone can craft a plan to do so which won't infringe on the rights of law abiding gun owners, I would be happy to support it.

---

[130] Wellford, Charles F., John Pepper, and Carol Petrie. "Firearms and Violence: A Critical Review." (Washington, DC: National Academies, 2004.)

[131] "Gun Control and the Second Amendment." <http://www.guninformation.org/>.

[132] Blackman, Paul, and Richard Gardiner. "Flaws in the Current and Proposed Uniform Crime Reporting Programs Regarding Homicide and Weapons Use in Violent Crime." Paper presented at 38th Annual Meeting of the American Society of Criminology; Atlanta, October 29-November 1, 1986.

Part 3: Random Objections Considered

Japan and Gun Control

Japan is commonly cited as a perfect model for gun control. Japan's gun policy is simple: "No-one shall possess a fire-arm or fire-arms or a sword or swords." Japan has the strictest gun laws while simultaneously having a homicide rate of 0.4 per 100,000 in contrast to the American homicide rate of five per 100,000 (both rates are for the year 2009).[133] The gap can be shortened slightly by showing differences in how murder rates in both countries are counted. In America, a criminal killed by a victim would still be counted as a homicide, as would an attempt to injure which accidently resulted in a death. Japan doesn't factor either of those two scenario's into their homicide rate. If Japan used the same system to count homicide in America, their murder rate would increase, but still leave a considerable gap between Japan and America. In addition to low murder rates, Japan also has fewer car thefts, robberies, rapes, and total crimes than America.

The murder and crime gaps between the US and Japan are nothing new. Japan's murder rates were either one half or one third of ours during the 1920s, and one fifth of ours in 1979.[134]

---

[133] "Intentional homicide, count and rate per 100,000 population (1995-2011)." *United Nations Office on Drugs and Crime.* <www.unodc.org/.../data.../statistics/crime/Homicide_statistics2012.xls>.

[134] Greenfield, Daniel. "Japan's Low Murder Rate Is Due to Its Immigration Policies, Not Its Gun Control." *Front Page Mag*, 16 Dec. 2012. <http://frontpagemag.com/2012/dgreenfield/japans-low-murder-rate-is-due-to-its-immigration-policies-not-its-gun-control/>.

Japan's low murder rate can't be explained by strict gun control measures; after all, Japan had a low murder rate before enacting these measures. Japan also has a lower non-gun crime rate than the states, which attests to a cause for Japan's low crime rate other than gun control. One factor would be Japan's conviction system, as Dave Kopel argues;

> Broad powers, professionalism, and community support combine to help Tokyo police solve 96.5% of murders, and 82.5% of robberies. In America, the police clear 74% of murders, but only a quarter of all robberies. 70% of all Japanese crimes end in a conviction; only 19.8% of American crimes even end in an arrest. A mere 9% of reported American violent crimes end in incarceration. Compared to the Japanese criminal, the American criminal faces only a minuscule risk of jail. Is it any wonder that American criminals commit so many more crimes?[135]

Japanese interrogation procedures are incredibly effective in forcing confessions among criminals and suspected criminals. One man falsely accused of child murder claimed to have been beaten into confession after being released from prison after serving 17 years. Toshihiro Futokoro, a man falsely accused of buying votes for his wife's cousin in an election attempted suicide twice after just three days of interrogation.[136] If there's over a 99 percent chance that you'll be thrown in jail just for being suspected for a crime, what are the odds that you would commit one? You don't even have to be near the scene of a crime to be a suspect, police in Japan regularly search people they find suspicious. In addition to all this, Japanese homeowners get a visit from a local police officer twice a year to update their file on

---

[135] Kopel, David B. "Japan: Gun Control and People Control." *Second Amendment Project*. Dec. 1988. <http://www.davekopel.com/2A/Foreign/Japan-Gun-Control-and-People-Control.htm>.

[136] Hogg, Chris. "Forced Confessions' in Japan." *BBC,* 29 Oct. 2007. <http://news.bbc.co.uk/2/hi/asia-pacific/7063316.stm>.

who lives there, their relation to one another, their jobs, their wealth, etc.[137]

The crime rate among Japanese Americans (who have access to firearms) is even lower than the Japanese living in Japan, which seem to indicate that Japanese culture plays a role in their lack of violence. As Gary Kleck noted, "21 of 48,695 arrests for murder and non-negligent manslaughter (in 1976-1978) were of Japanese-Americans, or 0.04 percent."[138] After adjusting for the Japanese-American population for those years, their homicide rate comes out to 1.04 per year.[139] Japan's homicide rate averaged 1.75 those same years.[140]

Mexico and the 90% Myth

One of the bigger statistical distortions in the gun control debate is the myth that 90 percent of the guns seized from Mexico and used in crimes originated from the United States. This myth has its origin in a 2009 study done by the Government Accountability Office (GOA). Of 30,000 guns seized from Mexico, 7,200 of them were sent to the U.S. Bureau of Alcohol, Tobacco, Firearms and Explosives (ATF) for tracing. Only around 4,000 of these 7,200 were even traceable (many of the guns didn't have serial numbers). Of the 4000 traceable guns, 3,480 were traced to the United States, which is nearly 90 percent. All this proves is that traceable guns tend to originate from the United States, but when put in larger context, those 3,480 guns equal less than 12 percent of all guns seized from Mexico in 2008.

---

[137] Poe, Richard. "The Seven Myths of Gun Control. (Roseville: Forum Prima, 2001), p. 59.
[138] Kleck, "Point Blank," p. 189.
[139] Ibid.
[140] See: "List of countries by intentional homicide rate by decade." *Wikipedia,* <http://en.wikipedia.org/wiki/List_of_countries_by_intentional_homicide_rate_by_decade>.

Of the untraceable guns, there is a number of possible origins for these guns other than the United States. There's also that obvious fact that certain kinds of guns are legal to purchase and own in Mexico. These include handguns smaller than a .357 magnum such as the .380 and .38 Special. .380 pistols are commonly used by cartel hit men for assassinations.[141] Other countries that supply Mexico with weapons include China, South Korea, Spain, Israel, and Russia.[142]

Three years after the bogus "90 percent" number was released, a *Huffington Post* article found it more believable to put the "real" number at around 70 percent.[143] No one will be less surprised than I when the number is revised to 60 percent or 50 percent within the next few years.

Guns and Public Shootings

It has been demonstrated that criminals fear nothing more than an armed victim. One concerned young man closely followed Colorado's gun legislation, openly voicing opposition to legislation that would allow concealed carry to be easier. The young man was Dylan Klebold – one of the two Columbine killers.[144] Coincidentally, the Columbine shooting took place on

---

[141] Burton, Fred, and Scott Stewart. "Mexico: Examining Cartel War Violence Through a Protective Intelligence Lens." *Stratfor*, 14 May 2008. <http://www.stratfor.com/weekly/mexico_applying_protective_intelligence_lens_cartel_war_violence>.

[142] Lott, Maxim, and William L. Jeunesse. "The Myth of 90 Percent: Only a Small Fraction of Guns in Mexico Come From U.S." *FOX News*, 2 Apr. 2009. <http://www.foxnews.com/politics/2009/04/02/myth-percent-small-fraction-guns-mexico-come/>.

[143] Stevenson, Mark. "Mexico Drug War: 70 Percent Of Guns Seized Originate In U.S." *Huffington Post*, 13 June 2011. <http://www.huffingtonpost.com/2011/06/14/mexico-drug-war-seized-guns_n_876653.html>.

[144] Belluck, Pam, and Jodi Wilgoren. "SHATTERED LIVES -- A Special Report; Caring Parents, No Answers, In Columbine Killers' Pasts." *The New York Times*, 29 June 1999. <http://www.nytimes.com/1999/06/29/us/shattered-lives-special-report-caring-parents-no-answers-columbine-killers-pasts.html?pagewanted=all&src=pm>.

the day that the bill was scheduled to pass.[145] Whether or not that was a mere coincidence, the same sort of thinking was apparent at the "Batman" shooting in Aurora, Colorado, where out of the seven theaters within twenty minutes of the killers apartment, the killer chose the one theater that banned moviegoers from carrying concealed firearms.[146] This is all consistent with a statistic I provided earlier, that nearly every mass public shooting has occurred in a place where guns were not allowed.

It's hard for the public to gauge the frequency that public shootings are prevented for many reasons. A public shooting where twenty people were killed will get covered in the media for days, and "spark a conversation over gun control," while attempted public shootings where the assailant is taken down quickly by an armed citizen will receive almost zero coverage. The latter reason isn't even because of the media's well-known general anti-gun bias, but because a mass shooting will generate better ratings over a longer period than brief stories about armed criminals being taken down.

The blog 'Classically Liberal' reported on one such occurrence in 2002 where a student attempted a shooting at his school. Two students heard shots, ran to their cars where they had handguns locked inside, then approached the shooter. The shooter dropped his weapon, and a third (unarmed) student joined the other two in restraining him until police arrived. An analysis of the reporting on the story determined that of the 88 stories reporting the incident, only two of them mentioned that the two students who confronted the shooter were armed.[147]

---

[145] Lott, John. "Did Colorado Shooter Single out Cinemark Theater Because It Banned Guns?" *FOX News*, 10 Sept. 2012. <http://www.foxnews.com/opinion/2012/09/10/did-colorado-shooter-single-out-cinemark-theater/>.
[146] Ibid.
[147] Eaves-Johnson, James. "Law school, guns, and a media bias." *The Daily Iowan,* 24 Jan. 2002.

The good news is that the data on public shootings shows they are on the decline. There were 42 in the 1990s, and 26 in the 2000s, which means that your chance of dying in a public shooting is about the same as being struck by lightning.[148] When we look at the effect of concealed carry on crime, public shootings fell faster and farther than any other form of crime. On average, from 1977-1999 multiple deaths from public shootings fell 60 percent when state governments decriminalized concealed carry of handguns, while total death and injuries fell 78 percent.[149]

Concealed Carry on Campus

A new phenomenon is an increasing number of colleges allowing students who have concealed carry permits to bring their firearms onto campus. Obviously, this has brought up many safety concerns. Even if you favor concealed carry in other situations, you probably recognize that there is a difference between allowing a college student and an adult to have a concealed firearm because many college students engage in heavy drinking or drug abuse. Statistics backing up this concern come from a 2007 Columbia University study estimating that around 5.4 million full time college students abuse drugs or alcohol each month.[150] I don't doubt this – but the evidence suggests that most alcohol consumption occurs between ages 18 and 21[151] – and therein lies the problem in this argument. The required age to obtain a concealed carry permit in most states is

---

[148] Fund, John. "The Facts about Mass Shootings." *National Review Online*, 16 Dec. 2012. <http://www.nationalreview.com/articles/335739/facts-about-mass-shootings-john-fund>.

[149] Lott, John R. "The Bias against Guns: Why Almost Everything You've Heard about Gun Control Is Wrong." (Washington, DC: Regnery, 2003), p. 323.

[150] "Wasting the Best and the Brightest: Substance Abuse at America's Colleges and Universities." *The National Center on Addiction and Substance Abuse at Columbia University*, Mar. 2007. <http://www.casacolumbia.org/templates/Publications_Reports.aspx#r11>.

[151] *National Institute on Alcohol Abuse and Alcoholism No. 29 PH 357*, July 1995. <http://pubs.niaaa.nih.gov/publications/aa29.htm>.

21, and the Columbia study never bothered to distinguish rates if substance abuse between underclassmen and upperclassmen.

Factors that would prohibit a student from obtaining a permit include the student having a prior conviction of a misdemeanor of domestic violence, failure to pass a mental health background check, or evidence of having addiction to any controlled substance.[152] These restrictions would at least help to weed out potentially dangerous students from obtaining permits. Still, organizations such as the Students for Gun Free Schools point to a Harvard study aiming to show that students who own guns are more likely to engage in any form of substance abuse, [153] which appears to contradict the general understanding that concealed carry permits holders are law abiding. However, when someone actually bothers to read the actual Harvard study he will find that it proves exactly the opposite of what the SGFS wants it to. What the study did in fact show was that only 5 percent of those gun owners were more likely to engage in substance abuse than were holders of concealed carry permits.[154]

As I have demonstrated, concealed carry can prevent crime in public, so how can anyone think that concealed carry on campus is an exception to the rule? Concealed carry should be given a chance to succeed on all college campuses. Between 2005-2007, 16,000 assaults and 10,000 sexual assaults were reported on campuses.[155] The evidence of concealed carry

---

[152] Snyder, Jeffrey R. "Cato Institute Policy Analysis No. 284: Fighting Back: Crime, Self-Defense, and the Right to Carry a Handgun." *The Cato Institute*, 22 Oct. 1997. <http://www.cato.org/pubs/pas/pa284.pdf>.

[153] Miller, Matthew, David Hemenway, and Henry Wechsler. "Guns and Gun Threats at College." *Journal of American College Health*, Vol. 51, No. 2, 2002. <http://www.hsph.harvard.edu/cas/Documents/Gunthreats2/gunspdf.pdf>.

[154] "Why Our Campuses Are NOT Safer without Concealed Handguns Rebutting the Rhetoric of Students for Gun Free Schools." *Students for Concealed Carry on Campus*. <http://www.concealedcampus.org/pdf/sfgfs.pdf>.

[155] "Department of Postsecondary Education Aggregated Data For Calendar Years 2005 – 2007." <http://ope.ed.gov/security/dataFiles/Crime2008.zip>.

nationwide at least suggests that concealed carry would cut down on the frequency of these crimes.

As of January 2011, 71 campuses have allowed concealed carry permit holders to bring their firearms on campus. Thirty-five of them have had this policy for over five years, and this gives us an opportunity to measure its effects. What we know is that there have been no reported firearm accidents or crime thus far.[156]

Criticisms of Self-Defensive Gun Use

Statistics demonstrating the usefulness of guns in self-defense don't exist without criticism. These criticisms differ from those posed by McDowall. In this case, critics of these statistics will accept that they're truthful, but will try to find other ways to attack them.

One of these criticisms was made by "Drug Czar" R Gil Kerlikowske. He argues that although guns are used in self-defense, there are far more cases of innocent people being shot when mistaken for intruders. He even tells a story about an acquaintance who was injured in a scenario.[157] On average, the number of innocent Americans killed per year by armed citizens who had mistaken them for intruders is a measly 30.[158] Thirty deaths is thirty too many, but this number is still smaller than the number of deaths and injuries per year from police mistaking innocent civilians for criminals. As previously cited, the percentage of shootings by civilians mistaking innocent persons for criminals is 2 percent, while 11 percent of police make the same mistake. There will be accidental casualties from gun use,

---

[156] Pelt, Tiffany. "Students Back Concealed Carry on Campus Bill in Austin." *KCBD*, 29 Jan. 2011. <http://www.kcbd.com/story/13933208/carry-guns-on-campus?redirected=trueT>.

[157] "Guns Reduce Crime." *Intelligence Squared*, 2008 Oct. 28. <http://intelligencesquaredus.org/index.php/past-debates/guns-reduce-crime/>.

[158] Poe, "Seven Myths of Gun Control," p. 105.

but the negatives are minor in comparison to the number of lives saved by using a gun in self defense correctly. In the United States, a country of 310 million people, the odds of being accidently shot and killed in the Kerlikowske scenario is about one in 10.3 million.

In one episode of Aaron Sorkin's 'The Newsroom', the show's main character, Will McAvoy (played by Jeff Daniels), finds a handgun in his date's purse. When questioned, his date removes the gun's clip, points it at him, and informs him that it's for self-defense. In turn, McAvoy informs his date that in all likelihood "this is going to happen" as he knocks the gun from her hand, grabs it midair, and points it back at her. Kerlikowske also raises a similar point, telling a story about a young police officer he knew who was shot to death with his own handgun.

When we look beyond anecdotes and to actual studies, we find that criminals only gain possession of a victim's gun around 1 percent of the time. Sixty eight out of a total of 600,000 police officers were killed in 1997, 8 of whom were killed with their own weapons.[159]

The salient point would seem to be that if cops are being harmed at a high rate with their own weapons (which we now know are not), then citizens must fare much worse. The statistics do show that some people who use guns in self-defense are injured during an attack – but that's only half of the story. Concealed carry permit holders are not trigger happy – as Gary Kleck points out, the majority of people do not use their gun in self-defense until after they are injured, at which point they are prompted to use their gun, and not vice versa.[160] Many people defending themselves with a gun will be injured, but since the

---

[159] Kleck, Gary. "Guns and Self-Defense." 1997. <http://www.pulpless.com/gunclock/kleck2.html>.

[160] "Guns Reduce Crime" (Intelligence Squared Debate).

injury occurred prior to pulling out their weapon the argument that gun use lead to injury falls apart. Even if these statistics didn't suffer from such flaws, 12 percent of those defending themselves with a gun are injured, while those offering no resistance are have a 27 percent chance of injury, and fleeing the scene results in a 26 percent chance of injury. Attempting to use a different weapon (such as a knife) increases the chance of injury to 30 percent.[161]

A study by Arthur Kellermann and Donald Reay in the New England Journal of Medicine claimed to find that keeping a gun in the home leads to the death of a member of the household or friend 43 times more than that of an intruder.[162] This study can be dismissed on the basis that most people scare off intruders with guns rather than shooting them, which gave this "43 times more likely" result. After looking at the statistics of this study in more depth, more problems arise and the conclusions of this study are put further in doubt. Kellermann and Raey included suicides in their statistics, which make up almost all of the deaths.[163] Gary A. Shade and Rob Murphy list multiple flaws in Kellerman and Raey's study in their critique, the most important being that only three counties were sampled (and the majority of counties have zero murders). A look at the participants in the study also found that 52.7 percent of Kellerman' s subjects had a family member with an arrest record, 31.3 percent had a history of drug abuse, and 31.8 percent had a household member injured in instances of domestic violence.[164]

---

[161] Kleck, "Targeting Guns," p. 190.

[162] Kellermann, Arthur and Donald Reay. "Protection or Peril? An Analysis of Firearm Related Deaths in the Home." *The New England Journal of Medicine*, vol. 314, no. 24, June 1986, pp. 1557-60

[163] Shade, Gary A., and Rob Murphy. "Statistical Misgivings and Lies." *Firearms and Liberty,* September 3, 2002. <http://www.firearmsandliberty.com/papers-shade/StatisticalMisgivingsandLies.PDF>.

[164] Ibid.

The analysis by Kellermann and Reay is still greatly flawed, and misunderstands the reasons that people may keep a gun in the home. By their way of thinking, we could also find that people who wear bulletproof vests are more likely to get shot, but that would completely misinterpret why people wear bulletproof vests.[165] It's also common for the police population to increase in an area following a surge in crime. Had Kellerman and Raey looked at that statistic, would they have concluded that more police leads to more crime?

How the Brady Campaign's Own Report Card Proves Nothing

Brady's Campaign against guns simply loses in this debate. The Campaign's YouTube channel doesn't allow ratings or comments on their videos, and dissenting comments on the group's Facebook page usually result in a ban on that commenter. There is even a "Brady banned me from their campaign" Facebook page! Is it any wonder that they have to censor any form of opposition, when even their own facts and measurements fail to prove a single point in their favor?

One thing unique to the Brady Campaign is their report card which ranks states based on their level of gun control. Regulations that aim to curb trafficking, limit bulk purchases, track handguns, report lost/stolen guns, and require background checks and permits to purchase a gun all increase a state's gun control ranking in the report card. The maximum rank a state can get for gun regulation is a score of 100 points. To put their ranking to the test, the table below lists all the states with the least amount of gun murders alongside the Brady Campaign's ranking for them for the year 2011:

---

[165] A similar case against the study was made in: Sowell, Thomas. "Ever Wonder Why? And Other Controversial Essays. (Stanford, CA: Hoover Institution, 2006), pp. 232-234.

Table 1.1: Ten States with Least of Gun Homicides Per Capita

State	Gun Homicides Per 100,000[166]	Brady Ranking[167]
Hawaii	0.07	50
New Hampshire	0.53	6
Rhode Island	0.57	44
South Dakota	0.68	4
Iowa	0.71	7
Vermont	0.75	0
Montana	0.76	6
Minnesota	0.82	14
Maine	0.9	7
North Dakota	0.93	2

It is worth noting that Vermont was ranked lowest in gun homicides in the year 2010[168] - and that state doesn't require a permit for concealed carry. The only restriction to concealed carry is that you don't carry with the intent to injure another human being, and be over the age of 16.[169] One of the reasons Vermont dropped down the list is because their firearm homicide rate doubled – from two murders to four!

Hawaii scores so well because the Aloha State enjoyed an 86 percent firearm homicide decline from the year prior. This

---

[166] Rogers, Simon. "Gun Crime Statistics by US State: Latest Data." *The Guardian*, 17 Dec. 2012. <http://www.guardian.co.uk/news/datablog/2011/jan/10/gun-crime-us-state>.

[167] "2011 STATE RANKINGS." *The Brady Campaign to Prevent Gun Violence*, <http://www.bradycampaign.org/xshare/stateleg/scorecard/2011/2011_Brady_Campaign_State_Scorecard_Rankings.pdf>.

[168] "Table 20: Murder by State, Types of Weapons, 2010." *Federal Bureau of Investigation*, <http://www.fbi.gov/about-us/cjis/ucr/crime-in-the-u.s/2010/crime-in-the-u.s.-2010/tables/10tbl20.xls>.

[169] "Vermont Concealed Carry Permit Information." *USA Carry*, <http://www.usacarry.com/vermont_concealed_carry_permit_information.html>.

wasn't due to any increased gun control measures, however, as Hawaii's Brady ranking was the same in their 2010 scorecard:[170]

Table 1.2: Ten States with Most Gun Homicides per Capita

State	Gun Homicides Per 100,000	Brady Ranking
District of Columbia	12.46	N/A
Louisiana	10.16	2
Mississippi	7.46	4
South Carolina	5.41	8
Michigan	5.06	25
Missouri	4.63	4
Arkansas	4.39	4
New York	4.12	62
Georgia	3.93	8
Tennessee	3.92	8

It is convenient (and self-serving) that Brady doesn't rank the District of Columbia, which happens to have some of the strongest gun laws in the country and the highest gun homicide rate. Ranked at 12 is California, which the Brady Campaign ranks as #1 in gun control with a score of 81.

Overall, the 2011 data show no correlation between strictness of gun control laws and firearm homicide rates.

Guns and Suicide

A supposed correlation between suicide and guns has become a modern argument for gun control. In 1999, guns were

[170] "2010 STATE RANKINGS." *The Brady Campaign to Prevent Gun Violence*, <http://www.bradycampaign.org/xshare/stateleg/scorecard/2010/2010_Brady_Campaign_State_Scorecard_Rankings.pdf>.

used in 67 percent of all suicides, resulting in 15,699 deaths.[171] A 2007 study by the Harvard School of Public Health examined the correlation between guns and suicide and discovered the suicide rate in the top 15 states with the most guns is double that of the 6 states with the least guns. One should be cautious when correlating anything with suicide rates, as a legitimate study has shown that the cities which play the most country music on the radio also have the highest suicide rates.[172] Like the previous study, the one put forth by Harvard is a prime example of correlation not implying causation. As Gary Kleck explains:

> Of thirteen studies, nine found a significant association between gun levels and rates of gun suicide, but only one found a significant association between gun levels and rates of total suicides. The only study to find a measure of "gun availability" significantly associated with total suicide... used a measure of gun availability known to be invalid
>
> This pattern of results supports the view that where guns are less common, there is complete substitution of other methods of suicide, and that, while gun levels influence the choice of suicide method, they have no effect on the number of people who die in suicides. [173]

It turns out that these states also coincidentally had higher non-gun suicide rates as well. While hosting the Rachel Maddow show, Ezra Klein reported that "in states where gun ownership is relatively high, so it turns out is suicide." He then completely contradicts himself within the next 30 seconds (unknowingly it seems), by pointing out that "even when you factor in suicides by

---

[171] "CDC- Injury – WISQARS – Fatal Data." *Centers for Disease Control and Prevention*. 11 Jan 2011. <http://www.cdc.gov/injury/wisqars/fatal.html>.
[172] Stack, Steven and Jim Gundalch. "The Effect of Country Music on Suicide." *Social Force*, Vol. 71, No. 1 (Sept., 1992), pp. 211-18.
[173] Kleck, "Targeting Firearms," p. 285.

other means… states with a higher rate of gun ownership still experience twice as many suicides."[174]

The average suicide rate in the United States relative to gun ownership contradicts expectations that a "more guns, more suicides" link exists. While the number of guns per capita has increased over 50 percent from 1972 to 1995, the average suicide rate has remained unchanged from 11.9 suicides per 100,000 in 1972 to 11.9 in 1995, fluctuating as high as 13 suicides per 100,000 once between 1972 and 1995.[175] Evidence from Canada can be used to form a similar conclusion. Research conducted by Martin Killias, John Kestern, and Martin Rindlisbacher found that in Toronto and Ontario, when firearms were restricted, suicides committed with guns decreased, but the overall suicide rate remained constant, as other methods of suicide such as jumping increased.[176]

Gun suicides allow all sorts of "more guns means more gun violence" statistics to be manipulated. The Violence Policy Center was able to "prove" that more gun ownership leads to more gun deaths only by including suicides in their data.[177] There is overall, in fact, zero correlation between gun ownership rates and gun homicide rates in the United States at the state level)[178]

If the number of firearms per capita correlates with high suicide rates, it makes no sense why a country like Japan, where

---

[174]The Rachel Maddow Show, MSNBC, July 23rd 2012.

[175] Kleck, "Targeting Firearms," p. 265.

[176] Martin, Killias. "Guns, Violent Crime, and Suicide in 21 Countries" *Canadian Journal of Criminology*, Oct. 2001. <http://rechten.uvt.nl/icvs/pdffiles/guns_killias_vankestern.pdf>.

[177] Langley, Marty. "States With Higher Gun Ownership and Weak Gun Laws Lead Nation in Gun Death." *Violence Policy Center*, 24 Oct. 2011. <http://www.vpc.org/press/1110gundeath.htm>.

[178] "United States Homicide Rate vs Gun Ownership by State." *Objectobot*, 19 Dec. 2012. <http://www.objectobot.com/?cat=186>.

virtually nobody owns a firearm, has a higher suicide rate than the US.[179]

Child Safety

Gun control advocates often cite child safety as a concern, and there is no doubt that this is a reasonable concern. As Richard Poe points out "Even the staunchest gun rights advocates shrink before this emotional argument."[180] Fortunately, the number of children who die per year due to firearms accidents is declining. Recent estimates put the amount of children that die annually from firearms accidents at 30-50 children per year.[181] Other estimates place the number around 250 deaths per year, but usually factor in people up to age 19, while the lower estimates include only children aged 1-14.[182] Of the top 18 causes of accidental death ranked by the Center of Disease Control in 2007, children aged 1-14 who died from accidental gunshots ranked 10th. Death by accidental firearm discharge ranked just behind death by falling, and was half as common as death by poisoning.[183] Death by motor vehicle caused nearly 42 percent of all accidental deaths that year, while firearms caused 1.7 percent.

To put the data in perspective, children are far more likely to be injured or killed in a bicycle accident then by a firearm accident. In 2007, the number of children under the age of 16 who visited the emergency room for bicycle accidents

---

[179] Taylor, Humphrey. "Gun Ownership: Two in Five Americans Live in Gun-Owning Households." *The Harris Poll #25*, May 30, 2001. <http://www.harrisinteractive.com/vault/Harris-Interactive-Poll-Research-Gun-Ownership-Two-in-Five-Americans-Live-in-Gun-Owning-Households-2001-05.pdf>.

[180] Poe, "Seven Myths of Gun Control," p. 120.

[181] D'Souza, Dinesh. "Letters to a Young Conservative." (New York: Basic Books, 2005), p. 133.

[182] Boyse, Kyla. "Gun Safety for Kids and Youth: Your Child." *University of Michigan Health System*, Nov. 2010. <http://www.med.umich.edu/yourchild/topics/guns.htm>.

[183] "Unintentional Injuries, Ages 1-14, All Races, Both Sexes, Total Deaths: 3,782." *Centers for Disease Control and Prevention*, <http://webappa.cdc.gov/sasweb/ncipc/leadcaus10.html>.

(approximately 250,000)[184] was 147 times higher than the number of children of in the emergency room as a result of a non-fatal gun accident that same year (1700).[185]

Despite the rarity of child gun accidents, some gun control advocates will go so far as to assert that 4,000 children die each year from some form of gun violence (mainly homicide),[186] but statistics like this factor in people in their early twenties as "children". An obvious problem with this is that it allows the high death toll of black and Hispanic young men involved in drug trafficking to be factored into the statistic. How many young victims of gun violence are gang members? A study in New York City found that 40 percent of teens shot were shot during a time they should have been in school, while a study in Los Angeles found 71 percent of teens injured in drive by shootings to be gang members.[187]

In the year 2009, for children 15 and younger, the average daily death rate is 0.9, and for children 10 and under, its 0.41 per day; these are all lower daily death rates then children killed in car accidents or drowning., And that's according to the data from the anti-gun Children's Defense Fund. [188]

---

[184] "Bicycle Helmet Statistics: Statistics from the US Consumer Product Safety Commission." *Bicycle Helmet Safety Institute*. <http://www.hetlmets.org/stats.htm>.
[185] "WISQARS Nonfatal Injury Reports." *Centers for Disease Control and Prevention*. <http://webappa.cdc.gov/sasweb/ncipc/nfirates2001.html>.
[186] "Million Mom March and Rosie O'Donnell's Gun Control Views." *ABC News with Cookie Roberts and Sam Donaldson*, May 14, 2000.
[187] LaPierre, Wayne. Chapter titled "The Threat of Guns in the Home Is Exaggerated" in "Gun Control." (Detroit: Greenhaven, 2007), p. 30.
[188] "Protect Children Not Guns 2012." *Children's Defense Fund*, 2012. <http://www.childrensdefense.org/child-research-data-publications/data/protect-children-not-guns-2012.pdf>.

The Ultimate Hypocrites

There will always be tragic stories of people being shot, and there will always be heroic stories of people having their lives saved by guns. As seen in the statistics, concealed carry permits don't turn citizens bad. On the other hand, it seems to be the gun control activists who are a threat to themselves.

It was barely a year after Rosie O' Donnell's "Million Mom March" when Barbara Graham (an organizer for the event) was convicted of shooting and paralyzing a man for life. When police searched her house, they uncovered three handguns and a TEC-9 submachine gun, which had been banned by the 1994 Assault Weapons ban.[189] Gun control activists can claim that banning guns will keep guns out of the hands of criminals all they want, but even they don't believe it, and some of them are in the best position to know this not to be true.

I suppose that anyone could claim that Graham's actions are that of just one individual in the gun control movement, but it also appears that O'Donnell enjoys the benefits of guns while trying to rob them from others. In Rosie's case, it was only days after the march that she applied for a concealed carry permit.[190] Such behavior seems to be quite common among the anti-gun lobby. While Media Matters for America's founder David Brock has taken in $400,000 from pro-gun control groups, he travels with an armed bodyguard.[191]

---

[189] Originally published as: George, Donna St. "Mother Gets 10 Years to Life for Trying to Take Revenge." *The Washington Post*. June 27, 2001; Page B01. An online version can be found at:
<http://www.tincher.to/mother.htm>.

[190] Dougherty, Jon E. "Rosie's Armed Bodyguard." *World Net Daily*, 26 May 2000. <http://www.wnd.com/?pageId=1999>.

[191] Chiaramonte, Perry. "Brock and the Glock: Armed Men Guarded Media Matters Boss as He Took $400,000 Gun Control Donation." *FOX News*, 16 Feb. 2012. <http://www.foxnews.com/politics/2012/02/16/brock-and-glock-armed-men-guarded-media-matters-boss-as-took-400000-gun-control/>.

Since even gun control advocates like their guns, I would encourage you to adopt the same position.

Chapter 2

The Health Care Imperative

"Unless we put medical freedom into the Constitution, the time will come when medicine will organize an undercover dictatorship. To restrict the art of healing to one class of men, and deny equal privilege to others, will be to constitute the Bastille of medical science. All such laws are un-American and despotic, and have no place in a Republic. The constitution of this republic should make special privilege for medical freedom as well as religious freedom."

- Reported to have been argued by Benjamin Rush, doctor and signer of the Declaration of Independence.

Paul Krugman's bestselling book *The Conscience of a Liberal* lays out plans for a "new-New Deal", with an emphasis on health care reform. Like most liberals, the position Krugman defends is what most refer to as "universal healthcare." I take issue with that term. Capitalist, Socialist, or otherwise, the goal of any health system should be to provide coverage to all its citizens at the lowest cost and with the highest quality. The debate truly lies in what is the best way to achieve this goal. While the term "universal healthcare" is itself associated with a government run bureaucracy, "socialized medicine" tends to be a much more appropriate definition for the system Krugman defends.

Advocates of a free market in health care like myself seek to achieve universal health care by allowing market competition to drive down the prices of care while sustaining or increasing quality. This isn't to say that a free market system would operate without a safety net. As a society we recognize that food stamps are necessary for the very poor to survive, but we don't also suggest socializing food. Such a view is similar to that of economist Friedrich Hayek in his seminal work *The Road to Serfdom* – that the state may aid in such matters, but only within the framework of a free market.[192]

In the US, we have seen attempts at universal coverage through mandating individuals to buy insurance. On the worldwide scene, every other first world nation except the US operates under socialized medicine. The purpose of this chapter is to tear down the arguments put forth by Krugman and others in favor of socialized medicine, while building the case for free market reforms in our current system. While my reforms propose

---

[192] Many people, including Paul Krugman, have taken Hayek's statements in *The Road to Serfdom* out of context to make it appear that he supported socialized medicine while he supported no such position. See: Hammond, Jeremy R. "Paul Krugman vs. Ron Paul and Friedrich Hayek." *Foreign Policy Journal*, 17 Sept. 2011. <http://www.foreignpolicyjournal.com/2011/09/17/paul-krugman-vs-ron-paul-and-friedrich-hayek/>.

a dramatic scale back in the role of government, the proper role of government in health care will also be examined.

Part 1: Healthcare Myths

The Myth of Free Market Care

In the healthcare debate, comparing America to other countries to evaluate "market vs. socialized" systems is a great mischaracterization of the reality of the current situation. For starters, American healthcare is not a free market. Our government already covers half of our health care costs, with private insurance covering the rest. A mere 12 percent of healthcare costs are paid out of pocket.[193]

Since American health care is not completely controlled by the government, market incentives still apply to some extent, even if they are heavily distorted. Basic functions of the price system are eroded by the influence of third parties. For example, what is the point of price shopping for healthcare if you are only paying 12 percent of the bill? While I defend the current system as still being superior to socialized medicine, in the long run the problem of rising costs will be the bane of American health care. Ironically, while America's health care system has market oriented aspects, the whole concept of cost control is lost due to the influence of third parties, including the government.

An annoying myth is that the health care debate is between our supposedly free market system and "free" universal health care, as if it was possible to make everything "free" by funding it through taxes. Those reaping the benefits of "free" healthcare in the UK have 11 percent of every pound they make between £100-£670 a week allocated to the NHS (their universal

---

[193] Mitchell, Dan. "The Real Healthcare 'Chart of the Day.'" 28 Dec. 2009. <http://danieljmitchell.wordpress.com/2009/12/28/the-real-healthcare-chart-of-the-day/>.

healthcare service) via taxes, and an additional 1 percent of every pound after £670.[194] In Germany, citizens pay between 12.2 percent-16.7 percent of income to "free" healthcare,[195] and in Canada 22 percent of all taxes went toward their universal healthcare system.[196] France fares slightly better, with employers paying 12.8 percent of wages for each employee, with employees paying an additional 0.75 percent of their income towards medical care, and both of those taxes exist in addition to a 5.25 percent General Social Contribution. After triple taxation, the French end up paying 18.8 percent of their income to medical care. Yet despite this, 90 percent of French still purchase private healthcare insurance.[197] I recognize that overall health care expenditures are higher in the US than in the countries listed here, but the point is that health care is hardly "free" elsewhere.

The "50 Million Uninsured Myth"

One apparent flaw in the American health care system is the extremely large number of uninsured individuals. Politicians pushing for more government control in health care usually cite the number of uninsured as being between 45 and 50 million. This number is incredibly overestimated and is easy to cut down to size, as bulleted on the next page. Note that there is overlap between groups.

---

[194] OECD, "Taxing Wages 2006/2007: Special Feature: Tax Reforms and Tax Burdens," 2008.

[195] "Costs of Health Care." *BigGovHealth*. <http://biggovhealth.org/resource/myths-facts/costs-of-health-care/>.

[196] Lehr, Jay. "Canadian Healthcare is No Model for US: Claims That Canada's Single Payer Health System Is More Efficient or More Compassionate than Ours are Just Plain Untrue," *The Heartland Institute*, 1 June 2004, <http://news.heartland.org/newspaper-article/2004/06/01/canadian-health-care-no-model-us.>

[197] Tanner, Michael D. "The Grass Is Not Always Greener." *The Cato Institute*, 18 Mar. 2008. <http://www.cato.org/pubs/pas/pa-613.pdf>.

- 9.7 million of those uninsured are not citizens of the United States.[198] Even under a system where every single American citizen purchased insurance, these non-citizens would give the false appearance of an uninsured group, and shouldn't be included in the statistic.

- 12-14 million are eligible for government assistance but haven't signed up.[199] If anyone in this category visits the emergency room, taxpayers pick up the tab. Around 70 percent of uninsured children are in this group.[200]

- 17 million have an annual income of over $50,000 a year, and eight million in this group make over $75,000.[201] If they were to fall ill or suffer an injury, they would be able to afford the costs of healthcare. This group represents the voluntarily uninsured.

- 7.9 million are aged 18-24, an age group which requires a small amount of medical care. Overall, the amount of deaths per year in this age group is declining. In the 2006-2007 period, deaths in this group dropped 2.8%.[202] Even if a person in this group were to require surgery, this age group has an average annual salary of $31,790, so most

[198] Klein, Philip. "The Matter With Myths." *The American Spectator*, July-Aug. 2009. <http://spectator.org/archives/2009/07/21/the-matter-with-myths>.
[199] Ibid.
[200] "A Randomized Trial of Effects of Parent Mentors on Insuring Minority Children." *ClinicalTrials.gov*, 20 Dec. 2010. <http://clinicaltrials.gov/ct2/show/NCT01264718>.
[201] Carmen DeNavas-Walt, Bernadette D. Proctor and Cheryl Hill Lee, "Income, Poverty, and Health Insurance Coverage in the United States: 2005," *U.S. Census Bureau, Department of Commerce*, August 2006, <http://www.census.gov/prod/2006pubs/p60-231.pdf>. (See Table 8)
[202] Xu, Jiaquan, Kenneth D. Koc hanek, Sherry L. Murphy, and Betzaida Tejada-Vera. "National Vital Statistics Reports: Table A. Percentage change in death rates and age-adjusted death rates in 2007 from 2006, by age, race, and sex: United States. *Centers for Disease Control*, 20 May 2010." <http://www.cdc.gov/NCHS/data/nvsr/nvsr58/nvsr58_19.pdf>.

> individuals in this group would be able to afford care.[203] Forcing this group to be insured is a difficult task. One third of those in Massachusetts who refuse to purchase health insurance (which is required by law) are in this age group.

It is also important when looking at the data to view the uninsured not solely as a statistical category, but as individuals. Out of the total number of uninsured, between 21-31 million individuals are uninsured for the entire year.[204] This means that anywhere between 15-25 million out of the 50 million will likely get insurance soon. The permanently uninsured make up a very small percentage of the uninsured, and only 16 percent of the uninsured remain uninsured for longer than 24 months.[205] Luckily, those so-called "permanently uninsured" are comprised mostly of people who can afford insurance but chose not to purchase it. From 1993-2003, those with household incomes under $25,000 a year showed the largest decline in the uninsured rate, with a 15 percent drop. Meanwhile, those making $25,000-$50,000 had a 13 percent increase in their uninsured rate, those making $50,000-$75,000 showed a 54 percent increase, and those making over $75,000 showed a 130 percent increase.[206]

There is a problem group of individuals who fall between the cracks, but the amount of people in this situation can be estimated to be below ten million based on the data I have provided. Keeping this in mind, it is important not to tie a lack of health insurance with a lack of health care. Appearing on 'Real Time with Bill Maher' during a defense of the Occupy Wall Street movement, former Congressman Alan Grayson claimed

---

[203] Ibid., Table 1 (sub heading Income and Earnings Summary Measures by Selected Characteristics: 2006 and 2007).

[204] Gratzer, David. "The Cure: How Capitalism Can Save American Health Care." (New York: Encounter Books, 2006), p. 85.

[205] Ibid., p. 86.

[206] Ibid., p. 88.

that fifty million Americans "can't even see a doctor."[207] While there is obviously a gap in health care spending between those with and without insurance, the uninsured are receiving care. In 2001, one study published in *Health Affairs* showed that with public and private/charitable contributions included, $1,587 is spent each year per uninsured person.[208]

The Bankruptcy Myth

A 2007 study conducted by Dr. David Himmelstein and researchers from both Harvard University and Ohio University claimed to find that 62 percent of all bankruptcies in the year 2007 were caused by medical costs.[209] If accurate, this would amount to 2.4 million bankruptcies per year solely due to medical costs. Elizabeth Warren is fond of quoting the conclusions reached in this study – because she is one of the researchers involved in conducting it.

Leaving the bias of Himmelstein aside, (he is the National Spokesperson for Physicians for a National Health Program, which advocates a single payer system) there are multiple red flags that provide reasons to be skeptical. For instance, the study claims that 78 percent of those bankrupt from medical expenses had health insurance.[210] While the problem of the underinsured does exist, Himmelstein's "discovery" that more insured people go bankrupt than those uninsured is questionable.

Some other claims made by the Himmselstein study are that medical related bankruptcies increased 50 percent between

---

[207] Real Time with Bill Maher, HBO, Aired October 7th 2011.
[208] Gratzer, "The Cure," p. 89.
[209] Himmelstein, David U., Deborah Thorne, Elizabeth Warren, and Steffie Woolhandler. "Medical Bankruptcy in the United States, 2007: Results of a National Study." *The American Journal of Medicine*, 2007. <http://www.pnhp.org/new_bankruptcy_study/Bankruptcy-2009.pdf>.
[210] Credit to Lee Doren for pointing this out. See the video on his YouTube Channel "HowTheWorldWorks" titled "The Young Turks are Clueless, Part 5 of 4076." Posted on November 19th 2009.

2001 and 2007, and that the majority of those bankrupt are middle class and well educated.

Some basic problems with the study stem from its small sample size and how bankruptcy is defined for the purposes of the study. Despite attempting to get a sample size of 2,314 individuals, only 1,032 were actually interviewed for the study. Himmselstein also links **all** medical debt with bankruptcy. Even if an individual were to be a dollar in medical debt, and went bankrupt for any reason, he is factored into the 62 percent statistic. While Himmselstein does specify that in 92 percent of medical bankruptcies the individual has debts of over $5,000, his methodology is still sloppy. The respondents themselves may give better testimony to the causes of their bankruptcy, as only 32 percent of them attributed it to medical expenses.[211]

Then we have competing studies. The most reliable study to date uses a sample size nearly 5 times that of Himmselstein's. This study, conducted by the Department of Justice, found that 54 percent of bankruptcies involve no medical debt, and 90 percent have debt under $5,000. In addition, a study based on the Survey of Consumer Finances published by the Federal Reserve demonstrated that medical debt only rose from 5.5 percent of all debt to 5.8 percent of all debt between 2001 and 2007.[212]

The study also took place during a year (2007) atypical of other years when it comes to bankruptcy procedures. As Megan McArdle of The Atlantic has documented, in 2005 a congressional bankruptcy reform bill was passed which made it more difficult to file for Chapter 7 bankruptcy (where you

---

[211] McArdle, Megan. "Considering Elizabeth Warren, the Scholar." *The Atlantic*, 22 July 2010. <http://www.theatlantic.com/business/archive/2010/07/considering-elizabeth-warren-the-scholar/60211/>.

[212] "Survey of Consumer Finances." *The Federal Reserve Board*, 2007. <http://www.federalreserve.gov/pubs/oss/oss2/scfindex.html>. Note: This source was obtained through Lee Doren's video.

liquidate your debts and are not required to go into a payment plan). As McArdle writes:

> This tightening was real, but rather exaggerated in the popular press (the overwhelming majority of people who need to file bankruptcy will have no problem qualifying for a Chapter 7). Perhaps for that reason, even bankruptcy experts were stunned by the number of people who rushed to file before the six month grace period in the law was up. They were also stunned by the magnitude of the decline, and how long bankruptcies took to start trending back towards previous levels.[213]

There was an enormous upwards spike in the number of people filing for bankruptcy before the law went into effect. Around 12,000 people filed daily shortly before the law went into effect, but this number then fell sharply to about 1,000 daily after the law took effect. After that, daily bankruptcy filings began to steadily rise from the 1,000 of October 2005 to around 7,000 in 2010.[214] Because of this, the study measures a period where bankruptcies rose due to changes in legal code, not increasing medical expenses.

A handful of other studies have contradicted the findings of Himmelstein. This includes studies by Aparna Mathur of the American Enterprise Institute, David Dranove and Michael Millsenson of Northwestern University, Scott Fay, Erik Hurst, and Michelle White from the Universitys of Florida, Chicago, and San Diego, and lastly by David Gross of Compass Lexecon and Nicolas Souleles of the University of Pennsylvania.[215]

---

[213] Ibid.

[214] Ibid.

[215] Furchtgoth-Roth, Diana. "Testimony before the Senate Committee on the Judiciary, Subcommittee on Administrative Oversight and the Courts." *Hudson* Institute, 20 Oct. 2009. <http://www.judiciary.senate.gov/pdf/10-20-09%20Furchtgott-Roth%20Testimony.pdf>.

The Lifespan Fallacy

If lifespan were the only way to measure the success of a health care system, we are not doing too well. It is no secret that the US lags behind most other first world countries in life span. When placed side by side with statistics showing how much more the US spends on health care, it appears that we spend thousands more than these countries for no added benefit. However, we must keep in mind that lifespan not the only way to measure a health care system, and it is in fact a rather deficient measurement.

If we want to determine quality and efficiency of healthcare, the best way to do this is to compare survival rates for certain life-threatening conditions between countries. This will be done later in the chapter, but here the causes of the apparent lifespan deficit between the US and other countries will be examined. The problem in using lifespan as an estimate is that while it is a good indicator a nation's health, other factors can alter estimates when doing close comparisons between countries. If "Nation A" has a lifespan of 80 years, and "Nation B" a lifespan of 40 years, it would be reasonable to conclude that the healthcare system of Nation A is superior. However when examining the difference in lifespan between first world nations, the difference is by either months or at most a few years. Factors beside medical care can affect the average lifespan by only a very small amount, but this amount is still enough to make us appear inferior from a statistical perspective.

I have identified four factors where the US ranks poorly compared to other nations that lower our lifespan statistic. With these factors considered, it really is no surprise that the countries charted alongside the US in the table below appear to live longer: our murder rate is more than triple most of theirs, our suicide rate is slightly higher, our obesity rate is higher, and we get in more car accidents.

Table 2.1: Average Lifespan vs. Other Variables (Using Most Recent Data up to 2011)

Country	Average Lifespan[216]	Murder Rate Per 100,000[217]	Suicide Rate Per 100,000[218]	Obesity Rate (% of population)[219]	Car Fatalities Per 100,000[220]
United States	78.57	4.7	12	28.5%	12.3
Canada	81.54	1.7	11.5	26.2%	9.2
Australia	79.2	1.16	9.7	26.8%	5.71
Cuba	78.29	4.6	12.3	11.8%	8.6
Switzerland	82.59	0.66	11.1	8.1%	5.7
Israel	82.05	2.1	5.8	15.7%	3.7
United Kingdom	80.49	1.17	11.8	24.8%	3.58

Fortunately, studies have been conducted on the specifics of what happens to the lifespan of citizens of a country once other variables are accounted for. According to Scott Atlas (a doctor himself), the US ranks 19th with variables unaccounted for – but

[216] "Life expectancy: Life expectancy by country." *World Health Organization.* <http://apps.who.int/gho/data/node.main.688?lang=en>.

[217] Each country is individually sourced at: "List of countries by intentional homicide rate by decade." *Wikipedia*, <http://en.wikipedia.org/wiki/List_of_countries_by_intentional_homicide_rate_by_decade>.

[218] "Suicide rates per 100,000 by country, year and sex (Table)." <http://www.who.int/mental_health/prevention/suicide_rates/en/index.html>.

[219] *OECD Berlin Centre*, <http://www.oecd-berlin.de/oecdwash/viz/obesity/slide1.php?cr=usa&lg=en>. The obesity statistics should be taken with a grain of salt. Nearly every source I found offering obesity statistics gave different figures, though the US ranked above all the countries in the table regardless of what the numbers were.

[220] Rates are individually sourced at <http://en.wikipedia.org/wiki/List_of_countries_by_traffic-related_death_rate>. All data regarding car fatalities uses the most recent figure.

#1 when factors except "fatal injuries" accounted for. [221] With only car accidents and murders accounted for, the US still ranks #1 in life expectancy, just by a larger margin.

Another way to demonstrate the effect of socialized medicine on lifespan, or lack thereof, is to look at the rate of acceleration in average lifespan in different countries before and after adopting such a system. To look at the UK; in all 48 years of the 20th century before the NHS was created in 1948, life expectancy rose from 47 years to 66 years. A rise of 19 years in real terms, or a 40.4 percent increase. By contrast, in the 48 years after the establishment of the NHS, life expectancy rose from 66 years to 77.5 years – only 11.5 years in real terms, a 17.4 percent increase.[222] The US showed similar increases in lifespan during both periods, plus or minus a few years[223] – which at least shows that we can't credit differences in life expectancy solely to differences in health care systems.

Infant Mortality Myths

Similar to argument discussed in "The Lifespan Fallacy," arguments comparing infant mortality in the U.S. vs. "socialized" countries are like comparing apples to oranges. According to the World Fact Book's estimate, the US ranks 46th in infant mortality, placing us behind the UK, Canada, and even third world countries like Cuba. This would be embarrassing if it were true, but again, the statistics lie.

---

[221] Atlas, Scott W. "The Worst Study Ever?" *Commentary Magazine*, Apr. 2011. <http://www.commentarymagazine.com/article/the-worst-study-ever/>.

[222] Dalrymple, Theodore. "Universal Mediocrity." *City Journal*, Summer 2012. <http://www.city-journal.org/2012/22_3_otbie-british-health-care.html>.

[223] See the table in: "U.S. Life Expectancy Lags behind 41 Nations." *USA Today*, 11 Aug. 2007. <http://usatoday30.usatoday.com/news/health/2007-08-11-life-expectancy_N.htm>.

There is simply no universal way that infant mortality is calculated, which allows certain variables to distort them. Some examples are listed below:

- The United Kingdom defines a stillbirth as "a child which has issued forth from its mother after the twenty-fourth week of pregnancy and which did not at any time after being completely expelled from its mother breathe or show any other signs of life."[224]

- In Canada, Germany, Ireland and Austria, premature babies weighing under 500 grams are counted as still births. In Australia, those weighing under 400g are stillbirths. These babies have a mortality rate of 869 per 1,000.[225]

- France requires a medical certificate that confirms that a child was born "alive and viable." This is not easy to obtain, nor is there any incentive to obtain one.[226]

- Most countries (with the exception of the United States) classify babies as "stillborn" if they survive less than 24 hours. The "stillborn" under that criterion make up 40% of all infant deaths.[227]

- In Hong Kong and Japan, children who die within 24 hours of birth are classified as "miscarriages." Nearly half of US infant deaths occur within the first 24 hours.[228]

---

[224] See: Births and Deaths Registration Act of 1953. Accessible online at: <http://www.legislation.gov.uk/ukpga/Eliz2/1-2/20>.

[225] Halderman, Linda. "The Doctor Is In: Infant Mortality Comparisons a Statistical Miscarriage." *Pajamas Media,* 3 Aug. 2008. <http://pajamasmedia.com/blog/the-doctor-is-in-infant-mortality-comparisons-a-statistical-miscarriage/>.

[226] Ibid.

[227] Ibid.

[228] Coulter, Ann. "A Statistical Regression Analysis of Maritime Unemployment Rates, 1946-1948. Just Kidding – More Liberals Lies About Health Care!" 30 Sept. 2009. <http://www.anncoulter.com/cgi-local/article.cgi?article=332>.

- Genetics also play a role; the infant mortality rate for blacks in the United States is 2.4 higher than that of whites.[229] This isn't due to inequalities in health care coverage, as Mexican Americans, who have the least access to health insurance, and are twice as likely to be born out of hospital, have lower infant mortality rates than do Native Americans and Blacks.[230] As a more ethnically diverse country, inequalities in mortality rates across races about American infant mortality rates negatively.

- Switzerland doesn't count the death of babies under 30 centimeters (11.8 inches) into their rate.[231]

Adjusting for even a single factor can change the outcome of the statistics a lot. Norway, which ranks 13th in infant mortality ranks equal with the US when weight at birth is accounted for.[232] Even with all the listed variables controlled for, other possibilities exist.

Underreporting can distort the figures of some countries. Countries do have a motivation to lie about these statistics, and this practice has been documented before. Cuba, in addition to underreporting statistics also has their doctors perform abortions on the unborn which would have otherwise been high risk births, most of which would have died and been added to Cuba's infant mortality rate had they been allowed to be born.[233]

---

[229] MacDorman, Marian F., and T. J. Matthews. "Recent Trends in Infant Mortality in the United States." *Centers for Disease Control*, Oct. 2008. <http://www.cdc.gov/nchs/data/databriefs/db09.htm>.

[230] Gratzer, "The Cure," p. 175.

[231] Eberstadt, Nicholas. "The Tyranny of Numbers: Measurement and Misrule." (Washington: American Enterprise Institute, 1995), p. 50.

[232] Halderman, "The Doctor is In."

[233] See John Stossel's "Sick in America: Whose Body is it Anyway?" Aired September 14th 2007 on 20/20.

Although determining the real infant mortality rate in other countries is difficult, comparisons can be made on how successful the US is in saving newborns in critical condition. For example, as rare as it is for a baby who weighs less than 400g to survive birth, the majority of survivors were born in the States. The "Tiniest Baby Registry" has tracked down 110 infants who we born weighing less than 400 grams at birth between 1936-2010. Eighty of them (73 percent) were born in the United States.[234] It also would appear that the United States has shown improvement and has an even larger share of credit when only <400g babies in the 21st century are measured. Forty-two of the 52 born after the year 2000 were born in the United States.[235]

We Rank 37th!

A myth recycled in Krugman's *Conscience* is that the United States ranks 37th in health care.[236] This number is based on a 2000 World Health Report from the World Health Organization[237] that ranks 191 different nations on health care. When examined, the study suffers from so many flaws that it brings into question whether or not Krugman had even bothered to read it

First, there are two different WHO rankings, overall attainment (OA) and overall performance (OP). Using OA, we rank 15th, but naturally Krugman chooses whichever looks worse. However, not all of the five factors the WHO uses when calculating the OP rank are relevant to how well a health system functions.

---

[234] Bell, E. F., and D. K. Zumbach. "The Tiniest Babies: a Registry of Survivors with Birth Weight Less than 400 Grams." *PubMed*, Jan. 2011. <http://www.ncbi.nlm.nih.gov/pubmed/21187314>.

[235] Ibid.

[236] Krugman, Paul R. "The Conscience of a Liberal." (New York: Norton, 2009), pp. 216-220.

[237] Christopher J. L. Murray et al., "Overall Health System Achievement for 191 Countries," *Global Programme on Evidence for Health Policy Discussion Paper Series no. 28* (Geneva: WHO, undated), http://www.who.int/healthinfo/paper28.pdf.

When the WHO study in question was published, the organization was under the control of the former Norwegian prince minister Gro Harlem Brundtland, a socialist. Speaking on the issue of healthcare, Brundtlant stated, "The ultimate responsibility for a country's health system's performance rests with the government, but the impact lies disproportionately on the poor."[238] In addition to these biases, the poor measurements used within the study reflect them, essentially being biased against any non-socialized system. The measurement criteria is bulleted below, with each factor's weight listed next to it.

1. Health Level (25%)

This factor is determined by a country's life expectancy. As previously discussed, this is an imprecise way of measuring a nation's health due to other variables. Lifespan certainly does play a large role and deserves to be included, but only with other variables adjusted for (such as the ones I have shown: murder rate, suicide rate, etc.), which WHO fails to do.

2. Healthcare Distribution (25%)

This does not actually measure the quality of medical care, just how unequal the care is given to different groups of individuals. To paraphrase what one Cato Institute report has pointed out; if "Group A" gets great medical care, while group B gets good medical care, they could rank behind "Group's C and D" even if both C and D got horrible care. Or to give a historical example, it would be like saying that the USSR was superior to the US simply because everyone in the USSR had the same living standards.

---

[238] Powell, Alvin. "Policies Can Combat Health-care Inequity: So say experts at SPH symposium honoring Fineberg, Hiatt." *Harvard University Gazette*, 3 Oct. 2002. <http://news.harvard.edu/gazette/2002/10.03/09-sph.html>.

3. Responsiveness (12.5%)

This measures speed of service, protection of privacy, choice of doctors, cleanliness of hospital services, and other miscellaneous features. Including these measures seems like common, but really is based on a subjective standard of a nation's "respect for persons." Subjective judgments have no place in objective analysis.

4. Responsiveness Distribution (12.5%)

Here returns the meaningless word "distribution." This factor suffers from the same flaws that "health distribution" does, both of which do not actually measure quality of health care.

5. Financial Fairness (25%)

This also depends on distribution. WHO calculates this by finding the percentage of income that households from different income brackets use for healthcare, and then measuring the difference paid across brackets. The poor and rich pay virtually the same amount on healthcare yearly, the top 20 percent paying $4,451 in 2003, and the bottom 20 percent paying $4,447.[239] Obviously, the poor are going to spend a larger percentage of their income on health care, as they do on literally every other good or service they pay for.

Since there is bound to be a gap, any economy that has some element of the market-driven healthcare system will thereby rank poorly worldwide according to this standard. The only way for us to rank better in this factor would be either to have greater government involvement in healthcare, or switch

[239] Samuelson, Robert J. "Getting Real About Healthcare." *The Daily Beast*, 5 Sept. 2008. <http://www.thedailybeast.com/newsweek/2008/09/05/getting-real-about-health-care.html>.

over completely to a single payer system. Either way, these two choices favor government intervention no matter what.[240]

Other Biases

Since the majority of these factors are irrelevant to measuring the quality of care, the ranking is rendered meaningless by any objective standard.

"Distribution" played a role in over one third of the standard. "Responsiveness distribution" was ranked twice as important as "responsiveness" itself. Adding to the bias towards socialized medicine, Brundtland writes:

> Where health and responsiveness are concerned, achieving a high average level is not good enough: the goals of a health system must also include reducing inequalities, in ways that improve the situation of the worst-off. In this report attainment in relation to these goals provides the basis for measuring the performance of health systems.[241]

It is reassuring however, that Brundtland writes in the paragraph following that "undoubtedly, many of the concepts and measures used in the report require further refinement and development."

Brundtland's views are not alien to the WHO, and indeed more recent studies have revealed the same level of bias. WHO's 2010 paper "Risk Pooling and Redistribution in Health Care: an Empirical Analysis of Attitudes Toward Solidarity" acts as a

---

[240] The bulk of information for the five factors is found in: Whitman, Glen. "WHO's Fooling Who? The World Health Organization's Problematic Ranking of Health Care Systems." *The Cato Institute*. February 28, 2008. 2 Aug 2011 <http://www.cato.org/pub_display.php?pub_id=9236>

[241] "Health Systems: Improving Performance." (Geneva: World Health Organization, 2000), p. viii.

global survey showing support for redistribution in health care (as the title implies).[242]

Part 2: The Pitfalls of Socialized Medicine

The American system is far from perfect, but there are many areas where it measurably exceeds the results that any socialized system can produce. In this section we will examine where the American system excels, where socialized systems fail, and the results of attempts at reform within the US at the state level.

Cancer Survival Rates

Rather than compare apples to oranges by arguing about overall life expectancy, what really matters in judging the results of a healthcare system is comparing how well it does at its primary goal – saving lives. The US excels when we use this standard to measure cancer survival rates. All cancer survival rate statistics discussed below are measured based on whether or not someone is alive 5 years after their diagnosis.

Overall Survival Rates

The overall cancer survival rate is highest in the United States. Currently, we have a survival rate of 62.9 percent. Only five European countries (Iceland, Sweden, Belgium, Switzerland, Finland) surpass 60 percent. Male survival rates trump Europe by an even a larger martin. The male survival rate stands at

[242] James, Chris, and William Savedoff. "Risk Pooling and Redistribution in health care: an empirical analysis of attitudes toward solidarity." *World Health Organization*, 2010. <http://www.who.int/healthsystems/topics/financing/healthreport/SolidarityNo5FINAL.pdf>.

66.percent in the US, but only one European country (Sweden) has a male cancer survival rate surpassing 60 percent. [243]

Survival Rates for Common Cancers

Of the 16 most common cancers, the US has the highest survival rate for 13 of them.[244] For American men, they have a nineteen percentage point lead in survival rates over the Europeans, while American women have a seven percentage point lead.[245] To give some specific examples, individual survival rates are charted in Table 2.2.

Table 2.2: Five Year Cancer Survival Rates of US vs. Europe

Cancer	**US Survival Rate (%)**	**Europe Survival Rate (%)**
Prostate	99.3	77.5
Skin Melanoma	92.3	86.1
Breast	90.1	79
Corpus Uteri	82.3	78
Colorectal	65.5	56.2
Non-Hodgkin Lymphoma	62	54.6
Stomach	25	24.9
Lung	15.7	10.9
All 16 Cancers (men)	66.3	47.3
All 16 Cancers (women)	62.9	55.8

Source: Mark Perry.[246]

---

[243] Martin, Nicole. "UK Cancer Survival Rate Lowest in Europe." *The Telegraph*, 21 Aug. 2007. <http://www.telegraph.co.uk/news/uknews/1560849/UK-cancer-survival-rate-lowest-in-Europe.html>.

[244] "Cancer Survival in Five Continents: A worldwide population based study (Concord)." *Lancet Ontology*, Vol. 9, August 2008.

[245] Ibid.

[246] Perry, Mark J. "5-Yr. Cancer Survival Rates: US Dominates Europe." 11 Aug. 2009. <http://mjperry.blogspot.com/2009/08/5-yr-cancer-survival-rates-us-dominates.html>.

Some more intelligent critics of this measurement may respond by pointing out that the when you adjust for age, the cancer survival rate has remained almost flat over the past half century. This seems like almost an unbelievable claim, since no one can believe that the health care system we enjoy hasn't improved in the past half-decade.

One conflicting statistic is that the cancer mortality rate for people ages between twenty and forty has declined by over 20 percent, yet still the cancer mortality rate has flat lined at 200 deaths per 100,000 people. In the book *Super Freakonomics* authors Steven D. Levitt and Stephen J. Dubner decided to tackle this issue and find a satisfying answer. Based on the fact that mortality from heart disease has been cut in half over the same period, they conclude that "many young people who in previous generations would have died from heart disease are now living long enough to die from cancer instead." As they point out, in the case of lung cancer, almost 90 percent of the newly diagnosed are over age fifty, and the median age of the newly diagnosed is seventy-one.[247]

Medical Technology

Even someone who buys into bogus statistics showing Cuba ranking above the US in terms of lifespan and infant mortality should have a hard time imagining that the quality of medical technology in Cuba is higher than that in America. The international statistics show that this indeed is hard to imagine for Cuba, but also for any other country in the world. As shown in the table below, the US far outperforms other OECD nations in terms of the availability of medical technology:

[247] Levitt, Steven D., and Stephen J. Dubner. "SuperFreakonomics: Global Cooling, Patriotic Prostitutes, and Why Suicide Bombers Should Buy Life Insurance." (New York: Harper Perennial, 2011), p. 86.

Table 2.3: Medical Technology in US vs. OECD Nations

	United States	OECD Average (US Excluded)
MRI's Per Million Population	25.9	12.7
CT Scanners Per Million	34.3	21.8
Mammographs Per Million	40.2	22.7
Radiation Therapy Equipment Per Million	11.3	6.9

Source: OECD.[248]

In addition to more and better medical technology in the US, it's also better utilized. In the US, for every 100,000 people per year, there are 203 who get coronary bypass surgery, but only 65 in Canada, and 41 in the UK. Three hundred and eighty eight (per 100,000) receive coronary angioplasty in the US, but only 81 in Canada, and 51 in the UK. The US has 87 dialysis patients per 100,000, while Canada has 46, and the UK has 27.[249]

Compounding the fact that medical technology is less abundant in other countries and poorly utilized, it is poorly maintained as well, and in some cases, outdated. For Canada in

---

[248] "OECD Health Data 2011 - Frequently Requested Data." *OECD*, <http://www.oecd.org/els/healthpoliciesanddata/oecdhealthdata2012-frequentlyrequesteddata.htm> Note: Some data was missing from the OECD's Health Data Statistics report. When calculating averages, I used the most recent data for each country, and excluded countries where no data existed.

[249] Goodman, John. "Five Myths of Socialized Medicine." *The Cato Institute*, Winter 2005. <http://www.cato.org/pubs/catosletter/catosletterv3n1.pdf>.

2007, 21 percent of bone densitometers, and 28 percent of SPECT units were over a decade old.[250] Bone densitometers carry out the task of measuring bone density of those with osteoporosis, while SPECT units are used in creating three-dimensional images of the human body. The same situation exists for many other types of medical equipment.

Other medical devices where a good portion are over a decade old in other countries include over 33 percent of gamma cameras (used for nuclear medicine imaging) and 25 percent of cardiac catheterization labs (used for heart ailments).[251] By the standards of the European Coordination Committee of the Radiological Electromedical Industries, no more than 10 percent of a country's health technology should exceed a decade in age, and 60 percent of medical technology should be under five years old.[252]

Physician Reduction

When the conditions that a doctor must work in worsen, it should come to no surprise that we see less doctors.

In the 1970's, before Canada's government takeover of medicine, they ranked second out of 28 countries on doctors per thousand people. Now, they rank 24th.[253] Even though Massachusetts attempted universal coverage just recently (in 2006), they are already experiencing doctor shortages in dermatology, general surgery, emergency medicine, and other areas.[254] All these problems have arisen despite Massachusetts ranking #1 in doctors per 100,000 residents, with 462 doctors per

---

[250] Pipes, Sally. "The Truth about Obamacare." (Washington DC: Regnery, 2010), p 11.

[251] Ibid.

[252] Ibid.

[253] Esmail, Nadeem, and Michael Walker. "How Good is Canadian Health Care? *The Heartland Institute*, 2004. <http://heartland.org/policy-documents/how-good-canadian-health-care?Email=yes>.

[254] Mitchell, Jennifer. "Doctor Shortage in Massachusetts, Some Wait 53 Days to See Doctor." 29 Oct. 2010. <http://actionforbetterhealthcare.com/?p=1436>.

100,000 in 2006.[255] While Massachusetts has retained its #1 ranking for now, their supply of doctors has now begun to lag behind demand. One hospital reported 1,600 people on their waiting list in 2008 and said it takes around 4 months for someone to have their first appointment.[256]

American programs that resemble socialized medicine in other countries – such as Medicare and Medicaid – already suffer from something similar to this problem of physician reduction. Since private insurers pay physicians more than Medicare and Medicaid, patients on these government programs have trouble finding physicians.. In Michigan, the number of doctors willing to see Medicaid patients has declined from 88 percent in 1999 to 64 percent in 2005. In Ohio, only 28 percent of doctors surveyed by the Ohio Coalition of Primary Care Physicians said they would continue to provide care to Medicaid patients on an unlimited basis without an increase in pay.[257] Like Michigan, Ohio also has followed a downward trend in doctors seeing Medicaid patients, with a decline from 93 percent in 1998 to 63 percent in 2002.[258]

Both programs cause doctors to work at a loss in some cases. One doctor at Hurley Medical Center named Dr. Mukkamala estimated that is cost him around $29 for every X-ray he takes. Medicaid pays him $20 per X-ray, Medicare pays $30, and insurers such as Blue Cross pay $33.[259] The Ohio

---

[255] "American Medical Association, Chicago, IL, Physicians Characteristics and Distribution in the U.S., annual (copyright)." Table 156, Statistical Abstract of the United States, 2009.

[256] Brown, Karen. "Mass. Health Care Reform Reveals Doctor Shortage." *NPR*, 30 Nov. 2008. <http://www.npr.org/templates/story/story.php?storyId=97620520>.

[257] "2002 Ohio Physician Medicaid Survey Key Findings." *The Ohio Coalition of Primary Care Physicians and the Ohio State Medical Association*, Jan. 2003. <ohiomedicaidreform.gov/pdf/Brian_Bachelder_PartI.pdf>.

[258] Ibid

[259] Fuhrmans, Vanessa. "Note to Medicaid Patients: The Doctor Won't See You." 19 July 2007. <http://mlyon01.wordpress.com/2007/07/19/note-to-medicaid-patients-the-doctor-wont-see-you/>.

Coalition study cited previously also found that 79 percent of doctors do not receive a large enough Medicaid reimbursement to cover their office overhead.[260]

Since many of the same health care "experts" that designed RomneyCare in Massachusetts also designed ObamaCare, there are more areas where these plans are similar than different. What has caused problems at a statewide level is bound to cause problems at the national level. Even prior to the passing of ObamaCare, many polls showed a reduction in the number of physicians to be inevitable. A survey of 270,000 primary care physicians in 2008 found that 76 percent already described themselves as "overextended or overworked." Because of this, 13 percent plan to look for a job that does not involve patient care, 30 percent plan to work part time or see fewer patients, and 11 percent plan on retiring.[261]

A survey conducted by the Physicians' Foundation nine months after ObamaCare was passed showed that 40 percent of physicians said they would drop out of patient care within the next 3 years by retiring, seeking a non-clinical job within healthcare, or seeking a job not related to healthcare.[262] I seriously doubt that someone who spends nearly a decade of their life in university obtaining a medical degree would truly seek employment in a non-medical field, but it at least it shows ObamaCare to be widely unpopular among physicians.

> A study by the Association of American Medical Colleges placed a number on the size of the predicted shortages. In summary, they found that by 2015 the predicted doctor shortage would be 50 percent worse with ObamaCare

---

[260] "2002 Ohio Physician Medicaid Survey Key Findings."

[261] "Obamacare Won't Survive Coming Doctor Shortage." *The Washington Examiner*, 28 June 2009. <http://washingtonexaminer.com/editorials/2009/06/obamacare-wont-survive-coming-doctor-shortage>.

[262] "Nation's Frontline Physicians Unhappy With Health Care Reform Measures." *Physicians' Foundation*, 18 Nov. 2010. <http://www.physiciansfoundations.org/PressReleaseDetails.aspx?id=250>.

> than without it.[263] People can rationally argue that many of these doctors are bluffing, but there are other fields that doctors can migrate to. These include specialties such as cosmetic surgery, Lasik, and others where the government does not involve itself. Since the ObamaCare bill would place a cap on reimbursements, doctors would rationally flee to these other specialties.[264]

In addition to physician reduction, many other problems exist. Fifty-nine percent said that ObamaCare would cause them to spend less time with patients, and 87 percent said they would have to close or restrict their practices to Medicare patients. Overall, 67 percent of physicians surveyed view the ObamaCare bill negatively.[265] ObamaCare is largely unpopular among physicians, who tend to know best what is in their best interests.

Waiting Lists

Economics 101's law of supply and demand still exists in the world of health care. Since pumping more money into the system does not help doctors work any faster, the combination of increased demand and decreased supply results in increased waiting times. Whatever way you look at it, waiting times are themselves a form of costs – and in many cases people would rather pay money to get around them.

To put some figures to the extent of these waiting times, we can look abroad to the "socialized" systems to see how they fare. Around 800,000 Canadian citizens are currently on a waiting list for surgery, and the time spent on that waiting list has

---

[263] "Health Reform to Worsen Doctor Shortage: Group." Ed. Peter Cooney. 30 Sept. 2010. <http://www.reuters.com/article/2010/09/30/us-usa-healthcare-doctors-idUSTRE68T67120100930>.

[264] Morrissey, Ed. "Study: ObamaCare Will Make Doctor Shortage 50% Worse by 2015." *HotAir*, 1 Oct. 2010. <http://hotair.com/archives/2010/10/01/study-obamacare-will-make-doctor-shortage-50-worse-by-2015/>.

[265] Nations Frontline Physicians Unhappy With Health Care Reform Measures.

grown longer over time. Over a fifteen year period the average wait time between getting a referral from a primary care doctor and getting treatment from a specialist doubled from nine weeks to over eighteen weeks.[266]

The UK's National Health Service (NHS) has the same problem, except they have a waiting list of nearly 615,000 (from April 2009-March 2010).[267] The UK's figures are incomplete however, because (a): there are patients waiting to even be able to get on a waiting list,[268] and (b): there are "hidden" waiting lists. While the official statistics in November of 2011 showed only 29,508 waiting over 18 weeks for care,[269] the NHS has been manipulating the numbers. One former nurse says that she "was told to cancel operations for anyone who was already waiting over 18 weeks, and instead to fill that theatre time with people closest to breaching the 18-week limit."

She continues, speaking of the NHS's tactics when "she was told to call a mother of three young children to offer her a short-notice slot for Christmas Eve, knowing she would refuse and so could be knocked off the list for refusing."[270] This practice occurs because the NHS has a target of treating 90 percent of patients in under 18 weeks, and knocking people off the list can

---

[266] Esmail, Nadeem, and Michael Walker. "How Good is Canadian Health Care?" *Fraser Institute*, November 2007. <http://www.fraserinstitute.org/commerce.web/product_files/HowGoodHC2007rev.pdf>

[267] "Inpatient and Outpatient Waiting Times Statistics." *Department of Health*. <http://www.dh.gov.uk/en/Publicationsandstatistics/Statistics/Performancedataandstatistics/HospitalWaitingTimesandListStatistics/index.htm>.

[268] Beckford, Martin. "Patients Struggle Even to Get on NHS Waiting Lists." *The Telegraph*, 29 July 2011. <http://www.telegraph.co.uk/health/healthnews/8671127/Patients-struggle-even-to-get-on-NHS-waiting-lists.html>.

[269] Campbell, Denis, and James Ball. "Number of NHS Patients Missing Waiting-time Target Soars." *The Guardian*, 19 Jan. 2012. <http://www.guardian.co.uk/society/2012/jan/19/patients-missing-nhs-waiting-time-target>.

[270] Toynbee, Polly. "How Cameron's NHS Cheats Waiting-list Figures." *The Guardian*, 20 Feb. 2012. <http://www.guardian.co.uk/commentisfree/2012/feb/20/cameron-nhs-cheats-waiting-lists>.

at least make the statistic confirm their goal. In reality, an estimated 250,000 have been waiting over 18 weeks for care.[271]

Liberal critics have attributed recent news of increases in waiting times to cuts in the NHS's budget, but it's unclear to what extent money alone can do to solve this problem. To deal with their waiting times, Canada devoted $6 billion trying to improve them. A report from the Wait Time Alliance (WTA) has tracked Canada's progress, showing minor improvement, but still lagging behind reasonable waiting times by a large margin. In some of the various medical procedures looked at, between 43% - 91% of people were waiting over 18 weeks for treatment, and for the average procedure listed from that group, 71.3 percent were waiting for that long.[272]

The gap in waiting times can in one sense, justify spending more on health care. Since an individual in America would be able to take less time off of work before his treatment due to the lower waiting time, he would be able to recover more income after a procedure than would otherwise be possible. Thomas Sowell gives an example on how this is accomplished:

> … if an American who gets an operation three weeks after being diagnosed by a primary care physician pays $2,000 more than a Canadian who gets the same operation fifteen weeks after being diagnosed by a primary care physician, then the question of whose full costs are higher depends on whether the lost pay is greater or less than about $167 a week, which is below the average rate of pay in either

[271] Smith, Rebecca. "Thousands Left for a Year on 'hidden' NHS Waiting Lists." *The Telegraph*, 17 Nov. 2011. <http://www.telegraph.co.uk/health/healthnews/8896182/Thousands-left-for-a-year-on-hidden-NHS-waiting-lists.html>.

[272] "Unfinished Business." *Wait Time Alliance Report Card*, June 2009. <http://www.waittimealliance.ca/June2009/Report-card-June2009_e.pdf>. This data was related to the wait times based on different procedures in seven specialties: ophthalmology, anesthesia, obstetrics and gynecology, nuclear medicine, gastroenterology, plastic surgery and orthopedics.

> country. This does not assume that either the American or the Canadian returns to work immediately after the operation, but only that the lost time after the operation is the same in both countries.[273]

Even a minimum wage worker who works thirty hours a week would benefit more in the US in the sort of scenario Sowell describes (without accounting for the opportunity cost of leisure time).

Drug Innovation

On average, it costs $1.3 billion to bring a new drug onto the market, and over a decade to research and develop the drug.[274] Despite the cost, new drugs bring pharmaceutical companies profit, and also provide cures to countless illnesses. In this aspect of medicine, the US ranks #1. If the profit motive is removed, who would risk $1.3 billion for no return on this investment?

Drug production is only possible at its current levels in America because of the lack of price controls on our drugs. Implementing price controls may appear to keep prices low, but these low prices are costly.[275] The cost of these price controls are paid in the lack of innovation that results by removing the profit incentive to produce new drugs. While other countries who have placed price controls on their drugs can keep their prices low, they also produce few new drugs while most of the new drugs they use are from the US. As unfair as the profit motive seems at first glance, it's still preferable to any alternative where either less or no innovation exists.

---

[273] Sowell, Thomas. "Applied Economics: Thinking beyond Stage One." (New York: Basic Books, 2009), p. 61-62.

[274] Herper, Matthew. "The Truly Staggering Cost Of Inventing New Drugs." *Forbes*, 10 Feb. 2012. <http://www.forbes.com/sites/matthewherper/2012/02/10/the-truly-staggering-cost-of-inventing-new-drugs/>.

[275] A quote from P.J. O'Rourke comes to mind: "If you think healthcare is expensive now, just wait until it's free."

The entire European Union, Switzerland, Canada, and Australia, with a combined population of 681 million, have won 41 Nobel Prizes in Medicine and Physiology, while the US, with under half the population, has won 57 (as of 2010).[276] When it comes to actual drug creation instead of just our Nobel Prize achievements, we fare even better. Fifteen times more money is invested in American biotech companies than in European companies.[277] As a result, the US is responsible for 90 percent of new drugs worldwide.[278] This has led quite obviously to the US becoming the largest seller of new pharmaceuticals to foreign countries. During the 1999-2005 period, the US sold 71 percent of new pharmaceuticals, while Japan and Germany (our largest 2 competitors) sold 4 percent each.[279]

Due to our monopoly on innovation, patients in the US tend to be treated with newer drugs more often than patients in other countries. To give two examples, the average age of American diabetes drugs used by patients is five years old, compared to 7-8 years in Canada, Germany, and the United Kingdom. For anti-psychotics, American patients' drugs are 8 years old on average, compared to 18-21 years in other countries. New drugs are estimated to have been responsible for 40 percent of increased life expectancy from 1986-2000,[280] which is something no one should try to prevent by any means, intentional or unintentional.

---

[276] "Nobel Prize in Physiology or Medicine Winners 1901-2010." <http://nobelprizes.com/nobel/medicine/>.

[277] Goldberg, Robert. "Don't Blame Canada." *Natonal Review Online*, 23 Dec. 2004, <http://www.nationalreview.com/comment/goldberg200412230817.asp>.

[278] Whelan, Elizabeth M. "The Drug Importation Hoax." *National Review Online*, 16 Jun. 2005, <http://www.nationalreview.com/comment/whelan200506160741.asp>.

[279] Barlow, Doug. "Saving Pennies, Costing Lives." *The Wall Street Journal Europe*, March 16, 2005.

[280] Litchenburg, Frank R. "The Impact of New Drug Launches on Longevity: Evidence from Longitudinal, Disease-Level Data from 52 Counties." *National Bureau of Economic Research*, June 2003. <http://www.ruf.rice.edu/~econ/conference/papers/lichtenberg.pdf>.

Evaluating State Level Reform

Attempts at health care reform on the state level gave us a look into what these reforms could look like at a national level. The emphasis in this section will be on RomneyCare, as its provisions are almost identical to that of ObamaCare.

RomneyCare

In 2006, Republican governor Mitt Romney made Massachusetts the first state to attempt universal coverage through what is known as an "individual mandate." Explained simply, the mandate forces everyone (or every employer with a business of a certain size) to purchase insurance or else face a fine as a consequence. Low-income earners are given subsidies with which to purchase insurance. While this may come as a surprise to many, the concept of an individual mandate has conservative origins. The concept was created by the Heritage Foundation and received the support of Newt Gingrich and other Republicans at the time. Regardless of its political origin, one of the lessons we can learn from its implementation is that it simply does not work.

RomneyCare was pushed through with the goal of insuring all uninsured citizens and controlling the cost of healthcare. In regard to the goal of insuring universal coverage, RomneyCare can be considered a success or failure depending on what your interpretation of the word "universal" is. Before RomneyCare, estimates placed the number of uninsured anywhere between 372,000 and 618,000. During the 2006-2008 period, 219,000 were insured by RomneyCare.[281]

We cannot know exactly what the rate of uninsured now is, because many have hidden their uninsured status to avoid penalty for refusing to enroll. The fine for not purchasing health

---

[281] Tanner, Michael. "Lessons from the Fall of RomneyCare." *Cato Policy Report*, Jan/Feb. 2008. <http://www.cato.org/pubs/policy_report/v30n1/cpr30n1-1.html>.

insurance was originally $219, and increased to $912 in 2008.[282] The Census Bureau's American Community Survey estimates that 4.1 percent of those living in Massachusetts are uninsured,[283] but this survery suffers from the problem of underreporting of the uninsured.

There were three ways in which respondents could answer this survey and hide their uninsured status; refuse to take the survey, lie about their coverage in the survey, or leave the question about coverage unanswered. Simply leaving something unanswered isn't uncommon, as questions about a person's income sometimes go unanswered as well.[284] A study by the Cato Institute found that no response to the question regarding health coverage did in-fact increase after RomneyCare was passed. Overall, if those who refused to respond to the question did so to hide their status as uninsured, it would increase the Massachusetts uninsured population by 2.1 percent versus what the official statistic shows.[285]

In the case of controlling prices, RomneyCare had essentially no effect. In 2006, the cost of family premiums in Massachusetts were 108 percent of the national average. No data exists for 2007, but in 2008 costs were 112.1 percent of the national average, and 113 percent in 2009.[286] Various liberal bloggers have pointed to the fact that this trend has slowed down

---

282 "Massachusetts Health Care Reform: Two Years Later." *Kaiser Family Foundation* May 2008. <http://www.kff.org/uninsured/upload/7777.pdf>.

283 Turner, Joanna. "A Preliminary Evaluation of Health Insurance Coverage in the 2008 American Community Survey." *U.S. Bureau of the Census*, 22 Sept. 2009. <http://www.census.gov/hhes/www/hlthins/data/acs/2008/2008ACS_healthins.pdf>.

284 Yelowitz, Aaron and Michael F. Cannon. "The Massachusetts Health Plan: Much Pain Little Gain." *The Cato Institute*, 20 Jan. 2010. <http://www.cato.org/publications/policy-analysis/massachusetts-health-plan-much-pain-little-gain>.

285 Ibid.

286 Suderman, Peter. "Is RomneyCare Working?" *Reason*, 28 Feb. 2012. <http://reason.com/blog/2012/02/28/is-romneycare-working>.

after 2009, and there are some reasons for this having to do with RomneyCare, and others not.

The State did attempt to control costs somewhat in 2010, as temporary price controls were put in place. Harvard Pilgrim Health Care made a deal with the state of Massachusetts not to raise premiums for the year, but only after a three month battle.[287] To save money, insurers in Massachusetts also began limiting access to expensive hospitals, which allowed them to keep premiums down, at least temporarily.[288] But as this was occurring, the increase in average premium growth declined nationally in 2010 from 5 percent to 3 percent so Massachusetts is hardly unique in having their costs slow for this one year.[289] At least the other 49 states didn't need price controls to accomplish this reduction.

As we have shown to be the case in other countries with socialized medicine, RomneyCare increased wait times. To quote Investors Business Daily, "the year before RomneyCare got into full swing, 64 percent of internists accepted new patients and the average wait time was 33 days. By 2010, those numbers were 51 percent and 52 days."[290]

RomneyCare is no model for the rest of the states to follow. Now consuming 40 percent of the Massachusetts budget, and showing 8 percent increases in health care spending each

---

[287] Weisman, Robert. "Insurer, State in Surprise Accord." *The Boston Globe*, 3 July 2010. <http://www.boston.com/business/healthcare/articles/2010/07/03/harvard_pilgrim_reaches_settlement_with_state_to_limit_rate_hikes/>.

[288] Suderman, "Is RomneyCare Working?"

[289] Ibid. This is due to the fact that health care premiums tend to decline during recessions.

[290] Hogberg, David. "RomneyCare: The Doctor Is Accessible — You Just Have To Wait." *Investor's Business Daily*, 3 May 2011. <http://blogs.investors.com/capitalhill/index.php/home/35-politicsinvesting/2601-romneycare-the-doctor-is-accessible-you-just-have-to-wait>.

year, applying this kind of plan nationwide fails to address the woes of the current system.[291]

Hawaii Attempts Universal Coverage

The lack of success Hawaii had in insuring all their citizens can be summed up in one short sentence: the program lasted 7 months. The program originated in 2007 with their Republican governor Linda Lingle.

An estimated 3,500 to 16,000 children lacked insurance, but it wasn't only the uninsured who got access to care. The program aimed to insure these children through the lure of "free" care, with the exception of a $7 fee for each office visit.

By the time of Keiki Care's demise, 2,034 kids were enrolled. The pro-Keiki Care "Hawaii Covering Kids" website uses a high estimate in stating that 16,000 children were uninsured before Keiki care was passed.[292] They likely opted for the high estimate to try to make their program seem all the more necessary, but in retrospect it makes their program look like an even greater failure. Since around 85 percent of the children enrolled in the program turned out to have been previously privately insured,[293] even covering 2000 kids can hardly be considered an achievement since most enrolled only to save money. Hawaii's failure on such a small scale foreshadows the consequences of a nationwide government takeover of medical care. Hawaii had the smallest number of people to insure, since their program only tried to insure uninsured children.

---

[291] Ibid.

[292] Luksch, Barbara. "Fact Sheet: Keiki Care." *Hawaii Covering Kids*, 21 Nov. 2008. <http://www.coveringkids.com/hot_happenings/KeikiCareInfo112408.pdf>.

[293] Atlas, Scott W. "Reforming America's Health Care System: the Flawed Vision of Obamacare." (Stanford, CA: Hoover Institution, 2010), pp. 122-123.

A bill attempting to bring Keiki Care back to life was put forward in 2009, but this time it was vetoed by Governor Lingle.[294]

Part 3: Fixing the American System

This chapter so far has mostly shown only the negatives of socialized medicine and some of the positives of the American system, though the chapter began by noting that our system is far from that of a free market. The greatest folly of the American system is that costs are spiraling out of control. In 2010, health care consumed 17.6 percent of our economy – compared to an average of 9.5 percent for other OECD nations.[295] It needs to be specified that various reforms will be recommended for different types of health care. These types that I identify are: routine medical care, catastrophic care, and care for the elderly.[296] Routine medical case encompasses doctor visits and basic treatments, while catastrophic care refers to more expensive care likely requiring surgery. Care for the elderly refers to both routine and catastrophic care, though the discussion on it will be concerned with reforming Medicare and controlling end of life costs.

[294] DePledge, Derrick. "Hawaii Climate Task Force, New Spending on Health Care Vetoed." Honolulu Advertiser, 11 July 2009. <http://the.honoluluadvertiser.com/article/2009/Jul/11/ln/hawaii907110331.html>.
[295] "OECD Health Data 2012 How Does the United States Compare." *OECD*, 2012. <http://www.oecd.org/unitedstates/BriefingNoteUSA2012.pdf>.
[296] A similar distinguishing of the different types of health care is made in: Murray, Charles A. "In Our Hands: A Plan to Replace the Welfare State." (Washington, D.C.: AEI, 2006), pp. 40-41.

Why is Health Care so Expensive?

Put briefly, American health care is so expensive because our system infuses capitalism with the worst of government intervention.

Third Parties

"Third parties" in health care are any outside force that prevents the consumer from feeling the full financial cost of the services he receives. Health insurance is the third party that most people use, while Medicare and Medicaid are third parties that the elderly and poor utilize. In the real world, everyone price shops, but is far less likely to do so when someone else is paying the bill. John Stossel gives the analogy of what a world with grocery insurance would be like:

> With your employer paying 80 percent of the bill, you would fill the cart with lobster and filet mignon. Everything would cost more because supermarkets would stop running sales. Why should they, when their customers barely care about the price?[297]

This isn't a perfect example, because in the case of healthcare, insurance and government is paying far more than just 80 percent of the bill! But either way, if we barely pay the price, why care if the price rises? Most people do not: one survey even showed that only 12 percent of people do any research on costs or quality of certain health care providers each year.[298]

Separating consumers from the cost allows hospitals to charge hefty markups on their services. The website "Hospital

---

[297] Stossel, John. "John Stossel: Health Insurance Isn't All It's Cracked Up to Be." *AbcNews*, 16 Oct. 2006. <http://abcnews.go.com/Health/PrescriptionForChange/story?id=2574980&page=1>.

[298] Cannon, Michael F., and Michael Tanner. "Healthy Competition: What's Holding Back Health Care and How to Free It." (Washington, D.C.: Cato Institute, 2005), p. 60.

Bill Review" suggests that anywhere "from 157 percent to 702 percent markup for procedures is commonplace."[299] To put this in perspective, the markups on hotel mini-bars go up to 400 percent, fountain soda between 300-600 percent, and around 300 percent for lattes.[300]

In his 2001 essay *How to Cure Health Care*, Milton Friedman attributed 60 percent of the increase in health care costs from 1946-1997 to tax exempt health benefits, Medicare, and Medicaid.[301] Friedman also calculates that if health care spending rose at the same pace it did from 1919 to 1940, which was 3.1 percent per year, per-capita health care spending would have been $1,751 in 1997 instead of $3,625.[302] These figures are inflation adjusted in dollars for the year 2002.

FDA Regulation

Along with the passage of the Kefauver Harris Amendment (also known as the Drug Efficacy Amendment) in 1962, the Food and Drug Administration increased its strength in the regulation of drug production. As of 1938, drugs had to pass a "proof of safety requirement," but the 1962 law added both a "proof of efficacy" requirement and removed time constraints the FDA had to respond to applications for new drugs pharmaceutical companies wished to have enter the market.[303]

Like most government agencies, there are good intentions behind the FDA's approval of drugs. By some estimates, their preventative policy saves 10,000 lives per decade. Putting together such an estimate is easy, but what is not easy is

---

[299] Pell, M.B. "Huge Hospital Markups Burden Patients." *Hospital Bill Review*, 20 Apr. 2011. <http://www.hospitalbillreview.com/blog.php?post=14>.

[300] Morad, Renee. "20 Products With Giant Markups." *Yahoo! Finance*, 27 Sept. 2012. <http://finance.yahoo.com/news/20-products-giant-markups-115730856.html>.

[301] Friedman, Milton. "How to Cure Health Care." *Hoover Institution*, 2001. <http://www.hoover.org/publications/hoover-digest/article/7298>.

[302] Ibid.

[303] Friedman, Milton, and Rose D. Friedman. "Free to Choose: A Personal Statement." (San Diego: Harcourt Brace Jovanovich, 1990), p. 205.

calculating the amount of lives lost due to the length of the FDA's drug approval process. In the 1990's, it took slightly over 15 years for a new drug to get through the FDA's approval process. Even if the drug ended up saving only 1,000 lives a year, the FDA's regulations saved a net zero lives that decade. The problem is that there is not one, but thousands of potentially lifesaving drugs delayed from entering the market. An additional side effect is that it deters drugs from entering the market in the first place.

As Milton Friedman and his wife documented in their 1980 book *Free to Choose*, from the onset of new regulation in 1962, the amount of "new chemical entries" into the market had declined by over 50 percent each year until the publication of their book. Another group that excessive regulation harms is patients with rare diseases, as pharmaceutical companies wouldn't be able to recoup costs in producing drugs to treat such a small segment of the population.[304]

Even when they are not preventing drugs from entering the market, the FDA prevents lifesaving information from doing the same. From 1974 to 1980, plenty of studies were published demonstrating that aspirin reduces the risk of both death and repeat heart attacks by 20 percent for heart attack victims. The FDA wouldn't allow aspirin makers to disclose this information to doctors until 1988. Another study showing that aspirin reduces the risk of death for heart attack patients with unstable angina (when the heart doesn't receive enough oxygen) by an astonishing 50 percent also was also banned until 1988. Another study from the same timeframe showed that when taken daily for the month after a heart attack, aspirin reduces odds of death by 23 percent. This information was hidden from the public until 1996. On the international scene, the European Union has banned the

---

[304] The government has attempted to get around this problem by passing the Rare Diseases Act in 2002, which would offer financial incentives for companies to produce drugs treating or curing diseases that less than 200,000 people have.

claim that water can prevent dehydration after conducting a three-year investigation into this claim![305]

As stated earlier in this chapter, the costs to produce a new drug averages around $1.3 billion. Milton Friedman commented on the role of the FDA in increasing this cost as well, noting that before new regulation in the 1950s and early 60's, it cost half a million dollars and 25 months to bring a new drug to the market. By 1978, it had cost $54 million and eight years to bring a new drug to the market. Clearly this trend had has no signs of slowing down.

The $1.3 billion cost from FDA regulation then translates into higher costs for the consumers of those drugs. Not only does the producer have to recoup over a billion dollars, their timeframe to do so is limited. The patent on a new drug lasts between seventeen and twenty years, so when it expires another company can easily produce a generic and sell it for a lower price. One hundred tablets of Xanax cost $0.024 to produce, and sell for $136.79. This is effectively a markup of 570,000%.[306] Xanax has the highest markup of any prescription drug I could find, but other drugs still have absurd margins. Prozac's markup is 225,000%, Norvasex's 134,500%, and the lowest I could find was Zestril, at 2,800%.[307]

Perhaps reducing the length of a patent could solve the problem of high markups? Reducing the length of a patent may sound good in theory, but all shortening monopoly status for a few years would accomplish is for the cost of drugs to be even higher for a slightly shorter amount of time, since firms would

---

[305] Ward, Victoria, and Nick Collins. "EU Bans Claim That Water Can Prevent Dehydration." *The Telegraph*, 18 Nov. 2011. <http://www.telegraph.co.uk/news/worldnews/europe/eu/8897662/EU-bans-claim-that-water-can-prevent-dehydration.html>.

[306] Traister, Jeffrey. "Prescription Drug Cost Vs. Sale Price." *Livestrong*, 27 Sept. 2010. <http://www.livestrong.com/article/260599-prescription-drug-cost-vs-sale-price/>.

[307] Davis, Sharon, and Mary Palmer. "Material Costs of Medical Compounds Investigative Research Reveals the True Costs of Drugs." *Rense*. <http://rense.com/general54/preco.htm>.

still need to recoup costs from their investment. Reducing patent times too drastically would stifle innovation of drugs that producers consider to be a risky investment. The best way to reduce costs with the least amount of unintended consequences would be to lower production costs for firms looking to enter the market so they could enjoy the same amount of profits while charging a lower price.

Price controls may have made certain drugs in other countries cheaper than they are in the US, but our generics are cheaper, as would be expected through competition. The profit incentives are completely reversed: in America drug producers have to make money by charging more for drugs since they have a small timeframe to do so, while drug companies under the socialized system have to make a profit by charging more for generic drugs not limited by price controls.[308]

Relieving the stranglehold the FDA has on pharmaceutical companies would decrease the costs of drugs and help maximize the number of lives they can save. This kind of reform could also encourage self-regulation inside the industry due to the threat of lawsuits that would arise from a harmful drug.

Mandates Within Insurance

Different types of mandates have been discussed in this chapter, thus far with a focus on mandated purchase of insurance. However, there are other forms of health care mandates. One form of mandate is one wherein the health insurance company itself forces people to purchase coverage for health procedures they are unlikely to ever need. Although the purpose of insurance is to contribute to a risk pool and thereby spread the risk, for

---

[308] Forbes, Steve, and Elizabeth Ames. "How Capitalism Will Save Us, Why Free People And Free Markets Are The Best Answer In Today's Economy." (New York: Crown Business, 2011), p. 227.

many of these procedures it is questionable as to whether insurance should even cover them.

Mandates for coverage of specific procedures have been on the rise. While only seven healthcare mandates existed in 1965,[309] there were 2,156 in 2010.[310] These mandates are found throughout the states, Idaho having the least amount of mandates (13), and Rhode Island having the most (69).

Forcing people to join any kind of risk pool comes at a cost. Forty five states mandate benefits for alcoholism, 48 states have a mandate for breast reconstruction, 40 states have mandates for general mental health issues, while 42 states have mandates for mental health-parity and 30 states mandate contraceptive coverage.[311] This adds up; the alcoholism mandate adds 1-3% in added costs, general mental health adds 1-3% in costs, mental health parity adds 5-10% in costs, and contraceptives add around 1-3% in costs.[312] Of course, if every mandate added such a large amount in costs, no one would be able to purchase health insurance, and luckily most mandates increase costs by less than 1%. However, even a small cost increase of 1% translates into a lack of affordability for some people – between 22,222 and 33,333 according to one estimate.[313]

The states that add the most mandates show the largest increases in their uninsured population. Even as early as the 1990's, when hundreds less mandates existed, this trend held true. The Heritage Foundation tracked the progress of the 16 states which attempted to implement the policies of the failed Clinton healthcare reform plan and in doing so passed the most

---

[309] Seiler, John. "Mandated Health-Care Socialism." *The Freeman*, Sept. 2007. <http://www.thefreemanonline.org/featured/mandated-health-care-socialism/>.

[310] Bunch, Victoria C. "Health Insurance Mandates in the States 2010." *Council for Affordable Health Insurance*, 2010. <http://www.cahi.org/cahi_contents/resources/pdf/MandatesintheStates2010.pdf>.

[311] Seiler, "Mandated Health Care Socialism."

[312] Ibid.

[313] Ibid.

aggressive mandates between 1990 and 1994. The results weren't pretty. In 1996, the 16 most regulated states saw their average uninsured population increase by 8.14%, while the other 34 states showed a drop in their uninsured population of 1.02%.[314]

Insurance Regulation

If private insurance companies could truly compete with one another, premium prices would decline dramatically. Imagine two towns next to each other, each containing multiple pizza stores. If the average price of a slice cost $2 in one of the towns and $10 in the other, it is obvious that everyone would purchase pizza from a store in the cheaper town. If it were made illegal to cross towns to purchase pizza, however, the town charging $10 would never have to change their price, and could even increase it if they wanted too. A similar scenario occurs among private insurance companies, but on the national level, and with much larger amounts of money involved.

Regulation of health insurance is felt by consumers in the form of increased premiums. Highly regulated states like New Jersey have premiums seven times higher than in Tennessee. States like Wisconsin have average family premiums of $3,000, while in Massachusetts the average cost is $17,000.[315] Yet people cannot buy health insurance across state lines.

If competition was allowed, it would be impossible for companies to charge as much in premiums – assuming they want to stay in business. Why pay $17,000 when you can pay $3000 instead? Of course, it would only be possible for states like New Jersey and Massachusetts to begin to compete if their state-level regulations were eased. Some of these regulations force the insured to insure themselves against certain things they don't

---

[314] Schriver, Melinda L., and Grace-Marie Arnett. "Uninsured Rates Rise Dramatically in States With Strictest Health Insurance Regulations." *The Heritage Foundation*, 11 Aug. 1998. <http://www.galen.org/fileuploads/THF_Uninsured.pdf>.
[315] Ibid., p. 264.

necessarily need – which would be akin to wanting to purchase insurance on a house but being forced to also purchase insurance on your non-home property as well, which would increase your premium above what it would have been had you only bought home insurance.

In addition to anti-competitive measures at the state level, other insurance regulations limit the gap between what different age groups can be charged for care. This may seem like good policy; in this way, older and less healthy individuals aren't charged too high a premium. But for this to work, costs are then pushed back on younger holders of insurance. Since these younger individuals are much less likely to have health problems, they can drop their health insurance policy without much worry.

The way insurance companies balance costs and turn a profit is through the process of cost averaging. In the US, the oldest users of private health insurance (under 65, when Medicare begins to be used), spent six times more on health care than the youngest users of health care. Community ratings are put in place to prevent the oldest from paying six times as much. ObamaCare uses a 3:1 community rating, simply meaning that the oldest users can't be charged premiums three times higher than the youngest users. This lowers the cost for older users, but only at the expense of younger users. As a result, many of the younger insured drop their coverage since they hardly use any medical care anyway, but this withdrawal from the insurance pool then increases the premiums of everyone else who remains in.[316]

Recently, one state acted against the general trend towards more regulation and as expected saw overall health insurance costs decline . Maine's deregulation focused only on reducing the gap between what different age groups could be charge. The gap in pricing of premiums could only be 1.5 to 1

---

[316] Roy, Avik. "Putting the 'Insurance' Back in Health Insurance." *Forbes*, 21 May 2012. <http://www.forbes.com/sites/aroy/2012/05/21/putting-the-insurance-back-in-health-insurance/>.

under prior regulations, but deregulation expanded this figure, reworking the ratio to a 3 to 1 gap. As the *Wall Street Journal* details:

> According to the Maine Bureau of Insurance, a married couple age 40 to 44 with one child will pay $1,919 a month for a policy with a $2,250 deductible in 2013 if they choose to re-up their current policy. If the same family switches to the new health plan, or buys the plan for the first time, their premium will fall to $920, a 52% decrease. A couple over 60 could buy the same policy for $1,290, down from $2,466 under the old system. Or a young adult 25 to 29 could buy a high $10,000 deductible plan for catastrophic expenses for $232, previously $665.[317]

The 52% decline in premium costs is an extreme example, but the article explained that most showed declines in the range of 10-20%, while some older customers did have increases in costs.[318]

Hospital Restrictions

In 1964, New York became the first state to pass a "Certificate of Need," or CON law. If someone were to propose building a new hospital, the state's government would determine whether or not there was sufficient need. Then President Richard Nixon passed CON laws nationwide in 1972, believing that reducing the supply of hospitals would reduce health care costs. As basic economics tells us, limiting supply has the exact opposite effect on cost.

---

[317] "ObamaCare in Reverse." *The Wall Street Journal*, 30 May 2012. <http://online.wsj.com/article/SB10001424052702304707604577426162012576398.html>.

[318] Ibid.

Since 1972, 14 states have repealed their CON laws, and for good reason. Numerous studies over the years have shown that CON laws have done nothing to reduce costs. In 1988, the Bureau of Economics Federal Trade Commission found that relaxing CON laws would cause total hospital expenditures to decline by 1.4%.[319] A 1991 study of 1,957 hospitals found that costs were higher in CON states.[320] Other miscellaneous studies show that CON laws have little or no effect on increasing costs, but do nothing to contain them.[321] Since we do not live in a world with too many hospitals and not enough patients, full repeal of CON laws would be a step in the right direction.

Malpractice Reform

Like CON laws, medical malpractice insurance accounts for a tiny sliver of our current health care costs. The CBO estimated in 2004 that malpractice insurance premiums totaled only 2% of all health care costs.[322] The way malpractice insurance increases costs comes from the expense itself as well as doctors performing "defensive medicine" when they perform additional unnecessary procedures "just in case" to avoid getting sued. While malpractice reform isn't necessary for the sake of keeping costs down, it can help prevent states from losing doctors.

On the other hand, one estimate shows that around 10% of the money you pay to a doctor goes towards their malpractice

---

[319] Sherman, Daniel. "The Effect of State Certificate-of-Need Laws on Hospital Costs: An Economic Policy Analysis." *Staff Bureau of Economics Federal Trade Commission*, Jan. 1988. <http://www.ftc.gov/be/econrpt/232120.pdf>.

[320] Bosse, Grant D. "Do Certificate of Need Laws Reduce Costs or Hurt Patients?" *The Josiah Bartlett Center for Public Policy*, Feb. 2012. <http://www.scribd.com/doc/81538887/Irrational-Do-Certificate-of-Need-Laws-reduce-costs-or-hurt-patients>.

[321] Ibid.

[322] "Limiting Tort Liability for Medical Malpractice." *Congressional Budget Office*, 8 Jan. 2004. <http://www.cbo.gov/ftpdocs/49xx/doc4968/01-08-MedicalMalpractice.pdf>.

insurance just in case you decide to sue them.[323] In 2003, Texas has placed a cap on the amount that can be rewarded from a medical malpractice lawsuit in order to solve these problems. Caps were placed limiting the amount one could be rewarded from a lawsuit to $250,000 ($750,000 in rare cases) for pain and suffering (known as non-economic damages), and up to $1.6 million in cases of death.

Many other states have limits on medical malpractice awards, but Texas' limits are more than twice as strict as those of other states. Indiana, Nebraska, and Virginia for instance have their non-economic damages in the millions.[324] Doctors in Texas have seen their malpractice premiums fall over 20% as a result of the cap.[325] This has been appealing to both aspiring doctors and current doctors in other states. The Texas Medical board licensed 10,878 new physicians during the 2003-2007 period, an increase from 8,391 in the four years prior,[326] while over 7000 doctors migrated to Texas.[327] Doctors cited their reasons for migrating as lower insurance premiums, faster profit growth due to lower regulations, and various other perks such as Texas not having an income tax and low costs of living.[328] The costs of medical malpractice aren't an uncommon motive for doctor migration –

---

[323] Furchtgott-Roth, Diana. "Reduce the High Cost of Medical Malpractice." *Reuters*, 6 Aug. 2009. <http://blogs.reuters.com/great-debate/2009/08/06/reduce-the-high-cost-of-medical-malpractice/>.

[324] Hyman, David. "Damage Caps and Medical Malpractice Litigation." *The Volokh Conspiracy*, 2 Dec. 2008. <http://volokh.com/posts/1228240927.shtml>.

[325] Goldstein, Jacob. "After Texas Caps Malpractice, Docs Move In." *The Wall Street Journal*, 5 Oct. 2007. <http://blogs.wsj.com/health/2007/10/05/after-texas-caps-malpractice-docs-move-in/>.

[326] Blumenthal, Ralph. "More Doctors in Texas After Malpractice Caps." *The New York Times*, 5 Oct. 2007. <http://www.nytimes.com/2007/10/05/us/05doctors.html?pagewanted=all>.

[327] Furchgott-Roth. "Reduce the High Cost of Medical Malpractice."

[328] Donnelly, Jon. "Malpractice Curbs Hailed, Faulted." *The Boston Globe*, 26 Nov. 2007. <http://www.boston.com/news/nation/articles/2007/11/26/malpractice_curbs_hailed_faulted/>.

as Pennsylvania lost one third of its surgeons from 1995 to 2002.[329]

Detaching Health Insurance from Work

The relationship between health insurance and work was initiated during World War II when wage controls were passed limiting peoples income. Business still needed a way to attract new employees, and as a way to evade these controls benefits were given to employees instead of additional income.

Health insurance's attachment to work is another competition preventing mechanism, as it limits choice in health insurance. This could even be considered an unintentional additional level of health insurance regulation.

A Libertarian himself, Whole Foods founder John Mackay replaced insurance for his employees with Health Savings Accounts (HSA) to get around this problem. A vote was taken among employees about implementing it, and 87% voted in favor. Under their HSA system, Whole Foods pays 100% of the premiums for all their members who work 30+ hours each week (89% of their employees), and deposits $1800 each year in health care dollars into an employee's Personal Wellness Account. Money not spent remains in the account and compounds over time.[330]

HSAs are growing in popularity. By January 2007, 4.5 million Americans were enrolled in an HSA – enrollment doubling between 2005 and 2006 and increasing another 50% between 2006-2007.[331] By 2011, over 11 million have been

[329] Sowell, "Applied Economics," p. 69.

[330] Mackey, John. "The Wholefoods Alternative to Obamacare." *The Wall Street Journal*, 11 Aug. 2009. <http://online.wsj.com/article/SB10001424052970204251404574342170072865070.html>.

[331] Stout, Mary Katherine. "Facts and Health Savings Accounts." *Texas Public Policy Foundation*, May 2007. <http://www.texaspolicy.com/pdf/2007-05-PB25-HSAfacts-mks.pdf>.

enrolled.[332] Since HSAs are not available to those eligible for Medicare, all enrollment in such programs is composed of people under the age of 65. Forty six percent of those enrolled are aged 40 or above, while the other 54 percent is split between the two age groups 0-19 and 20-39.[333] On average, 55% of enrollees don't take any money out of their account for medical expenses, while of those who do take out money, 90% goes towards medical expenses.[334]

Such data has led some to argue that HSAs lead people to avoid care to save money, but a United Health Group study which surveyed 50,000 people shows otherwise. They found that among those with a consumer driven healthcare plan (CDHP), there were 22% less hospital admissions and 14% emergency room visits annually, and preventive care increased 5%.[335]

Speaking of costs regarding CDHP's, a writer for Americans for Tax Reform comments that:

> In conjunction with high-deductible insurance plans, many people end up paying premiums up to one-third lower than a regular insurance option. Often, an employer will pay enough to cover the deductible into the

---

[332] Paul, James. "HSAs Increasingly Popular Despite Attacks from Obamacare." *American's for Tax Reform*, 20 June 2011. <http://www.atr.org/hsas-increasingly-popular-despite-attacks-obamacare-a6262>.

[333] Stout, "Facts and Health Savings Accounts."

[334] Dicken, John E. "Health Savings Accounts: Early Enrollee Experiences with Accounts and Eligible Health Plan." *United States Government Accountability Office*, 26 Sept. 2006. <http://www.gao.gov/new.items/d061133t.pdf>.

[335] "Three-Year Study Shows Consumer-Driven Health Plans Continue to Stimulate Positive Changes in Consumer Health Behavior." *United Health Group*, 12 July 2006. <http://www.businesswire.com/news/home/20060712005494/en/Three-Year-Study-Shows-Consumer-Driven-Health-Plans-Continue>.

> HSA, and additionally cover the high-deductible premium.[336]

HSAs are a cheaper alternative. While the average Blue Cross of California plan cost a family $8,460 annually, in addition to a $500 deductible per member, an HSA with similar coverage cost $3,936 annually with a $2,500 deductible.[337] The type of care HSAs take care of is routine medical care, for which I see no role for insurance.

Another problem of employer-based health insurance that is seldom mentioned is that it contributes to the oft-cited problem of "preexisting conditions," which many see government as the only solution too. As Thomas Sowell notes, "If individuals bought their own health insurance, with the same tax advantages, the fact that an illness occurred after they changed employers would not make it a 'pre-existing condition.'"[338]

Since in the case of employer based coverage, someone with a pre-existing condition can only be barred from obtaining insurance if they have had less than a year of prior coverage, this would at least cut down on the problem of pre-existing conditions. The use of "catastrophic insurance" to pay for expensive medical care will be discussed later in this chapter. As will be pointed out, catastrophic insurance will be so cheap that, the only people who may be unable to pay for it would be the poor – who would then be eligible for Medicaid, which would also take away the sting of a pre-existing condition.

---

[336] Pacini, Benjamin. "Health Savings Account (HSA's): Best Policy Solution Killed by Obamacare." *American's for Tax Reform*, 29 Oct. 2009. <http://www.atr.org/health-savings-accounts-hsas-br-best-a4118>.
[337] Gratzer, "The Cure," p. 97.
[338] Sowell, Thomas. "Risky Business." *Townhall*, 28 Aug. 2012. <http://townhall.com/columnists/thomassowell/2012/08/28/risky_business>.

Medicaid Reform

Clearly, there needs to be a safety net for the poor in any free market society, but this isn't to say that the current Medicaid system is desirable.

Medicaid's problem as a safety net comes from the fact that it inadequately allocates funds to the poorest. Incentives provided by the federal government encourage states to expand their Medicaid programs in a way that creates this misallocation. For every dollar that a state expands their Medicaid program by, the federal government will reimburse between 50-83% of the cost, depending on the state. The problem is that richer states tend to get larger reimbursements. In 2007, the five richest states averaged $5,405 in Medicaid spending per person, while the five poorest states averaged only $3,547.[339]

To avoid this problem, the Cato Institute's "Downsizing the Federal Government" project proposes block granting the system, where each state is given a fixed amount of money and can distribute it however they like. Cato also looked into the effects of block granting "acute care," which includes hospital care, doctor visits, and drug costs and altogether accounts for two-thirds of overall Medicaid Spending. Had block grants been implemented at the time of their analysis (2010), they would have saved $625 billion from 2010-2019.[340]

Catastrophic Care

My contention that health insurance shouldn't cover routine medical checkups should be no less controversial than my belief that car insurance shouldn't cover my gas and oil changes, or that home insurance shouldn't pay for a maid. No one would dispute the fact that the cost of car and home insurance would

---

[339] Edwards, Chris. "Medicaid Reforms." *Downsizing the Federal Government*, Sept. 2010. <http://www.downsizinggovernment.org/hhs/medicaid-reforms>.
[340] Ibid.

increase under those circumstances. The proper role of health insurance is for individuals to pool their resources together in case tragedy strikes. A doctor's visit doesn't fit this category – so it makes no sense for it to be covered by health insurance.

As will be seen later in this chapter, market-oriented health care (in addition to HSAs) does make prices cheaper. But if a surgery costs hundreds of thousands of dollars, what difference will it make if the cost comes down ten or twenty percent? For the average America, this means bankruptcy either way. The answer to this problem is to replace modern health insurance with catastrophic health insurance. Current catastrophic plans run around $3,000 yearly for a family of four.[341]

One role of the government in a catastrophic insurance based system would be to subsidize the poor by giving them vouchers to purchase catastrophic insurance themselves. A $220 billion tax subsidy is already granted towards the purchase of employer-provided health insurance, so it wouldn't be unreasonable to extend this to catastrophic insurance as well.[342]

Where Free Markets Can Be Found

In a *New York Times* article discussing health care in a free market, after acknowledging that there are plenty of viable systems other than single payer, Paul Krugman notes that "there are, however, no examples of successful health care based on the principles of the free market, for one simple reason: in health care, the free market just doesn't work."[343] Quite the contrary, in

---

[341] "Most Could Afford Catastrophic Health Coverage." *U.S. News*, 13 Dec. 2006. <http://www.usnews.com/opinion/blogs/erbe/2006/12/13/most-could-afford-catastrophic-health-coverage>.

[342] Feldstein, Martin. "A Better Way to Health Reform." *American Enterprise Institute*, 8 Oct. 2009. <http://www.aei.org/article/health/healthcare-reform/a-better-way-to-health-reform/>.

[343] Krugman, Paul. "Why Markets Can't Cure Healthcare." *The New York Times*, 25 July 2009. <http://krugman.blogs.nytimes.com/2009/07/25/why-markets-cant-cure-healthcare/>.

fact. Are there any successful examples of free market health care? Plenty, actually.

Lasik

One such example of free market health care is LASIK eye surgery, which is not covered by most health insurance plans. During the period of 1999-2004, the price of the LASIK procedure per eye dropped from $2,106 to $1,796 without adjusting to inflation. This translates to a drop to $1,626 in 2004 when adjusted for inflation in 1999 dollars, and $1,451 when adjusted for medical inflation.[344] By 2010, the average cost had "increased" to $2,170 per eye[345]- or $1,657.93 in 1999 dollars.[346] The unique thing about LASIK's drop in price is that it decreased during a period of heightened demand for the service.

Cosmetics

Overall, cosmetic surgery has showed a trend similar to LASIK, seeing their inflation-adjusted prices decline every single year from 1992-2001.[347] The decline has been so steep that during the 1992-2001 period, general inflation of all goods outpaced that of cosmetic surgery.

Cosmetic laser procedures to reduce the appearance of one's age has shown in increase in popularity. In the three years prior to 2009, such surgery showed large growth; an increase of 456% in males and 215% in females getting this surgery was

---

[344] Cannon, "Healthy Competition," p.7.

[345] Segre, Liz. "Cost of LASIK Eye Surgery and Other Corrective Procedures." *All About Vision*. <http://www.allaboutvision.com/visionsurgery/cost.htm>.

[346] Calculated using CPI Inflation Calculator: <http://data.bls.gov/cgi-bin/cpicalc.pl>.

[347] Ibid.

seen.[348] Back in 2003, before this surge, the average price was $2,317.[349] By 2010, the average price dropped to $2,232,[350] not adjusted for inflation. This amounts to a drop of $513 when adjusted for inflation.[351]

Pet Care

Veterinary care, while still regulated by the government, receives no subsidies from it.[352] Insurance for veterinary care receives even less regulation, and still receives no subsidies from the government. Lessons can be learned from veterinary care in terms of both the way it operates in practice and the way its insurance system works.

Health insurance for pets is, as one doctor explains, "a form of property and casualty insurance." Insurance for pets is rapidly growing, but still has large room for growth, as only around 1-5% of animals are insured.[353]

The number of insurance providers fosters more competition among these providers. In New Jersey for example, while only three companies offer health insurance for humans,

---

348 Massier, Sarah. "Record Number of Patients Seek Laser Treatments to Take Lightyears off Their Faces." *American Academy of Cosmetic Surgery*, 24 Mar. 2009. <http://www.eurekalert.org/pub_releases/2009-03/aaoc-rno032409.php>.

349 "Cost of Laser Skin Resurfacing." *A Board Satisfied Plastic Surgeon.* <http://www.aboardcertifiedplasticsurgeonresource.com/laser_skin_resurfacing/costs.html>.

350 "Cost: Surgeon Fees per Procedure." *The American Society for Aesthetic Plastic Surgery.* <http://www.surgery.org/consumers/consumer-resources/frequently-asked-questions/cost-surgeon-fees-per-procedure>.

351 $2,317 in 2003 had the same purchasing power as did $2,745 did in 2010. Subtracting the 2010 average procedure cost of $2,232 from $2,745 yields a decline of $513. Calculated using: CPI Inflation Calculator.

352 The "subsidy" I'm referring too in contrast with private insurance is tax incentives given for employer sponsored health insurance.

353 Bailin, Deborah. "Research and Commentary: Pet Insurance as a Policy Model." *The Heartland Institute*, 8 May 2012. <http://heartland.org/policy-documents/research-and-commentary-pet-insurance-policy-model>.

there are more than ten for pets.[354] For total coverage, pet insurance costs under $100 a month for total coverage, with only a $100 annual deductible and 10% co-pay.[355] A year's worth of insurance for a healthy animal simply receiving wellness care will only cost between $200 and $300 annually.[356]

Additionally, it's much easier to open up an animal hospital than a human hospital, as animal hospitals aren't affected by CON laws, which were discussed earlier as a barrier to entry. Ted Balaker of *Reason* reports, "It took one veterinarian 12 weeks to start his clinic, but would have taken him 20 times longer had his clinic been for human care."[357]

Medical Tourism

There are two different kinds of medical tourism that people are familiar with. The first kind is more well known by defenders of the American health care system; each year, tens of thousands of people come from other countries to get care in the US. Among these are leaders of foreign nations. An estimated 60,000-85,000 visit the US every year for the purposes of getting care in our system.. The second kind of medical tourism, more well known by critics of the system, is that of the increasing

---

354 Lehrer, Eli. "A Health Insurance System That Works." *The Weekly Standard*, 7 May 2012. <http://www.weeklystandard.com/articles/health-insurance-system-works_642193.html?nopager=1>.

355 Suede, Michael. "America Should Model Its Health Care Market After Pet Care." *Policymic*, May 2012. <http://www.policymic.com/articles/8230/america-should-model-its-health-care-market-after-pet-care>.

356 Bailin, "Research and Commentary: Pet Insurance as a Policy Model."

357 Balaker, Ted. "Reason.tv: Treat Me Like a Dog—What Human Health Care Can Learn from Pet Care." *Reason*, 25 Feb. 2010. <http://reason.com/blog/2010/02/25/reasontv-treat-me-like-a-dogmd>.

numbers of Americans getting care overseas to save money. An estimated 600,000 Americans did this in 2012 alone.[358]

Medical tourists are not taking advantage of socialized medicine, because medical tourists predominantly visit private (non socialized) hospitals, so this would not lend credence to the supposed superiority of other opposing systems. The incentives to travel abroad are purely monetary: prices for treatment range from one-half to one-fifth of the price for comparable treatment in the US. Some of the reasons cited for cheaper costs are undesirable, such as how the doctors, nurses, janitors, and orderlies working in those hospitals make much less money than they would otherwise make had they worked in the US. On the other hand, in countries that attract lots of medical tourism, a large percentage of health care is paid out of pocket, there are few regulations, malpractice liability is limited, and prices are easy to negotiate.[359]

Medical Cash Discounts

A telling fact about the deviation between how the price system operates in a free market and how it operates in one influenced by insurance is best seen in the case of medical cash discounts. This is similar to how some gas stations will charge less for people paying with cash than with credit or debit, except to a much larger extent, and to avoid a much larger hassle. As David Belk, a doctor who runs the website "The True Cost of Healthcare" explains, in the process of billing, hospitals will usually bill an insurance company some multiple of what a procedure actually costs, because the insurance company will

---

[358] Akitunde, Anthonia. "Medical Tourism: Why More Boomers Are Going Abroad For Treatment." *The Huffington Post*, 4 June 2012. <http://www.huffingtonpost.com/2012/06/04/medical-tourism-health-tourism-medical-travel_n_1551217.html>.

[359] Herrick, Devon M. "Medical Tourism: Global Competition in Health Care." *National Center for Policy Analysis*, 1 Nov. 2007. <http://www.ncpa.org/pub/st304>.

always try to pay a smaller amount.[360] This is similar to how lawyers will over sue, knowing that while they'll settle for a smaller amount, they at least started high and ended near their desired target.

Paying in cash removes the influence of insurance from the equation. The size of most cash discounts shows just the extent to which prices are inflated. St. Josephs Heritage Medical Group advertises on their website that they offer a 30% discount on transactions over $72 that is paid for in cash, credit, or check. They also give discounts ranging from 30% up to 60% on laboratory tests.[361]

Even larger discounts can be found at other hospitals. As the *L.A. Times* reports, while insurance would negotiate a person's contribution towards a CT scan as $2,400, the cash price would be $250. While the insurance negotiated price at six other hospitals cited in the article is the same, the cash price for the procedure is under $1,000 in all hospitals except one.[362]

Free Market Care in Oklahoma

Something interesting happens to the third-party payer problem when you put Libertarians in charge of running a hospital. ReasonTV reports on an uncommon practice of the Surgery Center of Oklahoma: they post their prices online.[363] The bill for one woman receiving carpal tunnel release surgery at this hospital was a mere $2,750, so low that her employer covered the

---

[360] Belk, David. "Hospital Billing." *The True Cost of Health Care*, <http://truecostofhealthcare.org/hospital_billing>.

[361] "Cash Discount." *St. Joseph Heritage Medical Group*. <http://www.sjhmg.org/About-Us/Urgent-Care/Cash-Discount.aspx>.

[362] Terhune, Chad. "Many Hospitals, Doctors Offer Cash Discount for Medical Bills." *Los Angeles Times*, 12 May 2012. <http://articles.latimes.com/2012/may/27/business/la-fi-medical-prices-20120527>.

[363] Epstein, Jim. "Oklahoma Doctors vs. Obamacare." *Reason*, 15 Nov. 2012. <http://reason.com/reasontv/2012/11/15/the-obamacare-revolt-oklahoma-doctors-fi>.

cost. By contrast, a nearby hospital charged $7,452 for the very same procedure.[364]

Jason Sigmon, an Otolaryngologist at the Surgery Center, also provides services at Integris health, Oklahoma's largest health care provider. The effect of low prices on the Surgery Center forces them to be more efficient. Because of this, he's able to treat twice as many patients per day at the Surgery Center than at Integris. The surgery center is also able to keep prices low by cutting out administrative costs, instead making human resources and building maintenance the responsibility of the head nurse, rather than of "administrators in three or four thousand dollar suits running around," as one doctor put it.[365]

Care for the Elderly

Since Lyndon B. Johnson launched his War on Poverty in the 1960s, the government has played a major role in providing health care for the elderly. Since the rising costs of health care affects spending on Medicare and therefore increases our nation's deficit, attacking this problem by reforming Medicare is a necessity for both health and budgetary reasons.

Basic Structural Problems of Medicare

It has been argued that Medicare has played a large role itself in the inflation of health care costs, but to eliminate the system overnight would throw senior citizens under the bus. Not only that, it would be politically impossible to get rid of the system.

While working under the assumption that Medicare serves a purpose, there are major structural flaws in the system that need to be remedied in order to sustain it.

---

[364] Ibid.
[365] Ibid.

When the program was originally created there were four workers supporting each Medicare recipient, and now there are 3.4. By 2030, when the rest of the baby boomers retire, only 2.3 workers will be supporting each recipient.[366] To give more perspective on the unsustainability of the status quo, if both spouses in a household worked their entire lives earning the average wage and retired in 2011, they would have paid $114,000 in Medicare taxes, but would receive $355,000 in benefits.[367]

Another problem with the system is fraud. It is questionable how much effort is put into preventing fraud, as only 3 percent of claims are reviewed before they are paid for by Medicare.[368] Rep. Cliff Sterns, who held a congressional hearing regarding this, described the system as a "pay and chase model."[369] The Government Accountability Office released a 2011 report estimating around $48 billion in "improper payments" each year, but this is likely to be underestimated. The same year the executive director of the National Health Care Fraud Association placed the number at around $75-250 billion annually.[370] With the Medicare budget topping $500 billion in 2010,[371] the fraud rate is 10 percent at minimum. While no improvement has been seen in reducing Medicare fraud, fraud in certain private sector industries has been reduced. For example, online merchants lost 3.6 percent of their sales to stolen and

---

366 Avik. "Saving Medicare from Itself," p. 35.

367 De Rugy, Veronique. "Medicare and Social Security: What You Pay In vs. What You Will Get (Maybe)." *National Review Online*, 3 Jan. 2011. <http://www.nationalreview.com/corner/256212/medicare-and-social-security-what-you-pay-vs-what-you-will-get-maybe-veronique-de-rugy>.

368 Suderman, Peter. "Medicare Thieves." *Reason Magazine*, October 2011. P. 39

369 Ibid.

370 Ibid., p. 35.

371 "Fiscal Year 2010 Budget in Brief Medicare." *U.S. Department of Health and Human Services*. <http://dhhs.gov/asfr/ob/docbudget/2010budgetinbriefl.html>.

fraudulent credit cards in 2000, but only 1.4% in 2007 despite internet sales increasing 20% each year from 2000.[372]

Similar to the problem of fraud, wasteful spending has unnecessarily bloated Medicare's budget. Somewhere around 30 percent of all Medicare spending is on unnecessary treatments that don't provide any contributions to health or happiness. [373] Likewise, 40 percent of Medicare dollars spent on cancer screenings are unnecessary.[374]

The Difficulty of Basic Reform

As has been done for Social Security, increasing the age one must wait to utilize Medicare's services would save money. This seems to be the only thing in the government's power that can be done to further Medicare's sustainability, aside from raising taxes. We know that problems caused by government are seldom solved by government.

There are now 0.7 less workers supporting each retiree than when the program was created, so raising the age requirement to receive benefits appears to be common sense. The savings from this would be marginal however, since the majority of Medicare's money goes towards care near the end of life. If the age were raised to 67, it has been calculated that this would only amount to a savings of $14.8 billion a year.[375] But even this is being generous, since it is estimated that it would consume $9 billion in Medicaid dollars as seniors swap use of one

---

[372] Meacham, Jennifer D. "Credit Card Fraud: How Big Is the Problem?" *Practical Commerce*, 23 Apr. 2008. <http://www.practicalecommerce.com/articles/720-Credit-Card-Fraud-How-Big-Is-The-Problem->.

[373] Cannon, Michael F., and Chris Edwards. "Medicare Reforms." *The Cato Institute*, Sept. 2010. <http://www.cato.org/pubs/handbook/hb111/hb111-12.pdf>.

[374] Sharpe, Rochelle, and Elizabeth Lucas. "Forty Percent of Medicare Spending on Common Cancer Screenings Unnecessary, Probe Suggests." *The Center for Public Integrity*, 7 Oct. 2011. <http://www.iwatchnews.org/2011/10/06/6898/forty-percent-medicare-spending-common-cancer-screenings-unnecessary-probe-suggests>.

[375] Fiegl, Charles. "CBO: Raising Medicare Age to 67 Would save $148 Billion over Decade." *American Medical News*, 23 Jan. 2012. <http://www.amaassn.org/amednews/2012/01/23/gvsa0123.htm>.

government program for another[376] – leaving us with enough savings to fund the federal government for an additional 12 hours!

Cracking down on fraud is something that the government has little control over. While reducing fraud is a noble goal, it's hardly cost efficient. A $77 million computer system developed by the government and rolled out in the summer of 2011 promised to crack down on Medicare fraud. By Christmas, only $7,591 in fraud actually ended up being prevented.[377] Programs that do catch fraud (without operating at a loss) fail to prevent an adequate amount of fraud. Another government anti-fraud program that changed the way medical equipment was paid for managed to save the taxpayers $202 million – but that's only 0.4% of the $47.8 billion made in fraudulent payments that year.[378]

The problems of Medicare are, in summation, similar to those of Social Security in terms of sustainability, similar to those of any socialist product in terms of quality, and similar to any bureaucracy in terms of waste. Some problems can be corrected by government, others have to be tolerated, and the rest have to be dealt with by the free market.

The Case for Vouchers?

Medicare vouchers were the central proposal of Paul Ryan in the 2012 election. Under a voucher system, senior citizens would be given a set amount of money that they can use

---

[376] "Should the Eligibility Age for Medicare Be Raised?" *The Wall Street Journal*, Tuesday, September 18, 2012. P. B6.

[377] Kennedy, Kelli, and Ricardo Alonso-Zaldivar. "APNewsBreak: Anti-fraud Effort Disappoints." *The Associated Press*, 23 Feb. 2012. <http://www.utsandiego.com/news/2012/feb/23/apnewsbreak-anti-fraud-effort-disappoints/?ap>.

[378] Suderman, Peter. "Medicare Anti-Fraud Pilot Program Saves $200 Million. Only $47.8 Billion in Improper Payments to Go." *Reason*, 19 Apr. 2012. <http://reason.com/blog/2012/04/19/medicare-anti-fraud-pilot-program-saves>.

towards purchasing health insurance, and they can keep any money they do not spend for themselves. Proponents of Medicare vouchers advocate that these vouchers should be spent on medical insurance (as opposed to paying for care in case), but all this does is exacerbate the third-party payer problem. I can't imagine any insurance provider turning a profit by selling insurance to senior citizens either, unless they charged absurdly high premiums.

This chapter argues that the proper role of insurance is to protect against a catastrophe, and to this end a more practical voucher proposal would have funds doled out with the intent of being allocated towards catastrophic insurance, with the rest being used to pay for other types of medical care in cash.

This voucher would be adjusted relative to age, health risk, income and other factors. Redirecting incentives in this manner solves many problems, as seniors will simultaneously search for the cheapest care and not undergo unnecessary treatment. Moreover, since we've seen that medical care is much more expensive when third parties are taken out of the equation, these cheaper costs will only be solidified since hospitals will now need to compete for seniors seeking the best deal.

Since vouchers have become a common campaign topic, most analysis done on their effects are not on the effects of vouchers per se, but on the effects of vouchers under a Romney presidency. A good deal of the "analysis" is clouded by partisanship as well. David Cutler, a Harvard economist who helped design ObamaCare estimates that a voucher system would end up costing a 29 year old living today an extra $331,200 in retirement costs down the road, since Romney's vouchers wouldn't keep pace with health care spending increases.[379]

---

[379] Kavoussi, Bonnie. "Romney-Ryan Medicare Plan Would Cost 29-Year-Olds $331,200: Report." *The Huffington Post*, 27 Aug. 2012. <http://www.huffingtonpost.com/2012/08/27/mitt-romney-paul-ryan-health-care_n_1833187.html>.

Meanwhile in 2012, Cutler wrote of "removing the status of [traditional] Medicare, and instead "moving the Medicare population into the exchanges." In Cutler's own words, this "would be the same as the voucher."[380] If Cutler has proposed vouchers in the past, he's capable of knowing that they would help contain costs – something his analysis made sure to overlook. Keep in mind that this is just one example of how politics have clouded quality discussion on this issue.

Existing Free Market Models in Medicare

Choice and competition has even made its way into government-controlled medicine. Medicare Part D incorporates consumer choice and competition into its formula. After being introduced in 2003 and enacted in 2006 the plan gave seniors a set amount of money to spend on whichever health plan they wanted, but if the costs of the health plan exceeded the amount of money they were given, they would have to compensate for costs out of pocket. Unlike Medicare as a whole, Medicare Part D is voluntary. Part D was initially met with some criticism, mainly that no one would actually enroll in the program and that private insurance companies wouldn't participate in the program.

As one would expect, because of choice and competition prices haven't exploded as a result of Part D, but actually came in at 42% below predicted costs.[381] The average annual per capita spending on Part D drug benefits averaged 1.2% during 2006-2010, and declined during the 2006-2008 period.[382]

The lesson of Part D is that costs can be controlled even in a government program if market principles are included. We

---

[380] McCarthy, Meghan. "Mixed Message From Obama Advisers on Medicare." *National Journal*, 10 Sept. 2012. <http://www.nationaljournal.com/healthcare/mixed-obama-message-on-medicare--20120910>.
[381] Capretta, James. "Ezra Klein's F on Medicare Part D." *The Heritage Foundation*, 16 June 2011. <http://blog.heritage.org/2011/06/16/ezra-kleins-f-on-medicare-part-d/>.
[382] Cited in Ibid.

have seen from the case of medical cash discounts that cutting out insurance is a step in the right direction when it comes to cost containment. Replacing the current Medicare system with Medicare savings accounts is a viable proposal. Dividing up the 2011 Medicare budget equally to its enrollees would put $11,700 in each of their accounts.[383] Like HSAs, money not spent would compound over time, and another potential feature would be to allow the funds to be transferred into the accounts of other family members after death.

End of Life Care

As is to be expected from a deterioration of health as an individual ages, the majority of health care expenses occur later in a person's life. The end of life care that takes up an extremely disproportionate amount of health care costs is care in the last year, months, or weeks of life.

One quarter of Medicare spending per individual is on the recipient's last year of life, and 10% is spent on care in the last month.[384] A dilemma emerges because: (a) an enormous sum of Medicare funds are being wasted, and (b) this fact far from justifies rationing since the government has no way of knowing if a patient is in their last days of life. Governments also do a questionable job in prioritizing what kinds of care to ration. Under the NHS in the UK, drugs used to treat cancer and Alzheimer's disease are among some of the things rationed,[385] as are procedures including knee and hip operations.

Determining what types of procedures qualify as being in the "end of life" period is an impossible task. No doctor

---

[383] Cannon, Michael F. "A Medicare Reform Model Everyone Can Love." *The Cato Institute*, 11 July 2011. <http://www.cato.org/publications/commentary/medicare-reform-model-everyone-can-love>.

[384] McKeown, Karen. "Empowering Patients as Key Decision Makers in the Face of Rising Health Care Costs." *The Heritage Foundation*, 27 Dec. 2011. <http://www.heritage.org/research/reports/2011/12/empowering-patients-as-key-decision-makers>.

[385] Cited in Ibid.

performing a hip surgery on an elderly patient will know how many months or years he or she has left to live. A savings account oriented system can help improve this problem, but solving it entirely is impossible since no one has perfect knowledge of the future.

Personal savings accounts allow seniors who want to use their expenditures on expensive surgeries in the end of life to be able to do so, but seniors who choose not to will be choosing to make a tradeoff between a few months or years of shorter life expectancy and to be able to transfer more money to their loved ones after their death. As bleak as this may seem to some, it is a much more moral alternative than government rationing, which leaves the individual hopeless in the hands of the State. This plan would instead put people in control of their own decisions.

Summary and Conclusion

Since this chapter presents much more data and jumps from topic to topic much more so than the other chapters in this book, I feel that a summary is appropriate.

The alleged strengths of socialized medicine are largely based on bad statistics, as was the case for lifespan and infant mortality rates. When true measures of the success of a health care system are measured (such as cancer survival rates) we dominate European nations. Other measures, such as waiting times and the quality and frequency of medical technology also demonstrate conclusively that the US is ahead. While we don't rank first in doctors per capita, it has been shown that in other countries and Massachusetts, a switch to socialized medicine results in less doctors per capita.

The only clear strength that socialized medicine did show was in cost, but then again it is possible to keep costs under control without changing to such a system. Small changes, like the removal of CON laws and reforms to medical malpractice would contain costs only by a few percentage points, but the big driver of costs is the third party payer problem, which exists unless we pay for our treatment free from interference by government and other third parties such as insurance companies. As shown with medical cash discounts, paying in cash and thereby removing the third party of insurance allows many to receive cheaper care. Permitting people to put money into health savings accounts would enable them to pay for treatment with their own dollars rather than using insurance. In the case of a disaster or freak accident, a person would be covered by catastrophic insurance, which would be much cheaper than current insurance since it would only be for rare cases and would lack many of the mandates currently in place.

For the US health care system to function as a truly free market, reducing the burden of regulatory barriers such as the FDA as well as regulations on insurance is required to bring down the cost of drugs and services.

In the case of Medicare, free market reforms are possible, as evidenced by the results of Medicare part D. Personal savings accounts are one way of making Medicare more market oriented. Even if such reforms didn't reduce costs, if they could at least contain costs they would still be an improvement from the status quo.

Chapter 3

The Role of Government in a Free Economy

The curious task of economics is to demonstrate to men how little they really know about what they imagine the can design.

- F.A. Hayek, The Fatal Conceit, 1988.

As seems to be the case historically, tough economic times have renewed the debate over government's role in the economy. The sort of debate that is spurred as a result of economic problems can lead in many different directions owing to political ideology. The Great Depression led to the rise of Keynesian economics as the dominant economic policy for decades to come, but the stagflation of the Carter years also created openness to Reagan's philosophy of trickle-down. The debate from our most recent crisis beginning in 2007 and peaking in 2008-09 has turned our economic policy towards to left, with bailouts, monetary stimulus and Keynesian style fiscal stimulus spending offered as aid.

This chapter examines the proper role of government in creating both the freest and most economically healthy society possible. We begin with the steps needed to build the foundation for a healthy economy with a discussion of economic freedom, income inequality, education, and a lengthy treatise on tax policy. The chapter concludes with a blueprint for Social Security reform and a plan to balance the federal budget.

The Importance of Economic Freedom

The decline and fall of communism near the end of the 20th century is a testament to the fact that capitalism is the only viable economic system currently available. Advocates for big government still exist, however, but these people support a big government which regulates business practices rather than controlling them in their entirety. Likewise, very few people would conclude from the fall of communism that pure anarchy is the logical solution (though for some reason, most anarchists are leftists). While neither extreme (communism vs. anarchy) is viable, trends do show that the more economically free a nation is, the more prosperous it is.[386]

---

[386] For a wonderful read on the correlation between economic freedom and personal freedom, see Friedman's "Free to Choose" (cited liberally throughout this book).

The Economic Freedom Index

Every year since 1995, the Heritage Foundation has released a study on the economic freedom of the world.[387] A nation's ranking comes from how well it performs in four categories, which are "rule of law" (property rights, freedom from corruption), "limited government" (government spending, fiscal freedom), "regulatory efficiency" (business freedom, labor freedom, monetary freedom), and "open markets" (trade freedom, investment freedom, financial freedom).

At the top of list in 2012 is Hong Kong, with a score of 89.9 (100 being maximum freedom). Both Milton Friedman and John Stossel have visited Hong Kong to demonstrate the efficiency of their system. Stossel was able to start his own business in one day![388] Hong Kong is quite possibly one of the free market's greatest success stories; one where a once impoverished city has transformed into one where the average citizen now has more purchasing power than the average American.[389]

As one reaches the bottom of the Heritage Foundation's list, what is noticeable is the high frequency of third world nations. Peru ranks 42nd with a score of 68.7 points. This doesn't seem like such a bad score, but even "two thirds" of complete freedom yields dismal results. Hernando de Soto, the Peruvian economist known for his work on developmental economics, along with a team of researchers, chronicled their challenges of opening a one person clothing stall in Lima. While they originally vowed not to pay bribes, they did pay them on two out of the ten times they were asked for them, and for good reason.

---

[387] Accessible at <http://www.heritage.org/index/ranking>.
[388] For Friedman's visit, see the episode titled "The Power of the Market" in the TV series "Free to Choose" (titled after the book). For Stossel's, see the mini-documentary titled "Is America Number One?" on 20/20 (from 1999).
[389] In 2011 Hong Kong had purchasing power parity (PPP) of $49,387, while the United States had PPP of $48,387 according to the International Monetary Fund.

The team had to work 6-hour days for 42 weeks to obtain 11 different permits from seven government bodies just to open their business. The monetary costs of these actions were $1,231 – which is 31 times the monthly minimum wage in Peru.[390]

Effects on Major Economic Indicators

Another similar index of economic freedom is released by the Fraser Institute. The Fraser Institute's 2012 Economic Freedom of the World report provided a compelling analysis between the most and least free nations.[391] The Economic Freedom project has broken down the results into an easily accessible info graphic. The results show that economically free nations far exceed the least free in terms of per capita income overall, per capita income among the poorest nations, child labor, gender equality and respect for the environment.[392]

In terms of per capita GDP, the top 25% of free nations averaged $31,501, compared to $4,545 for the least free 25% of nations. Even among poor nations themselves, those poor nations with more economic freedom were richer than poor nations lacking that kind of freedom.

Many of those in the media will accuse anyone advocating less regulation to want to return to the old days where child labor was common. Child labor had nothing to do with economic freedom per se, but reflects the fact that the nation was poorer as a whole, and as a result child labor was required at that time in order for families to get by. Since more economic freedom leads to higher per capita GDP, child labor is reduced over time. As the data shows, 39.4% of young children work in

---

390 Wheelan, Charles J. "Naked Economics: Undressing the Dismal Science." (New York: W. W. Norton, 2010), p. 300.
391 The study in its entirety can be found at: <http://www.freetheworld.com/2012/EFW2012-complete.pdf>.
392 All sources for the following statistics in this section are individually sourced at: Katharine Ham, Mary. "Study: America Falls to 18th in Economic Freedom." *HotAir*, 25 Sept. 2012. <http://hotair.com/archives/2012/09/25/study-america-falls-to-18th-in-economic-freedom/>.

the 25 least free nations, compared to 5.5% in the more free. Even among poor nations, the least free have child labor rates of 40%, while the most free poor nations are slightly lower at 37%.

All of these comparisons work on a state-by-state level as well, though there are some distortions since Frasier's measurement looks at unemployment rates between 2000-2009. During that timeframe, the 25 most free states had unemployment rates of 4.9% compared to 5.5% in the 25 least free states. State and local debt was also lower in the 25 most free states, averaging 15.7% of GDP, compared to 16.2% of GDP in the least free.

In terms of gender equality, the more economically free a nation is, the smaller the gap is between the earnings of men and women. As will be demonstrated in chapter four, the current male/female wage gap in the US is non-existent when other variables are controlled for.

Respect for the environment is also stronger when economic freedom is realized, since private property provides a strong incentive for valuing the environment. The fifty most free nations have increasing forest growth rates, while the least free have declining rates. Air pollution in the 20 least free nations is nearly three times higher than in the 20 most free. CO2 emissions in relation to GDP are also around 5 times higher in the 20 least free nations than the 20 most free. Another potential reason for the disparity is that richer nations can afford to comply with environmental regulations and poorer nations aren't be able to do.

Economic Freedom and Income Inequality (Traditionally Measured)

It would seem completely rational to believe that more economic freedom will only help those at the top, but as we will later see, it is actually regulations that help those at the top while threatening those at the bottom wishing to compete.

A nation's level of income inequality is determined by what is known as the Gini Coefficient. A nation with a Gini coefficient of zero has no inequality, and a nation with a Gini of one has complete inequality. The Gini is calculated based on the gap between a nation's richest 20% and poorest 20% of earners. While it has become much more popular today to discuss the growing gap between the 1% and the 99%, the rallying cry of the Occupy Wall Street movement actually wasn't coined until rather recently after studies by economists Thomas Piketty and Emannuel Saez documented the growing income of the top 1%. Piketty and Saez's studies are critiqued and criticized in chapter 4.

Before taxes and income transfers are accounted for, the US had a Gini of 0.486, and a Gini of 0.378 after taxes and transfers.[393] The US has the fourth highest Gini after taxes and transfers are accounted for, but not much more than Australia (0.336), Israel (0.371) and the UK (0.345).[394]

The 50 most free nations average a Gini of .358, compared to .425 in the 50 least free nations.[395] Still, the US is quite unequal based on the Gini score compared to other European nations. The various causes of this gap are worth investigating individually.

---

[393]"Income Distribution - Inequality." *OECD StatExtracts*. <http://stats.oecd.org/Index.aspx?QueryId=26067&Lang=en>.
[394] Ibid.
[395] Mary Katharine Ham, "Study: America Falls to 18th in Economic Freedom."

Natural Inequality

A good deal of inequality is natural. In any society where people are free to pursue their own interests, there will always be inequalities. Some entrepreneurs will be more successful than others, and engineers will earn more than artists. Intelligence is one of the natural factors that effects income inequality. What social scientist Charles Murray defined as the "very bright" (90th+ IQ percentile) earned a median personal income of \$36,000 in 1993, compared to \$7,000 for the "very dull" (less than 10th IQ percentile).[396]

Income was not always this strongly correlated with intelligence. The charts provided in Murray's short book *Income Inequality and IQ* indicate that the gap between the intelligent and dull began to accelerate starting in the early 1980s,[397] presumably created by technological advancement.

When it comes to measuring wealth inequality rather than income inequality, the fact that some people have been alive longer than others is going to play a role. The longer someone lives, the more time they have to accumulate skills and save money, thereby adding to their net worth. While polling shows that Americans see the ideal wealth distribution as the top 20% controlling 32% of all wealth, we could expect and see a much more uneven distribution under communism. Even if all Americans earned identical incomes and saved at the same rates, the top 20% would still control more than 32% of the nation's wealth simply by the fact that they are older and had more time to save.[398]

---

[396] Murray, Charles A. "Income Inequality and IQ." (Washington, DC: AEI, 1998), p. 8.
[397] Ibid., p. 7.
[398] "A Consumption Tax Is a Wealth Tax." *The Money Illusion*, 10 Mar. 2013. <http://www.themoneyillusion.com/?p=19884>.

Again in regards to wealth inequality, even Sweden (whose trademark is their desired extreme level of income equality) has high levels of wealth inequality. Calculating the 1%'s share of income in Sweden isn't an exact science due to tax evasion, but one estimate shows them controlling anywhere between 25-40% of their nation's wealth, which is quite similar to the levels of wealth inequality in America.[399]

Family Trends

There is another important non-economic factor effecting income inequality: family. John Deparle of the *New York Times* estimates that the rise of 1-parent households may account for anywhere between 15% and 40% of the rise in inequality since 1970. When comparing increases in inequality among the top 10% and bottom 10% among the past 40 years, the rise is much greater in households with children. When comparing all households in this categories, inequality increased by 31% from 1970-2012, but 121% for houses with children.[400]

As a result, the number of workers per household in the bottom 20% is much less than in the top 20%. The bottom 20% has 0.48 workers per household, while the top 20% has 2.1 workers per household.[401] This clearly affects the distribution of income. In 2002 the top 20% earned 49.7% of all income, and the bottom 20% earned 3.5% of all income.[402] But if we adjust for the amount of workers per household, then the bottom 20%

[399] Sanandaji, Tino. "The Upper Class and Wealth Inequality in Sweden." 30 Apr. 2013. <http://super-economy.blogspot.com/2013/04/the-upper-class-and-wealth-inequality.html>.
[400] Deparle, Jason. "Economic Inequality and the Changing Family." *The New York Times*, 14 July 2012. <http://economix.blogs.nytimes.com/2012/07/14/economic-inequality-and-the-changing-family/>.
[401] Moore, Stephen. "Who's the Fairest of Them All?: The Truth about Opportunity, Taxes, and Wealth in America." (New York: Encounter, 2012), p. 37.
[402] Ibid., p. 38.

would earn 9.4% of all income, and the top 20% would earn 39.6% of all income.[403]

While we still rank high in the Gini score even after transfers and taxes, these factors do make a huge difference. As Thomas Sowell writes, "in 2001…cash and in-kind transfers together accounted for 77.8% of economic resources of people in the bottom 20 percent." [404] Another reason the top and bottom 20% are so separated economically is due to the sheer size of people in each household. There are six times as many people in households of the top 20% than in the bottom 20%, and over twice as many heads of household.[405]

The best way to reduce inequality, aside from excessive taxes and transfers, would be to enact policies which encourage the bottom 20% to work more than they currently do since there are already four times as many workers per household in the top 20%. For those in the top 20%, those who do work, work much longer. The portion of men working over 50 hours per week increased from 15% of the top 20% in 1970 to 27% in 2006, while the percent of men working over 50 hours in the bottom 20% decreased from 22% in 1979 to 13% in 2006.[406]

Inequality vs. Mobility

Another factor to consider, and in my opinion the most important, is that of income mobility. As discussed earlier in context of income growth throughout different administrations, when an income bracket is measured over time, there are different individuals in that bracket at different times. As Ronald Bailey writes for *Reason*:

---

[403] Ibid., p. 39.
[404] Sowell, Thomas. "Economic Facts and Fallacies." (New York, NY: Basic, 2011), p. 144.
[405] Ibid., p. 143
[406] Conard, Edward. "Unintended Consequences: Why Everything You've Been Told about the Economy Is Wrong." (New York: Portfolio/Penguin, 2012), p. 86.

> Before they reach the age of 60, 85 percent of Americans will experience economic insecurity at some point. On the other hand, nearly 77 percent of Americans will have lived in a household earning more than $100,000 for at least one year, and 21 percent will have enjoyed living in households earning $250,000 for at least one year.[407]

According to a study by the Treasury Department, about half of taxpayers who began in the bottom 20% in 1996 moved up to a higher group by 2005. Meanwhile, the majority of those at the very top dropped to lower income groups. Of individuals in the top 1/100th of the top 1%, only 25% of them remained in this income quintile during that period.[408]

Critics will argue that income mobility has been declining in recent years. In fact, mobility today is actually about the same as it was in 1970 – but there are better objections to my mobility argument.[409] For example, one effective criticism could be that American levels of mobility are lower relative to European nations. While this is true, there are plenty of explanations for this disparity that aren't an indictment of the American economic system.

First and foremost, the American middle class is much wealthier than the middle class of European nations. As John Stossel notes, while income mobility from the lowest fifth to the middle class is higher in Sweden than in the US, it only takes $12,500 in additional income to move from the lowest fifth to the

---

407 Bailey, Ronald. "You Have an 85 Percent Chance of Being Poor." *Reason*, 3 July 2012. <http://reason.com/archives/2012/07/03/85-percent-chance-of-rich-poor>.

408 "Income Mobility in the U.S. from 1996 to 2005." *United States Department of the Treasury*, 13 Nov. 2007. <http://www.treasury.gov/resource-center/tax-policy/Documents/incomemobilitystudy03-08revise.pdf>.

409 De Rugy, Veronique. "Scott Winship on Income Mobility: Good News Edition." *National Review Online*, 25 June 2012. <http://www.nationalreview.com/corner/303904/scott-winship-income-mobility-good-news-edition-veronique-de-rugy>.

middle class in Sweden, but over $22,000 in the US.[410] Additionally, different races have different levels of mobility. Income mobility of blacks for instance, is quite poor relative to whites. As the *Wall Street Journal* reported, the Brooking's Institute determined from tracking children born in the 80's and 90's that 68% of whites but only 34% of blacks make it to the middle class.[411]

Income mobility for immigrants tends to be generational rather than in decade-long periods like the Treasury Department measured. Since the US is a nation of immigrants, this negatively impacts the official income mobility statistics.[412] Likewise, race plays a role in mobility, so a country as diverse as the US will be affected by this.

Another reason for higher mobility in Europe is noted by George Mason University economist Tyler Cowen, known for his blog 'Marginal Revolution'. His explanation is somewhat more far-fetched, however. He hypothesizes that "while many Europeans will not be ambitious to enjoy public goods and avoid excessive taxation," "Some of the children of their families have comparable smarts but higher ambition and so they rise quite a bit in income relative to their peers."[413]

Once again, education is a major factor in determining mobility. Children of rich parents will be better off later in life

---

[410] Stossel, John. "More "Media Matters" Deceit." *FOX Business*, 26 May 2012. <http://www.foxbusiness.com/on-air/stossel/blog/2012/05/26/more-media-matters-deceit>.

[411] Wessel, David. "Race's Role in Economic Fate." *The Wall Street Journal*, Thursday, September 20, 2012. P. A6.

[412] Miller, Monta. "Immigrants Still Climbing America's Economic Ladder, But Trends Suggest Progress Is Slowing." *The Pew Charitable Trusts*, 25 July 2007. <http://www.pewtrusts.org/news_room_detail.aspx?id=26782>.

[413] Cowen, Tyler. "Why Economic Mobility Measures Are Overrated." *Marginal Revolution*, 18 Jan. 2012. <http://marginalrevolution.com/marginalrevolution/2012/01/why-economic-mobility-measures-are-overrated.html>.

due to access to better schools, while the opposite will occur with poor children. On the other hand, while children of upper class parents will make more money overall, a lower percentage of them will make more money than their parents did as compared to their lower quintile counterparts. According to the Pew Research Center, 93% of people raised in the bottom 20% will earn more than their parents at a similar time in their life, compared to 84% of children with parents in the top 20%.[414]

There's still some data to make the argument however, that an increase in inequality will actually reduce mobility, which would undermine my arguments presented here. Economics call the correlation between an increase in inequality with a decline in mobility the "Great Gatsby Curve," named after the novel. The correlation is undeniable, but the causation remains established. In fact, it's a study that Emmanuel Saez contributed to which found that "tax credits for the poor and higher taxes on the affluent seemed to improve income mobility only slightly," while "income mobility was also higher in areas with more two-parent households, better elementary schools and high schools, and more civic engagement, including membership in religious and community groups."[415]

Sample Size

Forbes Columnist Tim Worstall points to differences in population as a cause of higher inequality in the US relative to Europe. At the micro level, in the States we see that New York is the most unequal state, and Wyoming the most equal state. Worstall says the explanation for this is quite obvious: "the larger your data set the more variance you expect to have in your data

---

[414] Rohac, Dalibor. "The Mirage of Income Mobility." *The American Spectator*, 9 Aug. 2012. <http://spectator.org/archives/2012/08/09/the-mirage-of-income-mobility>.

[415] Cowen, Tyler. "Where Is Income Mobility High and Low?" *Marginal Revolution*, 22 July 2013. <http://marginalrevolution.com/marginalrevolution/2013/07/where-is-income-mobility-high-and-low.html>.

set." We would rather expect to have greater income inequality between the 20 million odd in NY State than we would in the 500,000 in Wyoming."[416] In fact, Wyoming is the least populated state, and New York the third most populated.[417]

To give an example on the macro level, take the most populated country, China. Statistically China has about the same income inequality as the US does, but that excludes an enormous sum of hidden wealth in China. According to one estimate, with hidden income included, the top 10% of households in China earn 65 times more than the poorest 10%, compared to a ratio of 23:1 reported in the official statistics.[418]

Income Inequality vs. Consumption Inequality

Finally, despite all the hype regarding the rise in income inequality, inequalities in consumption have barely changed. Since most studies of income inequality neglect to look at the purchasing power of the dollar to determine the real wealth of the poor, it underestimates their well-being. As the British magazine *The Economist* quoted from one study:

> The relative prices of low-quality products that are consumed disproportionately by low-income consumers have been falling over this period. This fact implies that measured against the prices of products that poorer consumers actually buy, their "real" incomes have been rising steadily. As a consequence, **we find that around half of the increase in conventional inequality measures during 1994–2005 is the result of using the**

[416] Worstall, Tim. "The Amazing Thing About American Inequality: How Equal The Country Is." *Forbes*, 22 Sept. 2012. <http://www.forbes.com/sites/timworstall/2012/09/22/the-amazing-thing-about-american-inequality-how-equal-the-country-is/>.

[417] "Resident Population Data." *United States Census*, 2010. <http://2010.census.gov/2010census/data/apportionment-pop-text.php>.

[418] Davis, Bob. "China Tries to Shut Rising Income Gap." *The Wall Street Journal*, Tuesday, December 22, 2012. P. A14.

same price index for non-durable goods across different income groups.[419]

The great fallacy perpetuated by many in discussing inequality is that it is assumed that wealth is like a pie, with some people taking more at the expense of others. Thomas Sowell likes to criticize this sort of thinking by saying that "wealth isn't distributed, it's earned." I would make a similar observation with a subtle difference: wealth isn't distributed, it's created. Indeed, one particular argument against inequality inadvertently proves this point. A columnist for *The Atlantic* reports that Harvard researchers have discovered that levels of income inequality today now exceed what they were in 1774 – and that's with slavery factored in.[420] But as a society, are we poorer today than in 1774? Hardly.

Economic Freedom and Economic Inequality (99% vs. 1%)

As stated previously, while income inequality is traditionally measured by comparing the bottom 20% of earners to the top 20%, economists Piketty and Saez have taken a different approach. Their research wasn't heavily popularized (with some exceptions)[421] until the Occupy Wall Street movement took off. The Congressional Budget office also appears to confirm the basic tenets of their research.

The CBO Reports that from 1979 to 2007, the top 1% saw their share of the national income grow from 8% to 17.3%.[422] Another measurement shows that income of the top 1% quintile

---

[419] "Is Rising Inequality in America Exaggerated?" *The Economist*, 17 Sept. 2010. <http://www.economist.com/blogs/democracyinamerica/2010/09/inequality_myth>.

[420] Weissmann, Jordan. "U.S. Income Inequality: It's Worse Today Than It Was in 1774." *The Atlantic*, 19 Sept. 2012. <http://www.theatlantic.com/business/archive/2012/09/us-income-inequality-its-worse-today-than-it-was-in-1774/262537/>.

[421] For example, see Krugman's "The Conscience of a Liberal," pp. 153- 172.

[422] "Trends in the Distribution of Household Income Between 1979 and 2007." *Congressional Budget Office*, Oct. 2011. <http://info.publicintelligence.net/CBO-HouseholdIncome.pdf>.

rose 275% during this period.[423] This study, however, ends at a peak year before a recession – and the top 1% saw their share of income fall to around 11.3% in 2009.[424] That aside, it is important to understand the real causes of this increase.

Regarding the top 1%'s income, in 2007 approximately 43.7% of it consisted of capital gains, dividends, and interest.[425] Capital gains are much different from normal income: there is more risk incurred than by earning income through a salary, and that the resulting income is often realized differently than from regular income . For example, someone who invests $100,000 in the stock market, and cashes out $200,000 in capital gains ten years later will have an immeidate surge of $100,000 in his income for that year, but technically he made only $10,000 a year. This dovetails with my point that an individual's position in the top 1% is often a short-lived one. From 1996-2005, 41% of individuals in the top 1% saw their incomes fall by more than half.[426] Only 33% actually saw increases during that period.[427]

Alan Reynolds at the Cato Institute attributes the rise in income of the top 1% as being behavioral responses to lower tax rates, as opposed to being solely due to the fact that these individuals are able to keep more of their income since taxes on their income group have fallen over the years. His explanation is worth quoting in its entirety:

> In 1988, business income jumped to 16.5% of the reported income of the top 1%, from 8.2% in 1986. Why? As the CBO explains, "many C corporations... were

---

[423] Ibid.
[424] Reynolds, Alan. "Tax Rates, Inequality and the 1%." *The Cato Institute* December 6, 2011. <http://www.cato.org/publications/commentary/tax-rates-inequality-1>.
[425] Ibid.
[426] Matthews, Stephen. "Trends in Top Incomes and their Tax Policy Implications", *OECD Taxation Working Papers*, 2011. <http://dx.doi.org/10.1787/5kg3h0v004jf-en>.
[427] Ibid.

converted to S corporations which pass corporate income through to their shareholders where it is taxed under the individual income tax."

The CBO estimates top incomes from individual tax returns. So it looked like a big spurt in top income in 1988 when thousands of businesses switched to reporting income on individual rather than corporate returns as the top individual tax rate dropped to 28% from 50%.

In reality, it was just a switching between tax forms to take advantage of the lower individual tax rate. Such tax-induced switching from corporate to individual tax forms in 1986-1988 makes it illegitimate to compare top income shares between 1979 and 2007.

After the tax rate on dividends fell to 15% in 2003 from 35%, the share of income reported by top earners from dividends doubled to 8.4% in 2007 from 4.2% in 2002, according to similar tax-based estimates from economists Thomas Piketty and Emmanuel Saez. Top earners held more dividend-paying stocks in taxable accounts rather than in tax-exempt bonds, or they kept dividends in tax-free retirement accounts.

In short, what the Congressional Budget Office presents as increased inequality from 2003 to 2007 is actually evidence that the top 1% of earners report more taxable income when tax rates are reduced on dividends, capital gains and businesses filing under the individual tax code.

If Congress raises top individual tax rates much above the corporate rate, many billions in business income would rapidly vanish from the individual tax returns the CBO uses to measure the income of the top 1%. Small businesses and professionals would revert to reporting

> most income on corporate tax returns as they did in 1979.[428]

Keep in mind that the Reynolds passage is quoted only as an explanation of the top 1%'s growing income share.

Others can try to demystify the growing income share of the top 1% by pointing out that a decent chunk of the top 1% are doctors, lawyers, professors, and members of other professions that society generally respects. On the other hand, both the Tea Party and the Occupy Movement are correct when they criticize the relationship between government and big business. When it comes to the top 1%, I will defend around half of them, as I suspect a good deal of the other half has garnered their income through the practice of rent seeking. Briefly defined, rent seeking is when an individual or business attempts to receive money without creating any new wealth. Lobbying for federal funds is a perfect example of rent seeking.

Interestingly enough, when we look at the geographic location of the top 1%, we find that of the richest 1% of counties, 43% are in the D.C. area.[429]

Political Consequences

One oft-argued side effect of income inequality is that the well off tend to oppose government action that would benefit the lower class. One author writes that "as economic inequality increases, the better off perceive fewer and fewer shared interests with the less well off."[430]

---

[428] Reynolds, "Tax Rates, Inequality and the 1%."

[429] Stossel, John. "Mistake." *FOX Business*, 28 Mar. 2013. <http://www.foxbusiness.com/on-air/stossel/blog/2013/03/28/mistake>.

[430] Nye, John. (Contributor). "Inequality: Facts and Values." The Cato Institute, Location 412 of 1066.

While it is statistically well established that upper earners vote Republican, they're not necessarily conservative politically, according to Gallup. When it comes to party affiliation, of the top 1%, 33% identify as Republican, compared to 28% of those in the bottom 99%. Fifty-seven percent of the top 1% also report to lean Republican, compared to 44% of the bottom 99%. But when it comes to ideology, a larger percent of the top 1% identify as moderate than the bottom 99%. Additionally, 39% of the top 1% identify as "conservative," and 20% as liberal, compared to 40% and 21% respectively for the bottom 99%.[431]

If we actually look at the data from the previous election, we find that Obama won eight of the ten richest counties.[432] This is hardly surprising, as the research of Charles Murray has found that those living in what he calls "SuperZips" (those living in zip codes in the 95th to 99th income percentile)[433] are about split on politics, 30% being "doctrinaire conservatives" and 29% "doctrinaire liberals."[434] For SuperZips living in New York, Washington, Los Angeles, and San Francisco, 64% are "doctrinaire liberals" and a mere 10% "doctrinaire conservatives."[435]

The Thrifty Rich

A common argument regarding the consequences of income inequality is that the rich don't spend enough of their money to keep the economy functioning. This argument is derived from the concept of the velocity of money. A common

---

431 Saad, Lydia. "U.S. "1%" Is More Republican, but Not More Conservative." *Gallup*, 5 Dec. 2012. <http://www.gallup.com/poll/151310/u.s.-republican-not-conservative.aspx>.
432 Toscano, Paul. "Obama Wins 8 of the Nation's 10 Wealthiest Counties." *CNBC*, 7 Nov. 2012.
<http://www.cnbc.com/id/49726054/Obama_Wins_8_of_the_Nationrsquos_10_Wealthiest_Counties>.
433 Murray, Charles A. "Coming Apart: The State of White America, 1960-2010." (New York, NY: Crown Forum, 2012), p. 78
434 Ibid., p. 98.
435 Ibid., p. 99.

analogy offered to explain this concept is a scenario where a homeless man is given $5, who then immediately runs off and spends it, thus helping inject money into the economy. By contrast, if Bill Gates were given $5 it probably would just sit around collecting dust. Another concept relevant to this argument is the "paradox of thrift," which essentially turns the old saying "a penny saved is a penny earned" into "a penny saved is a penny unearned," since everyone's income is dependent on somebody else's spending.

This sort of argument may be applicable to millionaires and billionaires,[436] but not the typical upper income person. The *New York Times* reported in 2010 that the top 5% of income earners account for 1/3rd of consumer outlays.[437] By contrast, the same top 5% earned 21.3% of national income that same year – showing that they are by far overrepresented in consumer expenditures.[438]

Even if this argument were accurate – that income inequality slows down the velocity of money – it still neglects the reality that consumption isn't the only factor driving economic growth. Throughout more recent fluctuations in the business cycle, investment declined first, which then lead to declines in employment. Throughout the 2001 recession, consumption spending was on the rise.[439] We're not richer today than we were

---

[436] But not necessarily all millionaires and billionaires. Nearly the entire net worth of Bill Gates and Warren Buffet is tied up in stocks, which puts their money to work in various companies.

[437] Rich, Motoko. "Wealthy Reduce Buying in a Blow to the Recovery." *The New York Times*, 16 July 2010. <http://www.nytimes.com/2010/07/17/business/economy/17consumers.html?_r=2&>.

[438] "Share of Aggregate Income Received by Each Fifth and Top 5 Percent of Households, All Races: 1967 to 2011." *U.S. Census Bureau, Current Population Survey, Annual Social and Economic Supplements* <www.census.gov/apsd/techdoc/cps/cpsmar12.pdf>.

[439] Papola, John. "Think Consumption Is The 'Engine' Of Our Economy? Think Again." *Forbes*, 30 Jan. 2013. <http://www.forbes.com/sites/beltway/2013/01/30/think-consumption-is-the-engine-of-our-economy-think-again/2/>.

100 years ago because we consume more, we're richer because we produce more – and investment drives production. Even if a wealthy person doesn't directly invest in companies, his savings are loaned out by banks.

Regarding the paradox of thrift, the international data fails to substantiate it. Below is charted the gross savings as a percent of GDP and the growth rates of various OECD countries in 2007:

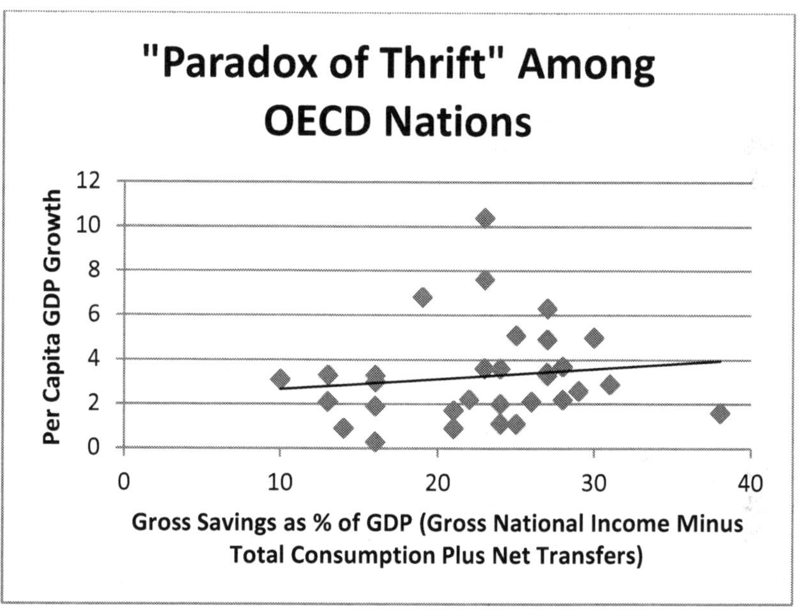

Source: The World Bank.[440]

The paradox fails by overstating the role that consumer spending has in the economy. The classic Keynesian equation states that

440 "Gross Savings (% of GDP)." <http://data.worldbank.org/indicator/NY.GNS.ICTR.ZS?page=1> and "GDP per capita growth (annual %)." <http://data.worldbank.org/indicator/NY.GDP.PCAP.KD.ZG>. Also note that in 1986, Franco Modigliana found a strong correlation between personal savings rates as a percentage of disposable income and compound annual growth in per capita disposable income. See: Skousen, Mark. "The Big Three in Economics: Adam Smith, Karl Marx, and John Maynard Keynes." (Armonk, NY: M.E. Sharpe, 2007), p. 179.

equilibrium income is composed of consumption, investment, and government spending (Y = C + I + G). Conventional wisdom states that consumption composes around 70% of the economy, but GDP only accounts for the final value of all produced goods and services, not the various intermediate states of production. Economist Mark Skousen created the concept of Gross Domestic Expenditures (GDE) to measure sales at all stages of production. The GDE shows that consumer spending accounts for only one third of the economy, and business spending (which Skousen defines as "investment plus goods in-process spending") composes more than half of the economy.[441]

The Role of Government in Education

My discussion on the importance of economic freedom cannot be further examined unless the role of education is also recognized. Combining education with a lack of economic freedom, or economic freedom with a lack of education will bring the same result, neither of which is desirable.

While it is well known that high school graduates earn more than high school dropouts, and that college graduates earn more than those with only a high school diploma, what is often overlooked is the effect that the *quality* of a high school education will have on future earnings.

The data indicates that the wealthier a family is, the better their child will do on the SAT.[442] It seems reasonable to conclude that this is mostly attributable to the fact that wealthier families can locate to more expensive areas with better schools, but there are other reasons as well, including the fact that some level of intelligence is inherited, and that higher income families may be

---

[441] Skousen, "The Big Three in Economics," p. 182-183.
[442] Rampell, Catherine. "SAT Scores and Family Income." *The New York Times*, 27 Aug. 2009. <http://economix.blogs.nytimes.com/2009/08/27/sat-scores-and-family-income/>.

more involved in their children's' academic activities than poorer families.

This brings up a major problem: the system produces merely "average" results for the average American, and absolutely cripples the poor and disadvantaged. As Michael Dougherty, a columnist for *Business Insider* reports:

> The three-yearly OECD Programme for International Student Assessment (PISA) report, which compares the knowledge and skills of 15-year-olds in 70 countries around the world, ranked the United States 14th out of 34 OECD countries for reading skills, 17th for science and a below-average 25th for mathematics.

He continues, noting that "out of 34 OECD countries, only 8 have a lower high school graduation rate." As the article noted, this is not due to a problem of funding, since the US ranks 4th highest in per-pupil spending.[443] Education spending in the US has produced poor results nationally and on the state by state level. Inflation adjusted public school spending per-pupil has doubled since 1970, while reading and math scores have stagnated. Furthermore, the high school graduation rate declined by around 4-5% during that same time period.[444] At the individual state level, we see no correlation between spending and results either.[445]

All the data available shows that trying to improve our educational system simply by increased funding would be futile. A more viable solution with proven results would be to provide

---

[443] Dougherty, Michael B. "If America Spends More Than Most Countries Per Student, Then Why Are Its Schools So Bad?" *Business Insider*, 7 Jan. 2012. <http://articles.businessinsider.com/2012-01-07/politics/30587761_1_oecd-countries-high-school-graduation-rate-spending>.

[444] Perry, Mark J. "Education Spending Doubled, Stagnant Test Scores." 9 Sept. 2009. <http://mjperry.blogspot.com/2009/09/education-spending-doubled-stagnant.html>.

[445] "The States That Spend The Most And Least On Each Student." *24/7 Wall St*, 31 May 2011. <http://247wallst.com/2011/05/31/the-states-that-spend-the-most-and-least-on-each-student/>.

school vouchers, a plan envisioned by Milton Friedman in the 1950s that severs the connection between a student's zip code and the school he is destined to attend. Under a voucher system, each student gets a voucher worth a certain amount of money. The theory behind the voucher system is that if a school wants to stay afloat, they'll need to compete for students. This would be disastrous for some schools – but the losers would be the worst schools, and the winners would be the best.

The data testing the success of vouchers exists only at a micro level right now, but the results are still promising. The New York Choice Scholarships Foundation offered $1,400 annually (in 1998 dollars) to 1,000 low income families with children in elementary school. Over 20,000 applied for the scholarship. To put the size of the voucher in perspective, the largest provider of private education in NYC was the Catholic archdiocese, which charged $1,728 a year at the time, and spent less than half per student as public schools did. In this case the voucher was funded by private donors to remove any problems of separation of church and state. A study of the effects this voucher program had on the 2,666 students who received vouchers showed it to be most successful for African-American students, who saw increases in full-time college enrollment of 31%, and a doubling of those accepted to selective colleges (which the study defined as requiring average SAT scores above 1100).[446]

To avoid any measurement errors in demonstrating the success of vouchers, it does need to be noted that students who attempt to get a voucher are much more academically rigorous than those who do not. But as evidenced by the D.C. Opportunity Scholarship Program (the first federally funded voucher program) the results of those who do attempt to get a voucher and succeed

---

[446] Chingos, Matthew M., and Paul E. Peterson. "A Generation of School-Voucher Success." *The Wall Street Journal*, 23 Aug. 2012. <http://online.wsj.com/article/SB10000872396390444184704577585582150808386.html>.

are still superior to those who attempt and fail. For example, the graduation rate in Washington D.C. is 56%, compared to 91% for students who receive a voucher, and compared to students who attempted to get a voucher and failed, who had a graduation rate of 70%.[447]

Government and College

In 2012, college debt totaled over $1 trillion, an average of $27,000 per graduate.[448] The large increase in college costs over the years can make something as large as the inflation of medical costs seem small: the rate of increase in college tuition tends to be around double that of general inflation.[449]

With numbers like this, clearly there are politicians with "solutions" to the problem. In the 2012 third party presidential debate, Green Party candidate Jill Stein called for both forgiving all current student loan debt and providing college tuition free of charge![450]

A basic way that government could attempt to control college tuition increases would be to place price controls on tuition, or caps on the amount that tuition is allowed to rise per year. Unfortunately, price controls never work out as intended in the real world. After price controls are placed on rent (rent control), less apartments are built, apartments are poorly maintained and housing shortages arise. Rent controls aren't the

---

447 Riley, Jason L. "Obama's War on School Vouchers." *The Wall Street Journal*, 14 Feb. 2012. <http://online.wsj.com/article/SB10001424052970204883304577223290975405900.html?mod=WSJ_Opinion_LEFTThirdBucket>.

448 Ellis, Blake. "Average Student Loan Debt Nears $27,000." *CNN*, 18 Oct. 2012. <http://money.cnn.com/2012/10/18/pf/college/student-loan-debt/index.html>.

449 "Tuition Inflation." *FinAid*, <http://www.finaid.org/savings/tuition-inflation.phtml>.

450 Third Party Presidential Debate, CSPAN, Thursday, October 23rd 2012.

only time price controls have failed – they've been around for thousands of years around the globe without a hint of success.[451]

Before we can alleviate the problem of rising tuition, a proper diagnosis is first required. There is a strong connection between federal aid and increases in tuition. Government subsidies of tuition create a cycle where tuition becomes artificially less expensive, which both increases demand and allows colleges to charge more, which then increases the demand for more subsidies. This theory was named the "Bennett Hypothesis" after Education Secretary William J. Bennett, who published a *New York Times* op-ed promoting this theory in 1987.[452] Government subsidies to college currently amount to about $43 billion a year, $28 billion of which is spent on Pell Grants and $13 billion of which is spent on government-guaranteed loans.[453]

Smart Money (a magazine published by the *Wall Street Journal*) reports that:

> Lesley Turner, a PhD candidate at Columbia University, looked at data on aid from 1996 to 2008 and calculated that, on average, schools increased Pell Grant recipients' prices by $17 in response to every $100 of Pell Grant aid. More selective nonprofit schools' response was largest

[451] Sowell, Thomas. "A Lesson From Venezuela." *Townhall*, 27 Feb. 2008. <http://townhall.com/columnists/thomassowell/2008/02/27/a_lesson_from_venezuela/page/full/>

[452] Bennett, William J. "Our Greedy Colleges." (February 18th 1987). *The New York Times*, http://www.nytimes.com/1987/02/18/opinion/our-greedy-colleges.html?pagewanted=all&src=pm

[453] Zingales, Luigi. "The College Graduate as Collateral." *The New York Times*, 13 June 2012. <http://www.nytimes.com/2012/06/14/opinion/the-college-graduate-as-collateral.html?_r=1&>.

> and these schools raised prices by $66 for every $100 of Pell Grant aid.[454]

So on net balance, college becomes cheaper for those receiving the grant, but increases in price for everyone else. Elsewhere, price discrimination is increasing the cost of college for those families in the top 60% of income earners. For example, a college can give a large financial aid package to a poor student, but only at the expense of a wealthier student. To quote from *Bloomberg News*:

> At four-year public universities, the average sticker price for tuition and fees has risen 127 percent in real terms, from $3,810 in 1992 to $8,660 in this academic year. But only $990 of this $4,850 increase in sticker price, or 20 percent, is due to increases in net cost. The remaining 80 percent is price discrimination.[455]

The story is similar at four-year private universities, with 28% of their cost tuition increases being due to net cost, and 72% to price discrimination.[456]

But can grants and price discrimination be justified? Just like our progressive tax system, we make those who earn the most pay more into the system so that those at the bottom can sustain themselves. In college, however, there is no guarantee that the subsidized recipients will use this advantage to their benefit. In fact, college students from low-income families have the worst track record in completing college.[457] The richest students with below average test scores complete college at a

---

[454] Hough, Jack. "Why College Aid Makes College More Expensive." *Smart Money*, 24 Feb. 2012. <http://www.smartmoney.com/spend/family-money/why-college-aid-makes-college-more-expensive-1330033152060/>.

[455] Soltas, Evan. "Misconceptions 101: Why College Costs Aren't Soaring." *Bloomberg*, 27 Nov. 2012. <http://www.bloomberg.com/news/2012-11 27/misconceptions-101-why-college-costs-aren-t-soaring.html>.

[456] Ibid.

[457] DeParle, Jason. "For Poor, Leap to College Often Ends in a Hard Fall." *The New York Times*, Sunday, December 23rd, 2012. Pp. 1, 30-31.

slightly higher rate than the poorest students with above average test scores.[458] In fact, the percentage of students from the bottom middle, or lowest end of the income distribution who score below average who will graduate from college is in the single digits – and this is who the bulk of the cost shifting benefits.[459]

A way to get around the problem caused by grants and also not cut off college as a possibility to intelligent low-income students would be to grant financial aid not based on need, but on intelligence and performance. In the state of Georgia, the Helping Outstanding Pupils Educationally (HOPE) Scholarship is the closest thing we have to a merit-based scholarship system. The scholarship was created in Georgia with the goal of lowering the number of students leaving their home state to attend out of state colleges.[460] The scholarship's criterion was that students must maintain at least a B average throughout high school, but there were no minimum SAT requirements.[461] In 2005-2006, the value of a HOPE scholarship was around $4,600 at top public universities, which is similar to that of a Pell Grant.[462]

While SAT scores weren't taken into consideration for the scholarship, SAT scores for incoming freshman did rise in the years after the scholarship was made available, which could indicate that when students became aware of the scholarship they worked harder and improved their grades, which subsequently allowed them to obtain higher SAT scores.[463] Merit-based systems also help reduce racial gaps in performance. As Jackson Toby writes "the quality-enhancement effect was considerably

---

[458] Ibid., p. 31.
[459] Ibid.
[460] Toby, Jackson. "The Lowering of Higher Education in America: Why Financial Aid Should Be Based on Student Performance." (Santa Barbara, CA: Praeger, 2010), p. 184.
[461] Ibid.
[462] Ibid, p. 185.
[463] Ibid.

greater for African American male and female students than for white male and female students."[464]

Sixteen other states have replicated Georgia's HOPE Scholarship so far, but the benefits would also help simplify the government aid process if adopted at a national level.[465] Awarding merit-based financial aid as an alternative to need-based aid would result in over 20 federal financial aid programs being replaced with one.[466]

An apparent disadvantage of this kind of policy is that less people would attend college as a result. This de-facto disadvantage overlooks the fact that we likely already have too many people in college, studying in areas with little or no job demand. I don't think that it would be difficult to tell our nation's 317,000 waiters/waitresses with bachelor's degrees, or the 5,000 janitors with Ph.D.'s that they didn't need to go to college to be qualified for their job.[467] Some might object that this is an unfair comparison, because it doesn't measure recent graduates. Maybe a good chunk of those hundreds of thousands of waitresses worked in a field related to their degree, and then were laid off or forced to find another job for various reasons. When we actually do look at recent graduates (under age 25), we find that 700,000 of the total 2,000,000 graduates are employed in jobs that don't even require a college degree![468] Similarly, 45% of those who graduated in 2009 are reporting earnings under $15,000 a year.[469]

---

[464] Ibid, p. 185-6.
[465] Ibid., p. 186.
[466] Ibid., p. 190.
[467] Vedder, Richard. "Why Did 17 Million Students Go to College?" *The Chronicle of Higher Education*, 20 Oct. 2010. <http://chronicle.com/blogs/innovations/why-did-17-million-students-go-to-college/27634>.
[468] Fairbanks, Amanda M. "Young, Educated, and Unemployed: A New Generation of Kids Search for Work in Their 20s." *Good Magazine*, 9 Oct. 2010. <http://www.good.is/posts/young-educated-and-unemployed-a-new-generation-of-kids-search-for-work-in-their-20s/>.
[469] Fairbanks, Amanda M. "College's Value Added." *The New York Times*, 7 Jan. 2011. <http://www.nytimes.com/2011/01/09/education/edlife/09books-t.html?_r=0&adxnnl=1&adxnnlx=1356562854-8jbVYpzupRf4ZHp3bzlj1A>.

Government Spending and Growth

As the size of government grows, the amount of resources taken from the private sector to finance it grows as well. If government expenditures cost of only pennies on the dollar relative to taxpayer earnings, it wouldn't affect the average person's purchasing power too substantially. No one would deny that education, police protection, and roads all add some economic value. But there does exist a cutoff point where government begins to impede growth and crowd out private investment.

There is no doubt that such a point exists – since countries with excessive government spending tend to have less economic growth than their small spending counterparts, and communist countries have virtually no net increase in living standards. To illustrate that such a cutoff occurs, a scholar named Richard Rahn at the Cato Institute devised the "Rahn Curve," as pictured below.

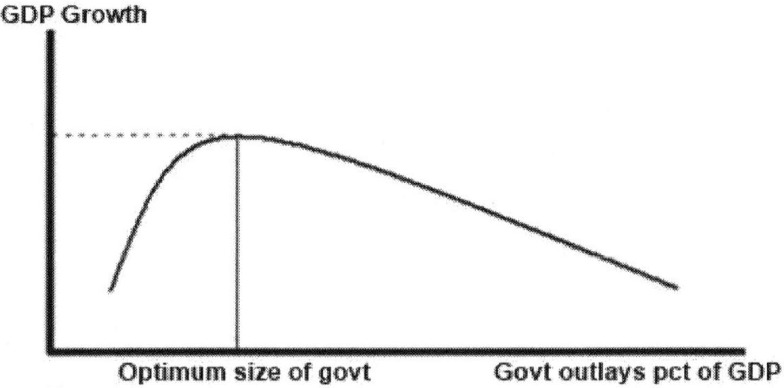

Source: Economics Help.[470]

[470] Picture sourced from <http://www.economicshelp.org/blog/447/economics/the-rahn-curve-economic-growth-and-level-of-spending/>.

The beginning upward slope of the Rahn curve comes from government spending on things that aid the free market, such as education, infrastructure, a safety net, minimal regulation, defense, etc. The downward slope comes from when the government overacts by over regulating, providing disincentives to work by offering a large welfare state, or crowding out private investment.

The best evidence for the Rahn curve comes from the fact that "small government" countries tend to grow faster than "big government' countries. "Small government" underdeveloped countries won't be used in this comparison, since any superior percentage increases in growth they have could be analogous tom why a thirteen year old grows in height at a faster rate than a thirty year old. This analysis looks at the 28 OECD countries which the International Monetary Fund has deemed to be advanced, and defines "small" government as having taxes and spending under 40% of GDP. From 1993-2002 "big government" countries grew an average of 3.1 percent annually, compared to 4 percent for "small government countries." The numbers for 2003-2012 were 2 percent for "big government," and 3.1 percent for small.[471]

Over a period of twenty five years, while the economies of "small government" countries would have more than doubled (a 115 percent increase), the "big government" countries would increased by only 64 percent.[472]

The data shows that smaller government is better for growth, but pinpointing where the Rahn Curve peaks isn't an exact science. The Adam Smith Institute estimates it to be around

---

[471] Knox, Tim, and Ryan Bourne. "To Get Growth, Shrink the State." *The Wall Street Journal*, 24 May 2012. <http://online.wsj.com/article/SB10001424052702304707604577423720925560872.html#articleTabs%3Darticle>.
[472] Ibid.

20 percent,[473] and some other estimates are similar - plus or minus a few percentage points. When all forms of government spending are accounted for (federal + state + local), government spending in the US totaled 40.27 percent of GDP in 2012. The last time government spending on all levels had fallen around 20 percent of GDP was in the 1940s.[474]

The Cost of Regulation

There are very few people who would argue for no regulation in the economy whatsoever, but the current costs of regulation bring into question whether or not the burden should at least be reduced.

If you try to justify regulations based on safety, capitalism has a far better track record of increasing workplace safety than any regulation could hope to achieve. Prior to the creation of the Occupational Safety and Health Administration (OSHA), workplace fatalities fell from 37 per 100,000 people to 18 between 1933-69. After OSHA, fatalities fell from 18 per 100,000 to 8 from 1969-93.[475] In other words, fatalities were falling at about the same pace before OSHA even existed.

It is easy to brand anyone who favors reducing labor regulations as wanting to "go back to the old days" where children would work hours on end, but what parent today would let that occur? The reason we have less child labor today is because we live in a richer society, one that doesn't need that additional labor simply to put food on the table. As was the case

---

[473] Worstall, Tim. "The Rahn Curve." *Adam Smith Institute*, 16 July 2011. <http://www.adamsmith.org/blog/tax-and-economy/the-rahn-curve>.

[474] See: <http://www.usgovernmentspending.com/past_spending>

[475] Mitchell, Daniel. "How Free Markets Keep Us Safe." *Townhall Magazine*, November 2012, p. 43.

with OSHA, the amount of child laborers in the workforce was already declining before any regulations were put into place.[476]

Regulations themselves can be considered a form of tax. Instead of money going directly to the federal government, a business sees additional regulatory costs that are pushed onto the consumer. The current cost of regulation in the US is estimated at around $1.75 trillion.[477] This is $650 billion more than the total amount of income taxes collected in 2011, and accounted for 11.5 percent of GDP that same year. Regulatory cost far exceeded the $1.3 trillion in pre-tax corporate profits in 2009. Regulations kill jobs in other ways, either by causing companies to eliminate existing jobs to save costs, or making new jobs too costly to create in the first place.

Deroy Murdock of the *National Review* estimates that in June of 2012, federal regulation had eliminated at least 780,000 potential jobs (enough jobs that would have brought the unemployment rate down half a percentage point, from 8.2% to 7.7%).[478]

Regulations are shown to be most destructive when their cumulative effects are measured. Since 1949, the drag on the economy by federal regulations has lowered GDP growth by an average two percentage points each year. A study published in the *Journal of Economic Growth* (which documented the prior statistic) determined that GDP in 2005 was only 28% of what it would have otherwise been had regulation remained at the levels they were in 1948. Extending their conclusions to today's numbers, they calculate that GDP in 2011 would have been $53.9

---

[476] Epstein, Richard A. "How Progressives Rewrote the Constitution." (Washington D.C.: Cato Institute, 2006), p. 5.

[477] Gattuso, James, and Diane Katz. "Red Tape Rising: A 2011 Mid-Year Report." *The Heritage Foundation*, 25 July 2011. <http://www.heritage.org/research/reports/2011/07/red-tape-rising-a-2011-mid-year-report#_edn1>.

[478] Murdock, Deroy. "Over-Regulation Is Pricey." *National Review Online*, 5 June 2012. <http://www.nationalreview.com/articles/301802/over-regulation-pricey-deroy-murdock>.

trillion in 2011, as opposed to $15.1 trillion! This means that median household income today would be $330,000, as opposed to $53,000 with regulation. There are obvious benefits to some regulations, and anyone objecting to this research should know that the study does take this fact into account.[479]

Regulations are demanded by the public for safety and demanded by big business for a different form of safety. The Public Choice School of economics reminds us that politics is a lot like a business itself, where big business can game the system at the expense of their competitors.

As Tim Carney discussed in a speech for the Cato Institute, the evidence does support the claim that the tendency of big business is to support regulation. Altria (which retains a majority of the cigarette market) supports federal regulation of tobacco. The specific regulation Altria supported would ban advertising for tobacco, which would essentially lock up their market share by preventing potential competitors from advertising their product. Nike, Alcoa, and General Electric support action against climate change. Nike doesn't make their shoes in the US, so they wouldn't be affected by these regulations – but their competitors would. Alcoa simultaneously fought against very similar regulations in Australia, where they actually produce their cars.[480] The companies that have lobbied for food safety regulation include McDonalds, Starbucks, and Kraft – and they have spent millions doing so.[481]

---

[479] Bailey, Ronald. "Federal Regulations Have Made You 75 Percent Poorer." *Reason*, 21 June 2013. <http://reason.com/archives/2013/06/21/federal-regulations-have-made-you-75-per>.

[480] Carney, Timothy. "Obamanomics: Is Obama Bankrupting America?" *ForaTV*, 12 Jan. 2010. <http://fora.tv/2010/01/12/Obamanomics_Is_Obama_Bankrupting_America>.

[481] Borowski, Julie. "Big Corporations and Big Government Go Hand in Hand." *FreedomWorks*, 25 July 2011. <http://www.freedomworks.org/blog/jborowski/big-corporations-and-big-government-go-hand-in-han>.

Tax Policy

Most discussions on the role of government seem to be confined to how much government should spend and tax. This is a simplistic approach to the issue, but does deserve an in depth look. How much the government should spend (and on what) will be discussed at the end of the chapter in a section on balancing the federal budget, while we will now discuss the proper role of taxation.

The Laffer Curve

The invention of supply side economics may best be credited to Andrew Mellon's 1924 book *Taxation: The People's Business*, but today, economist Arthur Laffer gets most of the credit for his invention, dubbed "The Laffer Curve."

The logic behind the curve works as follows: Imagine you were going to be taxed at a rate of 100%. Chances are you would not work at all, and thus the government wouldn't yield any tax revenue from you. This would thereby bring in the same amount of revenue as if the government had taxed you at 0%, the only difference being that you would more likely increase your work hours now that you wouldn't have to pay anything in taxes. The Laffer curve's logic is similar to that of a statement made by Andrew Mellon in 1924 that "the history of taxation shows that taxes which are inherently excessive are not paid. The high rates inevitably put pressure upon the taxpayer to withdraw his capital from productive business."[482]

---

[482] Mellon, Andrew W. "Taxation: The People's Business." (New York: Macmillan), p. 13.

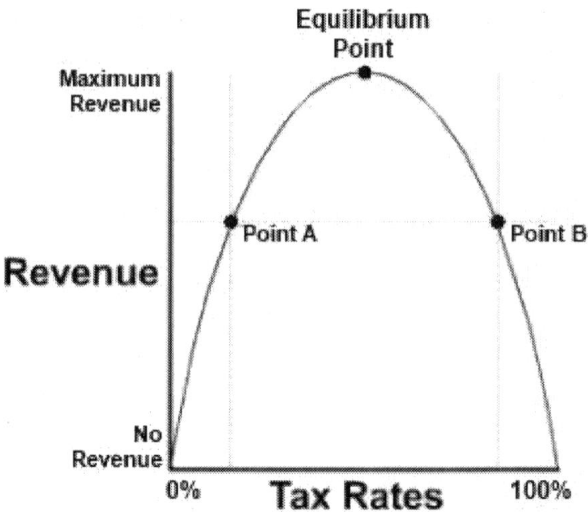

Source: Knowledge at CBSDU.[483]

As shown above, raising taxes raises revenue until the point of equilibrium is reached. After that point is reached any future tax increases decrease revenue since it creates work disincentives. Although the graph shown above is hypothetical because dozens of variants of the curve showing different points of equilibrium, it is useful in demonstrating the reasoning behind Mellon's statement. Any tax cut (when the tax rate is on the right side of the curve) will raise revenue. Points A and B represent two tax rates which would garner the same amount of revenue, but have different effects on the economy; point A being less damaging to economic growth than point B.

The Laffer Curve explains why work disincentives created by high taxes can lower revenue, and there are other ways higher tax rates lead to less revenue. Some of these other scenarios include:

---

[483] "Laffer curve-inside out!" <http://finxknowledgeatcbsdu.wordpress.com/tag/laffer-curve/>.

1) **Deduction.** People can consume tax-deductible goods in replace of nondeductible goods since higher tax rates translate to cheaper tax-deductible goods. This can happen even when these nondeductible goods are of lesser quality. In the 1970's, when the United Kingdom's top marginal tax rate was 98%, a business owner could purchase a £100,000 Rolls-Royce as a tax deductible business expense, thereby reducing his personal cost for that car to £2,000. Rolls-Royce sales fell dramatically after the top marginal tax rate was reduced to 70%, as it then cost that business owner £30,000 for that same car.[484]

2) **Sheltering.** Since high taxes deter investment, domestic investors will be more inclined to turn to ways to shelter their income from taxation. If one had to choose out of the three methods listed here to avoid taxation, sheltering would be the most preferable for economic growth as sheltering only affects tax revenues the government collects, rather than economic growth. As for other methods of sheltering, think Cayman Islands and Swiss bank accounts.

3) **Immigration.** Finally, based on what region (national, state, county, municipality) that a tax effects, a person could relocate to a different state or country to avoid the tax. At a national level, 180,000 people leave the UK each year due to high taxes alone.[485] On a state by state level, it is no wonder that New Jersey (which already has the highest property taxes in the nation) saw 302,780 households leave New Jersey between 2004-8 (with an

---

[484] Gwartney, James D., Richard L. Stroup, Dwight R. Lee, and Tawni H. Ferrarini. "Common Sense Economics: What Everyone Should Know about Wealth and Prosperity." (New York: St. Martin's, 2010), pp. 75-76.

[485] Worstall, Tim. "People Really Do Move Because of Tax Rates." *Adam Smith Institute*, 3 July 2011. <http://www.adamsmith.org/blog/tax-and-economy/people-really-do-move-because-of-tax-rates/>.

average income of $618,330) after that state introduced another "Millionaires Tax."[486] I put that in quotes because New Jersey has redefined the rules of math, with a millionaire being someone earning over $250,000.

This can even be seen on an even smaller scale in the sports world. Since the NBA has a salary cap limiting both the amount a team can spend on its players and on individual players' salaries, living in a no-income tax state helps these players save millions. Because of this, there is a pattern of talented players (generally the highest paid) migrating to states with small or no state income tax. This has even managed to create a direct correlation between state income tax and basketball playing ability - with players in the top 10 highest taxed states winning 39.3% of their games, the 10 mid taxed winning at a rate of 52.9%, and the top 10 least taxed winning 57.8% of the time![487]

Basketball isn't the only sport where this phenomenon occurs. In soccer, this happens at the national level. Tax cuts for foreign soccer players led to an increase in players emigrating to Denmark, Spain, and Belgium, while the quality of players in Italy declined. This policy has been named by some the "Beckham Law" because the famous British player David Beckham was one of the

---

[486] Kwoh, Leslie. "N.J. Loses $70B in Wealth during Five Years as Residents Depart." *The Star Ledger*, 4 Feb. 2010. <http://www.nj.com/business/index.ssf/2010/02/nj_loses_70b_in_wealth_over_fo.html>.

[487] Johnson, Drew. "How Tax Policies Determine Winners and Losers in the NBA." *Taxpayers Protection Alliance*, 4 June 2011. <http://www.protectingtaxpayers.org/index.php?blog&action=view&post_id=37>.

> people taking advantage of lower tax rates in other countries.[488]

It is important recognize that there are different kinds of taxes, the ups and downs of which effect incentives differently. In economics, the concept of elasticity explains how price increases and decreases affect different kinds of products differently. For example, the cost of this book increasing to $50 would cause sales to decline, which makes it an elastic book. By contrast, the cost of gasoline is inelastic, as the price increasing an extra dollar or two per gallon wouldn't harm sales because people need it in their everyday lives, usually to get to their job to earn income in the first place, and few substitutes exist. Elasticity can be applied to different kinds of taxes as well.

Put simply, different types of taxes have different levels of elasticity (or inelasticity). While the income tax is the most inelastic because everyone needs to earn income, changing rates does have effects on output. Taxes on capital gains (stocks, houses, land, etc.) and corporations are by far the most elastic. If the capital gains tax gets unbearably high, a person can simply chose not to invest in the stock market and put their money elsewhere. One pernicious problem of our country's high corporate tax rate is that it encourages production overseas to avoid the tax in the first place. Payroll taxes tend to be the most inelastic since they are the hardest to evade.

---

[488] Belsie, Laurent. "Do Tax Rates Affect Where People Live? Ask a Soccer Star." *Christian Science Monitor*, 11 Mar. 2011. <http://www.csmonitor.com/Business/new-economy/2011/0311/Do-tax-rates-affect-where-people-live-Ask-a-soccer-star>.

But Didn't We Use to Have High Taxes and Economic Prosperity?

It's common to hear the argument that some time in history, there were higher taxes than we have today, and an economy functioning in a much better fashion. Michael Linden of the Center for American Progress has "proven" that there is apparently little correlation between the top marginal tax rate and economic growth. After all, there's less growth under today's top rate of 35% than there was at Clinton's top rate of 39.6%. Moreover, it also appears that there was even slightly higher growth under top rates exceeding 75% in the country's past.[489]

The comparison between the economic records of Bush and Clinton are imperfect for various reasons. Growth under Clinton was largely attributable to a steadily inflating tech bubble, and the effects of the subsequent bursting of that bubble were felt mostly during the early years of the Bush presidency. Likewise, while some of the economic growth under Bush can be attributed to the housing bubble, the bursting of that bubble negatively impacted GDP growth during the final years of the Bush administration and first years of the Obama presidency. All of this would drag down the statistical measures of economic growth under a reduced 35% top marginal tax rate, even though it was in no way caused by the lowering of the top rate.

More important, however ,is the fact that top marginal tax rates and effective tax rates are not the same thing. Regarding the tax rates of the 1960s, Paul Krugman writes:

> Yet in the 1950s incomes in the top bracket faced a marginal tax rate of 91, that's 91 percent, while taxes on corporate profits were twice as large, relative to national

[489] Linden, Michael. "The Myth of the Lower Marginal Tax Rates." *Center for American Progress*, 20 June 2011. <http://www.americanprogress.org/issues/tax-reform/news/2011/06/20/9841/the-myth-of-the-lower-marginal-tax-rates/>.

> income, as in recent years. The best estimates suggest that circa 1960 the top 0.01 percent of Americans paid an effective federal tax rate of more than 70 percent, twice what they pay today.[490]

Well, not really. According to the Congressional Research Service, in the 1950s the top 0.01% of earners paid an effective rate of around 45%.[491] But this effective rate was dropping fast even without any cuts in the top marginal rate. In the 1960's, while top earners still faced a top marginal tax rate of 91%, this hardly reduced them to tax collectors working on a 9% commission! Due to all the deductions available, the top 0.01% of earners only paid an average of 31% of their income in taxes.[492] The same was true for the top 1% of earners in their entirety, who paid an average effective tax rate of 30.85% from 1966-70, and never saw their effective rate exceed 35%.[493]

There were also different economic conditions worldwide at this time that aided the US – and high taxes wasn't one of them: competing internationally tends to be much easier when many of your would-be competitors are suffering from the after effects of Second World War.

---

490 Krugman, Paul. "The Twinkie Manifesto." *The New York Times*, 18 Nov. 2012. <http://www.nytimes.com/2012/11/19/opinion/krugman-the-twinkie-manifesto.html?_r=0>.

491 Hungerford, Thomas L. "Taxes and the Economy: An Economic Analysis of the Top Tax Rates Since 1945." *Congressional Research Service*, 14 Sept. 2012. <http://online.wsj.com/public/resources/documents/r42729_0917.pdf>.

492 Domitrovic, Brian. "The Left's Dubious History of Income Inequality." *The Laffer Center for Supply Side Economics*, July 2012. <http://www.laffercenter.com/wp-content/uploads/2012/07/2012-07-TheLeftsDubiousHistoryofIncomeInequality-Domitrovic-LafferCenter.pdf>.

493 Cowen, Tyler. "Worthy of Further Investigation — What Were Tax Rates in the 1960s?" *Marginal Revolution*, 30 Nov. 2012. <http://marginalrevolution.com/marginalrevolution/2012/11/worthy-of-further-investigation.html>.

Aren't Taxes Already Low?

A popular talking point today seems to be that, despite the political rhetoric, taxes are actually the lowest they've been in decades. Bruce Bartlett writes in 2011 "the Congressional Budget Office estimated that federal taxes would consume just 14.8 percent of G.D.P. this year. The last year in which revenues were lower was 1950."[494] He's technically correct, but federal taxes aren't the only kind of tax paid. Total tax revenues at all level of government composed 22.7% percent of GDP in 1950, but 32.4% in 2011.[495]

Likewise, the average percentage that the median household pays is on the rise. In 1955, the median household paid 7.4% in personal income tax, and 4% in Social Security and Medicare taxes. By 2010, the median household pays 12.2% in personal income tax, and 13.3% on social security and Medicare taxes. [496] In other words, a jump from 11% of total income to 25% of total income, and this doesn't even include state and local taxes. The role of payroll taxes here is important. The *New York Times* published a lengthy article titled "Tax Burden for Most Americans is Lower than in the 1980s," and arrived at their conclusion by conveniently leaving out payroll taxes.[497] In the

---

494 Bartlett, Bruce. "Are Taxes in the U.S. High or Low?" *The New York Times*, 31 May 2011. <http://economix.blogs.nytimes.com/2011/05/31/are-taxes-in-the-u-s-high-or-low/>.

495 "Revenue As Percent Of GDP Fiscal Years 1900 to 2012." <http://www.usgovernmentrevenue.com/revenue_chart_1900_2012USp_13s1li011mcn_F0t_Revenue_As_Percent_Of_GDP#copypaste>.

496 "Historical Combined Income and Employee Tax Rates for a Family of Four." *Tax Policy Center*, 3 Apr. 2012. <http://www.taxpolicycenter.org/taxfacts/displayafact.cfm?Docid=228>. And "Historical Payroll Tax Rates." *Tax Policy Center*, 27 Sept. 2012. <http://www.taxpolicycenter.org/taxfacts/displayafact.cfm?Docid=45&Topic2id=50>.

497 Appelbaum, Binyamin. "Tax Burden for Most Americans Is Lower Than in the 1980s." *The New York Times*, 29 Nov. 2012. <http://www.nytimes.com/2012/11/30/us/most-americans-face-lower-tax-burden-than-in-the-80s.html?pagewanted=all>.

comments section of the article, the author defended doing so by defining payroll taxes as "insurance premiums."[498]

The Trickle-Down Myth

A surprisingly large amount of criticism of low tax rates is a beat down of a caricature that no one has ever advocated. In his nationally syndicated column, Thomas Sowell once challenged anyone to find an economist outside of a mental asylum who has ever advocated "trickle-down economics." The liberal watchdog Media Matters attempted to give it a swing. The only quotation they could provide came from former Reagan budget director David Stockman from an interview he had with *The Atlantic* in 1981 which he stated that "It's kind of hard to sell 'trickle down,' so the supply-side formula was the only way to get a tax policy that was really 'trickle down.' Supply-side is 'trickle-down' theory."[499]

So there we have it – over 80 years since Andrew Mellon invents supply side economics, Media Matters is able to find one example. Moreover, they deserve all the luck they can get in finding another example. As Sowell has pointed out, J.A. Schumpeter's 1,260 page history of economic analysis makes not a single mention of any sort of "trickle down" theory.[500] All that really followed from this was another column by Sowell appropriately mocking the Media Matters assessment under the title "Stupidly Tricking Down," and the hilariously titled response from the opposition; "Media Matters responds to Thomas Sowell's sound and fury."[501] Apparently nothing emits

---

[498] Ibid., comment posted on November 30th, 2012, at 6:09 p.m.

[499] Maloy, Simon. "Columnist Sowell Claimed 'no One Has Ever Advocated' Trickle-down Economic Theory; Reagan's Budget Director Would Disagree." *Media Matters for America*, 29 Mar. 2005. <http://mediamatters.org/research/2005/03/29/columnist-sowell-claimed-no-one-has-ever-advoca/132963>.

[500] Sowell, Thomas. "Trickle Down Theory and Tax Cuts for the Rich." (Stanford, CA: Hoover Institution, 2012), pp. 1-2.

[501] Foser, Jamison. "Media Matters Responds to Thomas Sowell's Sound and Fury." *Media Matters for America*, 1 Apr. 2005.

more rage to Media Matters than an economist who was in his mid-seventies at the time.

Still, the choice of Stockman because of his position in the Reagan administration seems almost too perfect, and Media Matters is indeed being disingenuous. This is the same David Stockman who later published the 1986 book "The Triumph of Politics, How the Reagan Revolution Failed." Stockman's interview with *The Atlantic* is actually discussed on page 1 of the book. Reagan reportedly said to Stockman; "Dave, how do you explain this... You have hurt me. Why?"[502] According to Stockman, the interviewer Bill Greider was a friend of his, who he would discuss with to "test 'our' arguments and learn 'their' objections. Stockman says that it was when they "had gotten so absorbed in the argument between our side and theirs that we hadn't clarified the ground rule about quotations. That's how the 'Trojan horse' slipped out."[503]

Bar Stool Economics

A popular way of lampooning calls for tax cuts is to label them to as "tax cuts for the rich." This kind of criticism works even when each income bracket receives the same percentage reduction in their tax burden. A tax cut of 1% is going to benefit someone with an annual salary of $250,000 more than it's going to benefit someone with a $50,000 salary. Even though this is common sense, an objection to nearly every tax cut is that the rich benefit most, mainly because they get the largest dollar amount back from any kind of tax cut. The analogy of "Bar Stool Economics" aims to give an analogy to illustrate both the logic and fairness of the rich benefiting the most from a tax cut. As

---

<http://mediamatters.org/research/2005/04/01/media-matters-responds-to-thomas-sowells-sound/132985>.

[502] Stockman, David Alan. "The Triumph of Politics: How the Reagan Revolution Failed." (New York: Harper & Row, 1986), p.1.

[503] Ibid, p.3.

articulated by economics professor David R. Kamerschen, Bar Stool Economics is as follows

> Imagine that every day, 10 men go to a bar and have a bill totaling $100.
>
> The first four men (the poorest) pay nothing. The fifth man pays $1. The sixth pays $3. The seventh pays $7. The eight pays $12. The ninth pays $18. The tenth pays $59.
>
> The bartender decides to give them a discount, now their total bill is only $80 – a 20% savings.
>
> Now the first five men pay nothing. The sixth pays $2 (33% savings), the seventh pays $5 (28% savings), the eighth pays $9 (25% savings), the ninth pays $14 (22% savings) and the tenth pays $49 (16% savings). Despite getting only as 16% savings, the tenth man saved $10, which was larger than the savings of everyone else combined.
>
> Despite six of the 10 men being in a more favorable scenario, they don't understand why the tenth man got the largest discount. "Only got a dollar out of the $20," declared the sixth man. He pointed to the tenth man, "but he got $10!" "Yeah, that's right," exclaimed the fifth man. "I only saved a dollar, too. It's unfair that he got ten times more than I!" "That's true!" shouted the seventh man. "Why should he get $10 back when I got only two? The wealthy get all the breaks!" "Wait a minute," yelled the first four men in unison. "We didn't get anything at all. The system exploits the poor!" The nine men surrounded the tenth and beat him up.

> But now the tenth man didn't show up for drinks the next day. Collectively the nine men couldn't even afford half of the bill.[504]

Kamerschen concludes the analogy "Tax them too much, attack them for being wealthy, and they just may not show up anymore. In fact, they might start drinking overseas where the atmosphere is somewhat friendlier."[505]

The Distribution of Taxes

Objections of the sort of thinking that bar stool economics advances argue that while the rich pay more in taxes, it's simply because they simply make more money and nothing else. Criticizing a column from David Brookes claiming that the top 10% of income earners pay 70% of all taxes, MSNBC host Chris Hayes attempts to debunk this by creating his own hypothetical society called "Inequalistan." Inequalistan has a population of only 10 people, nine of which earn $10 a year, and one who earns $100 a year. Inequalistan operates under a flat tax of 10%, which yields $19 in total tax revenue each year. $10 comes from the richest person, and $9 from the other nine people. Therefore, Hayes' conclusion is that in this society, the top 10% pay 50% of all income taxes, but only because that one earner is extremely rich compared to the other citizens.[506]

There is some basic element of truth to Hayes' analogy, but it doesn't compare to the US structure of income earnings and taxes paid. In Inequalistan, the "top 10%" makes 52.6% of the

---

[504] Kamerschen, David R. "Bar Stool Economics." <http://doc.cat-v.org/economics/bar_stool_economics>.
[505] Ibid.
[506] Up With Chris Hayes, MSNBC, Aired September 24th 2011.

income, and pays 52.6% of the taxes. In America, the top 10% earns 48% of all income, and pays 71% of all taxes.[507]

Regardless, while the logic of Hayes' "Inequalistan" is flawed, I've never found arguments concerning the distribution of taxes to be particularly convincing when it comes to the implications for raising or lowering taxes. I don't conclude from the data, like many do, that this justifies taxing lower earners more than they currently do.

Capital Gains Tax

The capital gains tax is much lower than both the income tax and corporate tax rate. The revenue maximizing point of the capital gains rate is also much lower than that of the income tax or corporate tax. The reason the revenue maximizing point is so much lower is due to the fact that while everyone needs to work to survive (and thus pay income tax), not everyone needs to invest in something subject to the capital gains tax (ex. stocks, precious metals, bonds, property).

One example of the Laffer Curve effect on capital gains comes from the Bush era. In addition to the income tax cuts, Bush also cut the capital gains tax in 2003. For those in the bottom 40%, their capital gains tax rate was cut from 15% to 5%, while the higher brackets had their capital gains tax cut in half from 20% to 10%. So were revenues from the bottom 40% cut by 66% and from everyone else in half? Not by a long shot - investors pay close attention to the capital gains tax rate, and the cuts encouraged more investment.

The cuts more than paid for themselves, totaling $110 billion in revenue in 2006[508] - which is 100% higher than they

---

[507] Moore, Stephen. "Who's the Fairest of Them All?: The Truth about Opportunity, Taxes, and Wealth in America." (New York: Encounter, 2012), p. 66.

[508] Congressional Budget Office, "The Budget and Economic Outlook: Fiscal Years 2008–2017,"
January 2007, p. 86, Table 4-3, www.cbo.gov/showdoc.cfm?index=7731&sequence=0.

had been in 2002 and nearly double the $63 billion that the CBO predicted would be collected *without* the cut.[509] It is significant that this was the CBO's prediction before the cut since they automatically assume that a lower tax rate yields less revenue.

Based off of data from the 1976-2004 period, Ohio State University professor Paul D. Evans has calculated that for each percentage point shaved off of the corporate tax rate, a 10.32% increase in revenues surfaces.[510] The data also estimated the revenue maximizing point to be at 9.69%.[511]

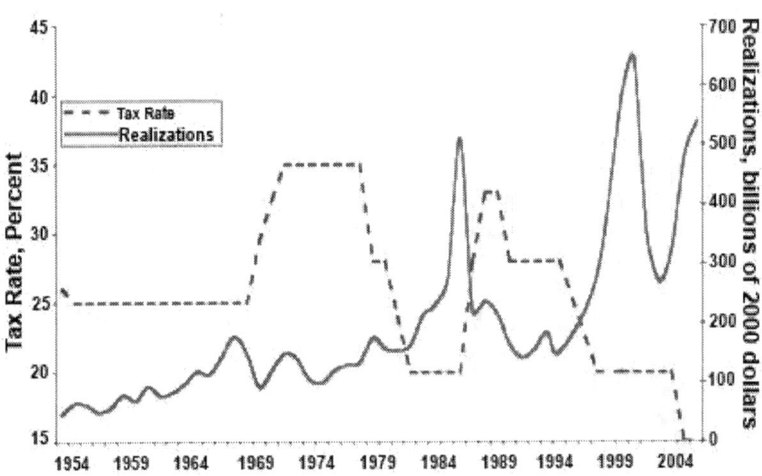

Source: Adam Smith Institute.[512]

---

[509] "Sign Up For CBO Emails Sign up for All CBO RSS Feeds An Analysis of the President's Budgetary Proposals for Fiscal Year 2004." *Congressional Budget Office*, 1 Mar. 2003. <http://www.cbo.gov/publication/14347>.

[510] Evans, Paul D. "The Relationship Between Realized Capital Gains and their Marginal Rate of Taxation, 1976-2004. *Institute for Research into the Economics of Taxation*, October 2009.

[511] Ibid.

[512] Ward-Proud, Liam. "The Effect of Capital Gains Tax Rises on Revenues." *The Adam Smith Institute*, 2010.

One myth that arises is that if the capital gains tax were to be either lowered or abolished completely, people would simply convert all of their income into capital gains to pay a lower rate. If it were that easy to do, everyone would already be doing it because the capital gains tax (1997 onward) has been lower than the one applied to the top four brackets of income. [513] But this isn't something that the average worker can do quite easily, and others realize that earning general income has no risk to it, while the stock market contains plenty.

There are countries with no capital gains tax, and it has had no effect on the amount of revenue collected from income tax. Australia's personal income tax collected just about the same amount of revenue when their capital gains tax was 0% as they did when they had the highest capital gains tax in the world. Income tax was 12.5% of GDP in 1980 with no capital gains tax, and 12% of GDP with the highest capital gains tax.[514] When Hong Kong had no capital gains tax, income tax receipts rose 17.8% annually during the 1984-1996 period while the US averaged a 7.1% annual increase with a capital gains tax ranging between 20% and 28%.[515]

Indexing the capital gains rate for inflation would be another way to lessen its burden. Unlike any other tax, the effective rate of capital gains can be harsher than the marginal rate. In 2007, the value of the dollar was roughly half of what it was in 1984, which leads Richard Rahn to propose the following thought experiment: "Assume you purchased a common stock in a company in 1984 for $100 a share and sold it in 2007 for $200 a share. Have you received any "income" from the sale of the shares of stock?" The purpose of this thought experiment is to

---

<http://www.adamsmith.org/sites/default/files/resources/capital-gains-tax.pdf>.

[513] In 1997 the Capital Gains tax was reduced to 20%. The tax was previously 28%.

[514] Ward-Proud, "Effect of Capital Gains on Tax Rises."

[515] Ibid.

demonstrate while the clear answer to the question is "no," the answer is still "yes" to the IRS.[516]

Corporate Taxation

In addition to a lowered income rate, a lowered corporate tax rate would be ideal. As any elementary business textbook will tell you, one downside of running a corporation is that its income is taxed at least twice. Corporations first pay taxes on their profits at the corporate level, then their employees pay income tax and state/local taxes, and shareholders pay tax on dividends.

Bruce Bartlett points out that corporate taxes average only 1.8% of US GDP, while the OECD average is 3.5%. Norway's stats are even as high as 12.5% of GDP, and Australia's at 5.9% of GDP.[517] The average OECD rate stands at around 26%,[518] while the high revenue gatherers like Norway and Australia's rates are at 28%, and 30%. To be specific, the US pays around 25% less than the OECD average in corporate taxes. All this evidence so far would suggest that the US corporate tax rate is especially low.

The actual amount of corporate taxes paid in the US appears low, but another to consider is the corporate tax *rates* in the countries being compared. How do these nations gather so much more revenue than the US? Bartlett gives the impression that it's because the US has a low corporate tax rate, but the data shows the exact opposite. Currently the US corporate tax rate is at 35%, which is the highest in the world.[519] Effective tax rates

---

[516] Rahn, Richard. "Inflation and the Tax Man." *The Wall Street Journal*, 17 Jan. 2008. <http://online.wsj.com/article/SB120053175732296095.html>.

[517] Bartlett, Bruce. "Are Taxes in the U.S. High or Low?" *The New York Times*, 31 May 2011. <http://economix.blogs.nytimes.com/2011/05/31/are-taxes-in-the-u-s-high-or-low/>.

[518] "U.S. Corporate Tax Rate Is Uncompetitive." *The Heritage Foundation*, 2011. <http://www.heritage.org/budgetchartbook/corporate-tax-rate>.

[519] "Michael McCaul Says U.S. Corporate Tax Rate Is World's Highest at 35 Percent." *PolitiFact*, 1 Nov. 2012.

are always lower than marginal rates, but even with that considered, a study by the American Enterprise Institute concludes that "the US statutory rate is nearly 10 percentage points higher than the effective average rate and nearly 17 percentage points higher than the effective marginal tax rate."[520]

The reason we have a higher corporate tax and lower revenue lends more credibility to the Laffer Curve than anything else. Facing a high corporate tax rate, American entrepreneurs can set up their corporation overseas to evade the rate. Compounding on this problem is that American entrepreneurs who set up overseas can't bring their money back to the States without it being taxed, so they often keep it overseas. Seventy US based companies that operate globally that were examined in one study were shown to hold $1.2 trillion in profits worldwide.[521] These companies are not paying zero taxes, the $1.2 trillion is leftover after taxes were paid to the governments in the countries that they set up business in.

In 2004 companies holding income abroad were given a tax holiday by Congress, which allowed them to bring back foreign income facing a tax of only 5.25%. This was done in hopes that they would bring foreign income (around $600 billion at this time) home.[522] Following the 2004 action by congress, 843 corporations brought $312 billion back into the country.[523] One downside of this was that less than one cent for every dollar

---

<http://www.politifact.com/texas/statements/2012/nov/01/michael-mccaul/michael-mccaul-says-us-corporate-tax-rate-worlds-h/>.

[520] Pethokoukis, James. "Sorry, Kevin Drum, Even the Effective U.S. Corporate Tax Rate Is Sky High." *American Enterprise Institute*, 22 Feb. 2012. <http://www.aei-ideas.org/2012/02/sorry-kevin-drum-even-the-effective-u-s-corporate-tax-rate-is-sky-high/>.

[521] Rubin, Richard. "Cash Hoard Grows by $187 Billion in Untaxed Overseas Profits." *Bloomberg*, 2 Mar. 2012. <http://www.bloomberg.com/news/2012-03-02/cash-horde-expands-by-187-billion-in-untaxed-offshore-accounts.html>.

[522] Forbes, "Flat Tax Revolution," p. 113.

[523] Peterson, Kristina. "Tax-Repatriation Holiday Gathers Some Steam." *The Wall Street Journal*, 23 June 2011. <http://online.wsj.com/article/SB10001424052702303339904576404183763158882.html>.

brought back was used for investment, though a good deal of the returned profits rewarded shareholders through dividends and stock buybacks.[524]

Pat Garofalo at Think Progress titles his piece on the 2004 holiday "FLASHBACK: Corporations Used 2004 Tax Holiday to Repatriate Billions, Then Laid Off Thousands of Workers."[525] He cites six companies who laid off workers after the holiday, but this is only 0.7% of all companies listed. It would be interesting to hear Garofalo explain the connection between bringing profits to the US and layoffs, but I don't expect to hear one. The reason that these six companies laid off workers probably had more to do with negative business conditions prior to the tax holiday. While there's almost no chance that another tax holiday would suddenly spur job creation, if the same setup occurred today (a 5.25% tax with about half of foreign income returning home), at least $30 billion in tax revenue would be raised and more money would be allowed to circulate in our economy.

This brings us to the question of what the perfect corporate tax rate is. The unanimous consensus among economists is quite low: zero percent.[526] Justifying this rate stems from the fact that the corporate tax is really just a layer of two separate taxes. But obviously it would be unwise fiscally while the government currently runs massive budget deficits. One 2007 study conducted by the American Enterprise Institute calculated the revenue maximizing point of the corporate income tax to be just over 25%,[527] though abolishing the tax completely down the

---

[524] Ibid.

[525] Garofolo, Pat. "FLASHBACK: Corporations Used 2004 Tax Holiday To Repatriate Billions, Then Laid Off Thousands Of Workers." *Think Progress*, 14 May 2011. <http://thinkprogress.org/economy/2011/05/14/173951/repatriation-flashback/>.

[526] "Tax Policy: In an Ideal World." *The Economist*, 24 July 2012. <http://www.economist.com/blogs/democracyinamerica/2012/07/tax-policy>.

[527] Brill, Alex, and Kevin A. Hassett. "Revenue-Maximizing Corporate Income Taxes: The Laffer Curve in OECD Countries." *American Enterprise Institute*, 31 July 2007. <http://www.aei.org/docLib/20070731_Corplaffer7_31_07.pdf>.

road would be ideal once the country is in a better fiscal condition.

The Case of Warren Buffet

No chapter advocating lower taxes would be complete without addressing what appears to be a multi-billionaire in opposition to it. I am referring to Warren Buffet, who claims that the tax system is unfair because he only pays 17.4% of his income in taxes while his secretary is paying a higher percentage of her income in taxes. The proposed "Buffet Rule" aims to solve this problem by requiring that those making over $1 million annually pay a minimum tax of 30% on their earnings.

Let us set aside the fact that the government is going to end up staking 55% of Buffet's fortune when he dies and examine why he only pays 17.4%. Buffet's income comes from two sources: personal income and dividends. Buffet salaries himself $524,000 that faces a tax rate of 35%, but the other $39.3 million of his income came from dividends that are taxed at 15%. Since Buffet is the largest shareholder and owner of Berkshire Hathaway, all of the income his company receives is taxed at the corporate level before he can receive dividends which are taxed again. Berkshire Hathaway paid $5.6 billion in taxes on $19 billion of earnings, and Buffet owns 37% of the company. Therefore, $2 billion of the taxes paid are technically Buffet's own money. If Buffet were to pay himself that money, he would technically face an overall tax rate of 52% when we factor in taxes paid at the corporate level plus the tax on dividends.[528]

If Buffet wanted to pay more in taxes, he wouldn't be the CEO of a company what openly admits that it owes taxes dating back to 2002. As the *New York Post* puts it: "If Buffett really thinks he and his 'mega-rich friends' should pay higher taxes,

[528] Schiff, Peter. "The Real Crash: How to Save Yourself and Your County." (New York: Saint Martin's Press, 2012), p. 137.

why doesn't his firm fork over what it already owes under current rates?"[529]

Around a month after his call for higher taxes on the wealthy, Buffet either back peddled or clarified his position. When asked about his call for higher taxes in an appearance on CNBC he said "my [tax] program would be on the very high incomes that are taxed very low – not just high incomes, not just some guy making $50 million playing baseball, his taxes won't change. Make $50 million appearing on TV, his income won't change." When asked if he considered $250,000 a year to be rich, he replied "No – that's another program that I won't be discussing. My program is to have a tax on ultra-rich people who are paying very low tax rates, not just all the rich people, and it would probably apply to 50,000 people." Luckily, research has been done on how many of the super-rich pay less in taxes (percentage wise) than their secretaries, and the number isn't anywhere close to 50,000.

Liberal columnist Dana Milbank claims that when he asked someone at the liberal Brookings Institution how many people would be affected by the Buffet Rule, the estimate he got was only around 1000 people. [530] The highest estimate seems to be around 4,000 people, according to the nonpartisan Tax Policy Center.[531]

---

[529] "Warren Buffett, Hypocrite." *The New York Post*, 29 Aug. 2011. <http://www.nypost.com/p/news/opinion/editorials/warren_buffett_hypocrite_E3BsmJmeQVE38q2Woq9yjJ#ixzz1WRoIlYSf>.

[530] Sheppard, Noel. "Liberal Think Tank: Almost 100 Percent of Millionaires Pay More Tax Percentagewise Than Lower." *Newsbusters*, 21 Sept. 2011. <http://newsbusters.org/blogs/noel-sheppard/2011/09/21/liberal-think-tank-almost-100-percent-millionaires-pay-more-tax-perce>.

[531] Rubin, Richard. "Buffett Rule or Not, Most Rich People Already Pay." *Businessweek*, 12 Apr. 2012. <http://www.businessweek.com/articles/2012-04-12/buffett-rule-or-not-most-rich-people-already-pay>.

Problems with Polling Data on "The Rich"

It is no secret that most Americans want "the rich" to be taxed more. Polling data from August 2011 even showed that slightly over half of republicans favor this.[532] This isn't to say however that Americans favor big taxes and big government – only 4% favor deficit reduction solely through tax increases, while 20% favor deficit reduction solely through spending cuts. [533] What the data does back up is most people supporting deficit reduction through both spending cuts and tax increases. I think that tax levels on the rich should stay at or around the same levels they are today, but this section aims to show how the polling data favoring high taxes on wealthier Americans is easily skewed.

The Obama administration has consistently defined households making over $250 thousand a year as rich, but everyone has a definition of their own. While a poll by the Reason Foundation concurred with other surveys showing that most Americans want higher taxes on the rich, the methods used in this survey differed. Instead of a simple yes or no question, people in different income brackets were surveyed on what income groups they think should pay more in taxes. Those making less than $25,000 annually defined rich between $100,000 and $500,000 a year. Those making $100,000-$199,000 defined this as being between $300,000 and $500,000. Those earning over $200,000 defined rich as being between $300,000 to $1 million. Those in the bottom 1% even thought that those making $50,000 a year should pay more in taxes.[534]

---

[532] De Pinto, Jennifer. "Polls Show Most Americans Support Raising Taxes on Wealthy." *CBS News*, 23 Sept. 2011. <http://www.cbsnews.com/8301-503544_162-20110458-503544.html>.

[533] Jones, Jeffrey M. "On Deficit, Americans Prefer Spending Cuts; Open to Tax Hikes." *Gallup*, 13 July 2011. <http://www.gallup.com/poll/148472/Deficit-Americans-Prefer-Spending-Cuts-Open-Tax-Hikes.aspx>.

[534] Ekins, Emily. "Tax the Rich?" *Reason*, 19 Sept. 2011. <http://reason.com/poll/2011/09/19/tax-the-rich2>.

To say that people want higher taxes only when it doesn't affect them is an understatement – as the statement holds true even when people have a better chance of getting struck by lightning then coming in contact with their money that could be taxed. In relation to the $656 million Mega Millions jackpot of March 2012, the *Wall Street Journal* publicized a survey conducted the month before on what people felt an appropriate level of taxation on lottery winnings were. The poll was based on winnings ranging from $1 million to $100 million. The results showed that less than a quarter chose a tax rate 30% of higher, and results averaged a rate of 15%. The averages by political affiliation showed that Republicans favored an average rate of 14%, and Democrats an average rate of 17% - a minor difference. The same exact poll showed that 62% support the Buffet Rule, and increased taxes on households earning over $250,000 a year.[535]

This remains true even when looked at from different angles. A 2011 survey conducted by *The Hill* asks 1000 likely voters what rate of taxation they would apply to high earners. Among respondents, 75% chose that the rich should be paying a rate under 30%, which would translate to a tax decrease from what the top marginal tax rate is currently.[536]

Everyone, including our friend Buffet is free to send a check to the government to help pay the nation's bills. Currently, the government gains an additional $3 million in revenue by this method. In a nation of over 300 million people, this amounts to less than a penny in revenue per person. For most people, this

---

[535] Gaines, Brian J., and Douglas Rivers. "Gaines and Rivers: What's a 'Fair' Tax for the Mega Millionaires?" *The Wall Street Journal*, 10 Apr. 2012. <http://online.wsj.com/article/SB10001424052702303772904577335351919453764.html?mod=rss_opinion_main>.

[536] "National Survey of 1,000 Likely Voters." *Pulse Opinion Research*, 23 Feb. 2012. <http://thehill.com/images/stories/news/2012/02_february/crosstabs_20120223_thehill.pdf>.

means when it's time to actually pay up, the government literally isn't worth their two cents.

After all this, all that comes to mind is a great quote by Buffet himself: "A public-opinion poll is no substitute for thought."

The Welfare State

Few would disagree that the government should have at least some sort of role in providing a safety net for citizens in the event that an unlikely circumstance puts them in financial danger. A point of difference between the American Right and Left is on how big we make that safety net, and at what point a safety net becomes a hammock.

The Incentives Trap Prior to Clinton

The greatest flaw in the early welfare system before Clinton-era reform was the lack of a work requirement. This problem was most influentially laid out in Charles Murray's book *Losing Ground*,[537] but other intellectuals such as Milton Friedman, Thomas Sowell, and Walter Williams also pointed at the problem.

This flaw was patched in 1996 when the welfare system was reformed by a combination of President Bill Clinton and his Republican House. The Urban Institute received plenty of media attention for its claims that this reform would throw an estimated 1.1 million children into poverty,[538] but six years after taking effect nearly three million less children were living in poverty.[539]

---

[537] Murray, Charles A. "Losing Ground: American Social Policy, 1950-1980." (New York: Basic, 1984).

[538] Goertzel, Ted. "Why Welfare Research Fails." *Rutgers University*, Aug. 1998. <http://crab.rutgers.edu/~goertzel/fail2.html>.

[539] Rector, Robert, and Patrick F. Fagan. "The Continuing Good News About Welfare Reform." *The Heritage Foundation*, 6 Feb. 2003. <http://www.heritage.org/research/reports/2003/02/the-continuing-good-news>.

The number of welfare caseloads was almost cut in half and 3.5 million fewer people were living in poverty overall.[540]

The Incentives Trap Today

An impoverished person on welfare can face a higher tax rate on their income than the richest American, and it isn't because of the tax code. It's because at a certain point, as an impoverished person earns additional income, they begin losing benefits. If an additional dollar in earnings lead to a reduction of 50 cents in benefits, the incentive to work is substantially reduced, especially when the cost of gas, child care, and eating outside of the home is taking into account.

An interesting post on Greg Mankiw's blog showed that for a hypothetical family of three living in Virginia, as that family's earned income rises from $15,000 to $30,000, the amount of total income (earned income + transfers) is stagnant.[541]

There have yet to be any viable welfare proposals that would fix this problem. Milton Friedman advocated replacing all welfare programs with a guaranteed minimum income (or negative income tax as it's also known). The Wikipedia page for "Guaranteed Minimum Income" cites support for the proposal from all sides of the political spectrum, including Thomas Paine, Martin Luther King Jr., F.A. Hayek, John Kenneth Galbraith, Francis Fox Piven, and others.[542] This sort of program would aim to reduce the work disincentive that welfare produces. For example, if the poverty line was at $10,000, with a negative tax rate of 50%, someone who earns $5,000 would receive a $2,500

---

[540] Ibid.

[541] Mankiw, Greg N. "The Poverty Trap." 11 Nov. 2009. <http://gregmankiw.blogspot.com/2009/11/poverty-trap.html>.

[542] "Guaranteed Minimum Income." <http://en.wikipedia.org/wiki/Guaranteed_minimum_income>. Accessed May 18th 2013.

check in the mail. The goals of this system were to incentivize work until that person no longer would need assistance when they hit the poverty line.

The evidence the NIT within the US is poor. Large experiments with the NIT between 1968 and 1979 have failed to provide any evidence that work disincentives were removed. Husbands reduced their hours worked by 9% on average, while wives did the same by 18%.[543] It was also found that the NIT did nothing to prevent family breakup, a charge which many rightly list as a consequence of the pre-Clinton welfare system.[544]

While the guaranteed minimum income and negative income tax are terms used interchangeably, many guaranteed minimum income proposals differ from the negative income tax. While the NIT cuts people a check for a certain gap between their income and the poverty line, the GMI gives the same cash payment regardless. Charles Murray's GMI proposal includes giving all Americans aged 21 and over $10,000 a year for life, the money for which comes from ditching all other welfare programs (including entitlements).

Welfare, Taxation, and Charity

Many liberals will argue that lowering taxes will leave less revenue to be spent on social programs which help the poor. The logic of this is hopelessly flawed because our government already spends much more than it brings in, and has done so for quite a while. On another level, this argument is flawed because private charity functions much more effectively, and with much less overhead than do government anti-poverty programs.

According to the Capitalism Institute, 70% of money given to private charity gets used on programs, while only 30% of tax dollars allocated for government aid programs actually gets

---

543 Allen, Jodie T. "Negative Income Tax." *Library of Economics and Liberty*, <http://www.econlib.org/library/Enc1/NegativeIncomeTax.html>.
544 Ibid.

used on programs. In other words, according to this estimate private charity is 150% more efficient than government aid.[545] According to a conflicting estimate from the *NonProfit Times*, private charities overhead is around 40%, which still makes it at least twice as efficient as government aid.[546]

While the 30% figure may seem questionable, it becomes much more believable when put in perspective. Whether it be Ronald Reagan in the 1960s or Milton Friedman in the 1970s, conservatives have long argued that if we took the amount of money that we spend on welfare programs and distributed it in the form of cash to every poor person, we would eliminate poverty. In 2011, $950 billion was spent on means-tested welfare programs at the federal and state level, and there were 49 million people classified as poor. Divided equally, this would provide each poor person with $19,400, or $77,600 for a family of four (while the poverty line for a family of four is $22,350).[547] On a related note, part of the logic behind the negative income tax is that it would help relieve some of the bureaucratic overhead that the current system has.

But getting back to the main point, private charity should also have an increasing role in public welfare. We already know that America is a highly charitable nation – the most charitable in the world to be exact.[548] In 2011, charitable donations totaled

---

[545] Connell, Shaun. "This Picture Shows What's Wrong With Government "Charity"." *Capitalism Institute*, 13 Dec. 2012. <http://www.capitalisminstitute.org/private-charity-infographic/>.
[546] Sullivan, Patrick. "Survey: Charities Should Spend 23% On Overhead." *The NonProfit Times*, 15 Aug. 2012. <http://www.thenonprofittimes.com/article/detail/survey-charities-should-spend-23-on-overhead-4804>.
[547] Heath, Hadley. "Welfare and Charity: Two Different Things." *Independent Women's Forum*, Dec. 2011. <http://c1355372.cdn.cloudfiles.rackspacecloud.com/9a090ecd-9aad-4cce-b335-95f4e847aa78/Newsletter%20December%202011%20Proof%204.pdf>.
[548] Peralta, Eyder. "Survey: U.S. Takes Top Spot As Most Charitable Nation." *NPR*, 20 Dec. 2011. <http://www.npr.org/blogs/thetwo-way/2011/12/20/144035063/survey-u-s-takes-top-spot-as-most-charitable-nation>.

nearly $300 billion.[549] The value created from volunteering can also be classified as a form of charity. The Bureau of Labor Statistics reports that between September 2011 and September 2012, 64.5 million Americans volunteered for a median time of 50 total hours in that period.[550] If we were to value a volunteer hour at the federal minimum wage of $7.25, these volunteer hours would have produced roughly $23.4 billion in benefit.[551]

According to one sociologist, the relationship between income and charitable donations is inversely related since American households with incomes under $10,000 give 5.5% of their incomes to charity, while those making over $100,000 give only 2.9%.[552]. 5.5% of 10,000 is $550, while 2.9% of 100,000 is $2900, so the claim that poor people give more to charity than the rich is hilariously flawed. Percent and actual dollar amount are not the same thing. Besides, there are other income groups than those making 10,000 and those making 100,000. Over 95% of millionaires donate to charity, and give an average 9% of their income in doing so.[553]

The relationship between taxes on the wealthy and charitable donations is somewhat less clear. While higher taxes mean less income, it also increases the size of a charitable donation's tax write-off.[554] Regardless, 56% of 150 billionaire

---

[549] Nichols, Michelle. "U.S. Charitable Giving Approaches $300 Billion in 2011." *Reuters*, 19 June 2012. <http://www.reuters.com/article/2012/06/19/us-usa-charity-idUSBRE85I05T20120619>.

[550] "Volunteering in the United States, 2012." *Bureau of Labor Statistics*, 22 Feb. 2012. <http://www.bls.gov/news.release/volun.nr0.htm>.

[551] 64,500,000 x 50 x 7.25

[552] Ore, Tracy E. "The Social Construction of Difference and Inequality: Race, Class, Gender, and Sexuality." (Boston Massachusetts: McGraw-Hill Higher Education, 2009), p. 638.

[553] Frank, Robert. "Millionaires Give Nine Percent of Income to Charity." *CNBC*, 29 Oct. 2012. <http://www.cnbc.com/id/49596515/Millionaires_Give_Nine_Percent_of_Income_to_Charity>.

[554] Frank, Robert. "Tax Hikes on Rich May Increase Charitable Giving." *CNBC*, 15 Jan. 2013.

attendees to the Forbes 400 Summit on Philanthropy polled claimed that taxes would negatively affect their personal charitable giving.[555] Though at the same time, 70% of those same billionaires surveyed claimed to give due to their "personal values,"[556] which only goes to show that taxes are one factor in many that drive charitable giving.

In case you're wondering the role that political affiliation plays in charitable giving, the research shows that conservatives have average annual incomes 6% less than their liberal counterparts, yet give 30% more to charity than liberals.[557]

Rethinking Retirement – Reforming Social Security

Texas governor Rick Perry created a storm of controversy at the Republican presidential debate in September of 2011 when he claimed that Social Security is a Ponzi scheme.[558]

Perry's comments are far less controversial than people wanted to make them out to be. Paul Krugman of all people published an article in the *Boston Review* in 1997 accusing Social Security being as such.[559] Since Krugman's piece got a good deal of attention following Perry's comments, Krugman naturally rushed to his blog to offer up an explanation about what he "really" meant. In his defense piece he claims that he only used the "Ponzi" term because another economist had done the same.

<http://www.cnbc.com/id/100380899/Tax_Hikes_on_Rich_May_Increase_Charitable_Giving>.

555 Frank, Robert. "Tax Hikes a Threat to Charitable Giving, Say Billionaires." *CNBC*, 19 Sept. 2012. <http://www.nbcnews.com/business/tax-hikes-threat-charitable-giving-say-billionaires-1B6053392>.

556 Ibid.

557 Brookes, Arthur C. "A Nation of Givers." *American Enterprise Institute*, Mar.-Apr. 2008. <http://www.american.com/archive/2008/march-april-magazine-contents/a-nation-of-givers>.

558 This was spoken at the Reagan Library Republican Presidential Debate, which occurred on September 7th 2011.

559 Krugman, Paul. "What Consensus?" *Boston Review*, Jan. 1997. <http://www.bostonreview.net/BR21.6/krugmann.html>.

[560] He does quote a paragraph from the 1997 "Ponzi" piece, and the last sentence states that "today's young may well get less than they put in." The best that Krugman can really argue at this point is that he doesn't think Social Security is a Ponzi scheme, but that it's instead just an awful deal from an investors perspective.[561] The latter would better describe my position when trying to argue for reforming Social Security.

Private Retirement vs. Social Security

The difference in outcomes between private investment and the current Social Security model is undisputed. The Cato Institute's study "Still a Better Deal" notes that despite the 2008 downturn in the stock market, someone who invested privately for the past 40 years (preceding 2012) would still yield average yearly returns of 6.85% from the S&P500, 3.46% from corporate bonds, or 2.44% from government bonds.[562] The study charts the difference between social security and private retirement plans using monthly returns in Table 3.1.

Table 3.1: Social Security vs. Private Retirement

	Monthly Benefit		
Investment Package	Poor	Wealthy	Average
Stocks	$1,287	$4,586	$2,621
50/50*	$1,096	$3,562	$2,067
Bonds	$896	$2,539	$1,565
Current	$891	$2,033	$1,358

*50% U.S. Treasury Bonds, 50% Moody's AAA corporate bonds
Source: "Still a Better Deal," *Cato*.

[560] Krugman, Paul. "The Ponzi Thing." *The New York Times*, 14 Sept. 2011. <http://krugman.blogs.nytimes.com/2011/09/14/the-ponzi-thing/>.
[561] Perhaps another contradiction; Krugman argues on p. 174 of "The Conscience of a Liberal" that the bottom 60% of income earners will receive more from Social Security than they put in, while the top 20% will lose on their "investment."
[562] Tanner, Michael D. "Still a Better Deal: Private Investment vs. Social Security." *The Cato Institute*. 13 Feb. 2012. <http://www.cato.org/publications/policy-analysis/still-better-deal-private-investment-vs-social-security>

Current Models: Chile and Texas

In the 2012 Republican presidential primaries, both Herman Cain and Newt Gingrich mentioned the Chilean model as one to base Social Security reform off.[563] Another model mentioned by Gingrich was the county Galveston, which is one of three counties in Texas to privatize their retirement systems (the other two are Brazoria and Matagorda).[564]

Prior to reform in 1981, Chile's Social Security model was similar to that of the United States in the sense that it was a pay-as-you-go system. Beginning in 1981 (coincidentally on the same date Ronald Reagan was sworn into office), the Chilean system has operated using personal accounts. All new workers were forced into the reformed system, while preexisting workers were given a choice between the two systems.

Workers in the new system are required to contribute 10% of their wages into their account. Workers pick their pension fund, and their payout comes in the form of either inflation-protected annuities or gradual withdrawals.[565]

Prior to reform, Chile had a problem with workers retiring early, since postponing retirements wouldn't increase their pension's payout (though luckily the US system does). Since reform, the labor force participation rate in Chile has grown higher than in the US for all age groups 40 and above, but the largest gap in participation is with the elderly. One study found that:

---

[563] Cain made mention of the Chilean model while campaigning. Gingrich cited the model in the South Carolina primary debate.

[564] Gingrich mentioned Galveston in the South Carolina Debate. Herman Cain previously mentioned it in the CNN/Tea Party Express debate in Tampa Florida, September 2011.

[565] My data on the structure of Chile's reformed system comes from: James, Estelle. "How to Keep Seniors Working: Lessons from Chile." *National Center for Policy Analysis*, 24 Aug. 2010. <http://www.ncpa.org/pub/ba718>.

> The biggest change in labor force participation was for individuals who had started receiving benefits from their retirement accounts: Participation rates rose by 15 percentage points for pension recipients in their late 60s. Rates rose by 28 percentage points for those in their 50s and early 60s. Among all pension recipients under age 70, the proportion who continued working more than doubled.[566]

Objectors to Chile's system point to many different apparent defects to make their case. One commonly cited statistic by opponents states that roughly 1/3rd of all money privately invested goes towards administrative costs. The source for this statistic is, of all places, AARP.[567] A 1996 study by the US Social Security Administration on the Chilean system reported that only around 3% of "worker's earnings for each contribution made" are used to "pay for disability and survivor benefits and for administrative expenses" under the Chilean system.[568]

Returns on private accounts outperformed original estimates, with workers yielding returns of 12% on average between 1981 and 1995, but some critics have argued that this is a fluke, since Chile's economy boomed during this period due to rampant privatization, something that can't happen indefinitely.[569] They have a point there, but even extending measurements from 1981 to 2010, real returns still average above 9%. The initial predicted return by Jose Pinera (the then labor

---

566 James, Estelle. "How to Keep Seniors Working: Lessons from Chile." *National Center for Policy Analysis*, 24 Aug. 2010. <http://www.ncpa.org/pub/ba718>.
567 One study citing the statistic can be found at: "Chile's Privatization Failures." *Century Foundation*, 25 Apr. 2005. <http://tcf.org/commentary/pdfs/nc962/chilefactsheet.pdf>.
568 Kritzer, Barbara E. "Privatizing Social Security: The Chilean Experience." *Division of Program Analysis, Office of Research, Evaluation and Statistics, Social Security Administration*, Fall 1996. <http://www.ssa.gov/policy/docs/ssb/v59n3/v59n3p45.pdf>.
569 Schalch, Kathleen. "Examining Private-Account Pensions in Chile." *NPR*, 7 Apr. 2005. <http://www.npr.org/templates/story/story.php?storyId=4580360>.

minister who proposed privatization) was a compounded annual 4%.[570]

Risk

The major stock market downturns of the pre-depression 1929 crash, the bursting of both the tech bubble in the early 2000s and the housing bubble in 2008 definitely make the stock market seem like a gamble. Despite the markets greatest downturns, it's still offset by its increases. Someone who invested the entirety of their retirement funds in the stock market at the market's highest point in 1929 right before the crash would still have an average annual return of 4.9% by the time their retired after 45 years in 1974.[571] Likewise, someone invested all of their funds in 1887 and pulled out their money in 1932 after the market bottomed out after the crash of '29 would still have annualized returns of 4.3%. [572]

Still complete privatization is still something that will never fly politically. Newt Gingrich mentioned that Chile bails out people who lose money on their private investments, but this would require a decent amount of central planning to prevent fraud, and plus, true capitalism required privatized profits and loses, not privatized profits and socialized losses. A more palatable solution politically would be partial privatization, whereas a person could allocate 1/3rd of their Social Security funds to an investment of their choice. That way, even if someone were to have their private funds eliminated completely, they would still have 2/3rds of their funds to fall back on once they retire – and we don't have to socialize the losses.

---

570 "The Chilean Model." *Investor's Business Daily*, 27 Dec. 2010. <http://news.investors.com/article/557939/201012271907/the-chilean-model.htm>.

571 Murray, Charles A. "In Our Hands: A Plan to Replace the Welfare State." (Washington D.C.: American Enterprise Institute, 2006), p. 29

572 Ibid., pp. 29-30.

Balancing the Federal Budget

In 2012, the federal government brought in $2.469 trillion in revenue, yet spent $3.796 trillion dollars, creating a $1.327 trillion deficit.

The Big Four

One of the few times I found myself in agreement with Ezra Klein is when he described the American government as an insurance conglomerate protected by an army. During the GSA scandal of 2012, while everyone in congress spent their time outraged over the hundreds of thousands of dollars wasted by the GSA, I couldn't help but wonder why no one was focusing on the hundreds of billions of dollars wasted in other areas of government which actually are contributing towards our bankruptcy as a nation.

In 2012, $716.3 billion was spent on defense, $484.486 billion on Medicare, $361.625 billion on health (non-Medicare), $778.574 on Social Security, and $579.574 billion on income security. This accounts for 2.92 trillion in spending itself, far exceeding our current tax receipts, and composing over three fourths of the federal budget.

Stopping cuts to defense at all costs is generally seen as a Republican ideal, but as Reason Magazine's editor in chief Nick Gillespie points out; "attacking the Military-Industrial Complex is a Republican Virtue – and good politics." Aside from the Eisenhower reference, he points out that recent Republican budget proposals have advocated spending less on the military than Obama has.[573] Rhetoric aside, the United States does already account for nearly half the world's military spending. We even spend billions more on military than the next top 14 military

---

[573] Gillespie, Nick, and Meredith Bragg. "3 Reasons Conservatives Should Cut Defense Spending Now!" Reason, 10 Jan. 2012. <http://reason.com/blog/2012/01/10/3-reasons-conservatives-should-cut-defen>.

spenders combined – many of which are allies.[574] As Gillespie also points out, after World War II, the Vietnam War, and the Cold War, military spending decreased. Now, with the Iraq war over, and the threat of Al Qaida, for the most part, neutralized, it is time to do the same. Assuming that the war in Afghanistan would also be ended, simply reducing military spending to what it was in the year 2000 would translate to roughly a $339.47 billion reduction in spending.

Defenders of our current levels of military spending have a few tricks up their sleeve to make military spending seem small. Among them are measuring defense spending as a percentage of the budget, and as a percentage of GDP. During the February Republican Primary debate in Arizona, Rick Santorum claimed that "when I was born (in 1958), defense spending was sixty percent of the budget. It's now seventeen percent. If you think defense spending is the problem, you need a remedial math class to go back to."[575] When measuring defense spending against GDP, American Enterprise Institute scholar Nicholas Eberstadt concludes that "in 2010 the national defense budget amounted to 4.8 percent of current GDP," which was "lower in 2010 than in almost any year during the four-plus debates of the Cold War era."[576]

Well actually, it's Santorum who apparently needs to take remedial math, and Eberstadt's measurement makes no sense. Eberstadt is measuring the defense budget's size against the size of our economy, instead of against historical real defense spending, or population size. When adjusted for inflation, the defense budget today is higher than during the peak of the

---

[574] De Rugy, Veronique. "World's Top Military Spenders: U.S. Spends More than Next Top 14 Countries Combined." *Mercatus Center*, 9 Dec. 2011. <http://mercatus.org/publication/worlds-top-military-spenders-us-spends-more-next-top-14-countries-combined>.

[575] Arizona Republican Presidential Debate in Mesa, Arizona on February 22nd 2012.

[576] Eberstadt, Nick. "A Nation of Takers: America's Entitlement Epidemic." (West Conshohocken, PA: Templeton, 2012), pp. 70-72.

Korean War, Vietnam War, and the Reagan build up during the Cold War.[577]

For Social Security, Doing something as basic as raising both the early and regular retirement ages would be a large cost saver. The case for raising the age is quite strong. Since people have been living longer without the retirement age increasing, they've been receiving benefits for longer periods of time. As a report for the Urban Institute showed, in 2008 the average expected length that workers collected Social Security increased by 5.1 years for men and 6 years for women since benefits began going out in 1940. During this same time period, the average age at which workers took up social security decreased from age 68.5 to 63.6.[578] With both variables accounted for, the amount of time recipients receive benefits is now approximately 17.9 years for men, and 20.5 for women.[579]

In practice, the Social Security retirement age would be raised in a way to not affect either new retirees, or those about to retire soon. Beginning in 2012, raising the early retirement age from 62 to 64 at a pace of 2 months per year (until 2025) would save around $144 billion over the next decade. Applying the same method to the normal retirement age to raise it to 70 would take until 2035, and would produce $120 billion in savings over the next decade.[580] Applying both savings measures would amount to around $26.4 billion in savings per year.

---

[577] Sharp, Travis. "Current U.S. Defense Spending vs. Spending Since 1948." *The Center for Arms Control and Non-Proliferation*, 26 Feb. 2009. <http://armscontrolcenter.org/issues/securityspending/articles/022609_fy10_topline_growth_since48/>.

[578] Favreault, Melissa M., and Richard W. Johnson. "Raising Social Security's Retirement Age." *Urban Institute*, July 2010. <http://www.urban.org/UploadedPDF/412167-Raising-Social-Security.pdf>.

[579] Ibid.

[580] "Raising Eligibility Ages Is Good For The Budget...And the Economy: A Look at CBO's Report on Raising Eligibility Ages." *The Committee for a Responsible Federal Budget*, 11 Jan. 2012. <http://crfb.org/blogs/raising-eligibility-ages-good-budgetand-economy>.

In addition to the cost savings to the country from raising the retirement age, this is also a great boost for the overall quality of retirement for workers in general. As one analyst for FOX Business reported; "By expanding upon the National Retirement Risk Index, analysts at CRR, including Webb, determined that 85% of us would have the financial resources needed to maintain the standard of living were enjoyed prior to retiring if we worked until age 70."[581]

Lastly in regards to healthcare as was discussed in chapter 2, block granting Medicaid would produce around $62.5 billion in annual savings.

In total, these cuts discussed would gut $428.37 billion from the federal budget.

Drug Policy Reform

While the drug war which began under the Nixon administration may have been good intentioned, so are most of the government's actions. Over a trillion dollars has already been spent on the drug war, yet the drug addiction rate remains unchanged from when it began.[582]

The benefits from legalization would arise from both the resources saved from lack of enforcement costs, and sin taxes placed on the drugs themselves. Harvard economics Professor Jeffrey Miron estimates in his book *The Budgetary Impact of Ending Drug Prohibition* that around $41.3 billion would be saved each year in enforcement costs (25.7 for state and local

---

[581] Buckner, Gail. "Easy Fix for Retirement Problems: Work Longer." *FOX Business*, 25 June 2012. <http://www.foxbusiness.com/personal-finance/2012/06/25/not-so-easy-path-to-secure-retirement/>.

[582] "AP IMPACT: After 40 Years, $1 Trillion, US War on Drugs Has Failed to Meet Any of Its Goals." *FOX News*, 13 May 2010. <http://www.foxnews.com/world/2010/05/13/ap-impact-years-trillion-war-drugs-failed-meet-goals/>.

governments, $15.6B for federal government), and would bring in $46.7 billion annually in tax revenue.[583]

The reduction in enforcement costs is based off savings from eliminating (non-crime related) drug arrests, the savings in the judicial area for convicting users, and the reduction in correctional resources for those imprisoned. The estimate on how much tax revenue will be garnered assumes that drugs are taxed at comparable rates to tobacco or alcohol. Additional tax revenue would be collected through the income tax, assuming producers of drugs make money from it.

On net balance, these reforms reduce the federal deficit by $62.3 billion.

Corporate Welfare

It's estimated by the Cato Institute that nearly of $100 billion of the federal budget consists of corporate welfare. Slightly over $25 billion comes from the department of agriculture, and around $4.7 billion comes from defense, so this money would already be cut from the other spending reductions proposed. There still exist sizeable chunks elsewhere; including the Departments of Commerce ($4.095B), Energy ($16.041B), Interior ($2.608B), State ($5.201B), Transportation ($2.024B). Other miscellaneous programs and agencies account for an additional $20,441B in spending.[584]

On net balance, gutting all forms of corporate welfare not already included in other proposed cuts would lead to a net savings of $90.3 billion.

---

[583] Miron, Jeffrey A., and Katherine Waldock. "The Budgetary Impact of Ending Drug Prohibition." (Washington, DC: Cato Institute, 2010), p. 1 (executive summary).
[584] DeHaven, Tad. "Corporate Welfare in the Federal Budget." *The Cato Institute*. 25 July 2012. <http://www.cato.org/publications/policy-analysis/corporate-welfare-federal-budget>

Department Eliminations and other Miscellaneous Cuts

This section will focus on smaller departments of government which, while they don't contribute enormously to the overall debt, are not worth the cost.

First on the list is the $56.25 billion spent on "international affairs," or foreign aid. The spending would have been defensible if it were spent fighting global poverty, but foreign aid dollars tend to be seized by warlords, not the poor. Following the law of unintended consequences, there is additional evidence that foreign aid harms economic development abroad. In Micronesia, Bangladesh, India, Egypt, Haiti, Guatemala, and Kenya, foreign aid has driven those countries local producers out of business. The governments of Peru, Haiti, and Guatemala have even either refused food aid, or asked the US to restrict aid.[585]

Second comes the Department of Agriculture, which comes with a price tag of $145 billion. This is one department that I wouldn't argue for total elimination, since it includes food stamps and school lunch programs, which act as safety nets. Moderate cuts could still be made to those programs with little consequence, as we've seen in recent times that obesity, not starvation, is a growing problem among the poor. Also, forty percent of those eligible for food stamps do not participate, which far from being a failure of the program, shows that many eligible for it don't need it.[586]

Around $30 billion of those cuts would be to subsidies – which would translate to better agriculture overall. Subsidy free farming is a place where we have a testable model – as this is

---

[585] Osterfeld, David. "The Failures and Fallacies of Foreign Aid." *The Freeman*, Feb. 1990. <http://www.thefreemanonline.org/columns/the-failures-and-fallacies-of-foreign-aid/>.

[586] Edwards, Chris. "Food Subsidies." *The Cato Institute*, July 2009. <http://www.downsizinggovernment.org/agriculture/food-subsidies>.

what has occurred in New Zealand since 1984. Farm productivity prior to 1984 averaged an increase of 1% per year, but increased to 4% per year post-reform. As one New Zealand farmer whites, "The agriculture sector in New Zealand has actually grown as a percentage of our GDP, from slightly more than 14 percent of GDP in 1986-87 to 16.6 percent in 1999-2000. This is almost unheard of in any other developed country."[587]

As "Downsizing the Federal Government," a project of The CATO Institute shows, cutting food subsidies in half, while ending all other functions of the Department of Agriculture would save $86.4 billion a year.[588]

Government employees simultaneously work less and earn more than their private sector counterparts. It's estimated that simply requiring public sector employees to work as many hours as private sector employees would save over $130 billion annually in labor costs.[589] That savings are without cutting anyone's salaries of benefits, just making them work longer to gain them, which, given the differential between public vs. private hours work, would be around an extra three hours a week for public employees. It's impossible for me to calculate just how much money would be saved in my budget plan, since many federal employees would lose their jobs as a result, and therefore not be part of the group working an extra three weekly hours.

---

[587] Lambie, Thomas. "Miracle Down Under: How New Zealand Farmers Prosper without Subsidies or Protection." *The Cato Institute*. February 7, 2005. <http://www.cato.org/publications/free-trade-bulletin/miracle-down-under-how-new-zealand-farmers-prosper-without-subsidies-or-protection>

[588] Edwards, Chris. "A Plan to Cut Spending and Balance the Federal Budget." *The Cato Institute*, Apr. 2011. <http://www.downsizinggovernment.org/balanced-budget-plan>.

[589] Biggs, Andrew G. and Richwine, Jason. "The Underworked Public Employee." *The Wall Street Journal*. Wednesday, December 5th, 2012. P. A17.

Cost Shifting[590]

Two proposed department eliminations will cut the federal deficit, but not lower the net cost of government to the taxpayer because they'll reappear at a state level. These two departments are Education and Transportation.

Third comes the Department of Education, whose complete elimination I would argue for. Ronald Reagan even campaigned on that, yet we unfortunately still have today. The disclaimer for these cuts is that I advocate them only because they would operate better at a state and local level. This would cut $139.21 billion from the federal budget overall. State and local governments can determine which functions that the Department previously completely that they determine are worthwhile funding themselves.

Eliminating the Department of Transportation would save $102.55 billion. Like education, this isn't to say that its function would cease to exist – but instead reappear at a state level. Without the Department dispersing funds, states can decide what method they want to collect revenue and how to spend it.

The Emphasis on Cost Cutting over Tax Increases

In total, roughly $1.033 trillion in cuts have been identified, and that is without factoring in any potential savings that would be realized from Medicare reform, or savings from cutting the hours of federal employees. The $1.033T figure isn't a perfect estimate because the spending cuts would technically cost some tax revenue in the short run. For example, if a hypothetical government worker is salaried $50,000 and pays $10,000 in taxes, cutting his job shrinks government expenditures by $50,000, while the net benefit is $40,000.

[590] I got the idea of cost shifting these departments to the states from John Medaille's book "Towards a Truly Free Market" (Wilmington: Intercollegiate Studies Institute, 2011), pp. 172-173.

The only form of tax increase that I would defend would be an end to the mortgage-interest deduction. If it were to be ended, it would've brought in an estimated $83.7 billion in revenue in 2012.[591] Another way to raise revenue without technically raising tax rates would be to place caps on itemized deductions. Putting this cap at $50,000 would raise an estimated $74.9 billion in revenue a year, 79.9% of which would come from the top 1% of earners.[592]

In the short run, large cuts in government spending and tax increases could be harmful until the economy adjusts. We do know however that tax increases are more harmful in the short-run than spending cuts,[593] which is why my deficit reduction plan emphasizes so heavily on spending cuts. One fact regarding revenue is that since the year 2012 was characterized by unemployment over 8%, the government will gather more revenue over time simply from the unemployment rate coming down.

The revenue gains from the unemployment rate simply decreasing would probably be enough to show some of the possible tax increases proposed unnecessary. In fact, as Daniel Mitchell has shown, if we had simply froze spending at 2011 levels, the budget would balance itself before 2018. If we were to increase spending 2% a year to keep up with inflation, it would take a little over a decade to do so.[594]

---

[591] Saunders, Laura. "Tax Breaks Under Fire." *The Wall Street Journal*, Saturday/Sunday, November 3-4, 2012. Pp. B7 and B9.
[592] Mankiw, Greg. "How To Raise Tax Revenue From The Rich Without Increasing Tax Rates." 10 Nov. 2012. <http://gregmankiw.blogspot.com/2012/11/how-to-raise-tax-revenue-from-rich.html>.
[593] Rugy, Veronique De. "Which Hurts More, Tax Increases or Spending Cuts?" *National Review Online*, 15 Nov. 2012. <http://www.nationalreview.com/corner/333447/which-hurts-more-tax-increases-or-spending-cuts-veronique-de-rugy>.
[594] Mitchell, Daniel J. "New CBO Numbers Re-Confirm That Balancing the Budget Is Simple with Modest Fiscal Restraint." *Cato at Liberty*, 27 Jan. 2011. <http://www.cato-at-liberty.org/new-cbo-numbers-re-confirm-that-balancing-the-budget-is-simple-with-modest-fiscal-restraint/>.

Chapter 4

Contemporary Economic Myths

In the department of the economy, an act, a habit, an institution, a law, gives birth not only to an effect, but to a series of effects. Of these effects, the first only is immediate; it manifests itself simultaneously with its cause – it is seen. The others unfold in succession – they are not seen: it is well for us, if they are foreseen. Between a good and a bad economist this constitutes the whole difference – the one takes account of the visible effect; the other takes account both of the effects which are seen, and also of those which it is necessary to foreseen.

– Frederic Bastiat, That Which is Seen and That Which is Not Seen, 1850.

Chapter 4

In 1850, French economist Frederic Bastiat penned his influential essay *That Which is Seen and That Which is Unseen.* The essay relays the simple fact that economic policy "gives birth not only to an effect, but to a series of effects." In applying this statement to his criticism of various economic fallacies, Bastiat shows how the alleged benefits of a certain policy can crumble with its hidden unintended consequences also taken into account.

The myths presented in this chapter for not only the reason that they provide falsehoods, but because they still manage to influence public policy. Bastiat's wisdom has influenced me greatly in writing this chapter. Many of the myths debunked appear to be true at face value, until more digging is done.

Myths will be divided into three different sections: basic economic myths, historical myths, and big government myths.

Part 1: Basic Economic Myths

Minimum Wage

Americans like the minimum wage. As a matter of fact, 71% support raising it to $9 an hour, a clear majority that includes both Democrats and Republicans.[595] It seems like a great idea too because of the immense difficulty one would face in trying to support themselves on only a minimum wage job. The myths regarding the minimum wage are that it would help the poorest among us by acting as a floor to wages, and some have even argued that the minimum wage helps the economy in other ways.

Who's who?

Since most people support raising the minimum wage due to the impossibility of living on a low minimum wage, its first necessary to understand whom exactly earns this wage. A so-called "living wage" is going to be much different for a teenager living with his parents than for an adult.

Out of 72.6 million wage earners in 2009, only 980,000 earned the minimum wage.[596] There are around 2.6 million workers classified as earning below the minimum wage, but this is misleading. Although earners such as waitresses technically earn less than the minimum wage, this is only because tips aren't

---

[595] Hanrahan, Tim. "Poll: Strong Support for Raising Minimum Wage." *The Wall Street Journal*, 21 Feb. 2013. <http://blogs.wsj.com/washwire/2013/02/21/poll-strong-support-for-raising-minimum-wage/>. Republicans, Independents, and Democrats all had majority support for the hike. Only those who identified with the Tea Party opposed it by a majority.

[596] "Characteristics of Minimum Wage Workers: 2009." *Bureau of Labor Statistics*, <http://www.bls.gov/cps/minwage2009.htm>.

factored into this statistic. Even if tips don't push them over $7.25 an hour in income, their employer is required by law to compensate them for the difference due to the Fair Labor Standards Act.[597] Tipped workers earned an average of $8.23 per hour in 2009, so nearly all of those included in the 2.6 million actually do earn equal to or over minimum wage.

Now out of those earning the minimum wage, around half are under age 25.[598] As reported by the Heritage Foundation, of all minimum wage earners aged 25 and under:

- 67% are working part time
- 17% live at or below the poverty line, while 65% have family incomes more than double the poverty line.
- Around 37% are college students who haven't yet completed their degree. This accounts for many of the non-teenage minimum wage earners.
- 36% have not completed high school. This group includes both current high school students and dropouts.[599]

Even for minimum wage earners aged 25 and over, reality isn't so bleak. Fifty six percent of them are only working part time, and although 23% live in poverty, 45% earn over double the poverty line.[600] Only 6.1% of them are single parents working full time.[601]

Earning the minimum wage is temporary anyway. Based off data from 1977-1997 period, 65.2% of workers had their salaries increased to above the minimum wage within their first

---

[597] "Fact Sheet #15: Tipped Employees Under the Fair Labor Standards Act (FLSA)." *U.S. Department of Labor Wage and Hour Division*, Revised March 2011. <http://www.dol.gov/whd/regs/compliance/whdfs15.pdf>.

[598] "Characteristics of Minimum Wage Workers: 2009," Tables 1 and 7.

[599] Hederman, Rea A., and James Sherk. "Who Earns the Minimum Wage - Single Parents or Suburban Teenagers?" *The Heritage Foundation*, 4 Aug. 2006. <http://www.heritage.org/research/reports/2006/08/who-earns-the-minimum-wage-single-parents-or-suburban-teenagers>.

[600] Ibid.

[601] Ibid.

year of employment. For college graduates, they on average see a 20% salary increase when put above the minimum wage.[602] There is a historical decline of the amount of people earning equal to or below the minimum wage. In 1979, 13.4% of workers were in such a position, but this declined to 5.2% in 2011.[603]

Unintended Consequences

All the data so far shows that those who earn the minimum wage are not in dire need of a raise to meet their basic needs. The problem with the minimum wage is that even if they were in need of a raise, it would create then harm people in need of a job. In recent years, the minimum wage has faced three hikes – up to $5.85 from $5.15 in 2007, to $6.55 in 2008, then finally $7.25 in 2009. To no surprise, this wasn't without a cost. As Cassy B. Mulligan of the *New York Times* estimated in July of 2011, by that point the hike to $7.25 had cost 800,000 jobs.[604] Of course, many of these losses were due to the fact that the minimum wage was risen in bad timing – during a recession.

Recessions aside, hikes in the minimum wage have a history of increasing unemployment. It's estimated that a 10% increase in the minimum wage results in around a 0.19% decrease in employment.[605] These declines in unemployment are primarily focused on the youth, and those with little education. If we do a comparison between states that set their minimum wages

---

[602] Evan, William. "Rising Above The Minimum Wage." *Economic Policies Institute*, Jan. 2000. <http://epionline.org/study_detail.cfm?sid=16>.

[603] "Characteristics of Minimum Wage Workers: 2011." *Bureau of Labor Statistics*, <http://www.bls.gov/cps/minwage2011.htm>.

[604] Mulligan, Casey B. "Where a Minimum-Wage Increase Would Bite." *The New York Times*, 13 July 2011. <http://economix.blogs.nytimes.com/2011/07/13/where-a-minimum-wage-increase-would-bite/>.

[605] Hicks, Michael J. "Did the Increase in Minimum Wage Cause Our Unemployment Rate to Rise?" *Ball State University Bureau of Business Research*, 24 Sept. 2008. <http://cms.bsu.edu/-/media/WWW/DepartmentalContent/MillerCollegeofBusiness/BBR/Publications/Wage Employ.pdf>.

at the federal minimum and those who set their minimum wages above the minimum, we find that youth unemployment is nearly four percentage points higher in those setting above the minimum.[606]

Higher Wages, More Employment?

"If the minimum wage is higher, people will have more money to spend, and therefore the economy will grow" – or so the argument goes in a *Huffington Post* piece by David Sirota criticizing former ABC host John Stossel.[607] Sirota's *Huffington Post* article was nothing more than a hit piece, calling Stossel a "pathological liar" in the title of the article, "down right stupid," and a "hypocrite" who pollutes the airwaves "without giving so much as a smidgeon of airtime to experts who would actually challenge this pathological liar with the facts."

Sirota ended up appearing on CNBC's Kudlow Report a month later debating Stossel face to face on the subject, repeating many of the same talking points. A statement that really stands out from Sirota is that experts would challenge Stossels' assertion. I decided to see what the experts had to say – and they didn't disagree with Stossel. Harvard economist and blogger Greg Mankiw has conducted polling data on economic experts over various issues – one of them being the minimum wage. In response to the statement "a minimum wage increases unemployment among young and unskilled workers," 79% of the experts agreed.[608]

Anyway, if we bother to look into the facts and figures, one study by the Economic Policy Institute estimates that the

---

[606] Murphy, Robert P. "I Get Empirical on Minimum Wage." *Free Advice*, 16 Feb. 2013. <http://consultingbyrpm.com/blog/2013/02/i-get-empirical-on-minimum-wage.html>.

[607] Sirota, David. "John Stossel Is A Pathological Liar." *The Huffington Post*, 30 May 2006. <http://www.huffingtonpost.com/david-sirota/john-stossel-is-a-patholo_b_21903.html>.

[608] Mankiw, Greg. "News Flash: Economists Agree." 14 Feb. 2009. <http://gregmankiw.blogspot.com/2009/02/news-flash-economists-agree.html>.

2009 minimum wage hike generated $5.5 billion in consumer spending nationwide.[609] This appears to aide Sirota's argument at first, but becomes less convincing when you realize that it only amounts for 0.0054% of the $10.1 trillion in consumer spending that year – hardly enough to spur job growth.[610]

Solutions

There exist many solutions to the problem of the minimum wage. Among them are abolishing it, decreasing it, altering its terms, or keeping it unchanged. Abolishing or decreasing the minimum wage would likely generate a lot of political pressure against it, which is why I proposed the third option. One way to prevent the job-killing aspect the minimum wage has on the unskilled would be to allow employers to pay their workers under the minimum wage for a specified training period, which could last anywhere from a few days, weeks, or months depending on the difficulty of the job.

After the training period would be over, the employer would be forced to pay the minimum wage to that employee – but they would have the skills to be worth the minimum wage after the training has ended. In reality, the length of a training program should be kept small. If the period were to be anywhere over a few months for all industries, many could hire employees, train them in a few days, then have them work for extremely low wages before firing them as the training period ends.

Despite the oft-cited myth of Australia's $16 an hour minimum wage and low youth unemployment rate, the reason they're able to have such low youth unemployment is because they have a graduated minimum wage. The minimum wage for those under age 16 is $5.87, $7.55 for those age 16, $9.22 at age

---

[609] The Study was cited on The Ed Show, MSNBC, Aired February 13 2013.
[610] Marron, Donald. "Consumer Spending Is Not 70% of the Economy." 27 May 2010. <http://dmarron.com/2010/05/27/consumer-spending-is-not-70-of-the-economy/>.

17, $10.90 at age 18, $13.17 at age 19, and $15.59 at age 20.[611] This may be a more preferable way of structuring the minimum wage, since lowering it for younger workers helps eliminate the job destroying effect that it has on low skilled workers. Lastly, regarding the fact that Australia's minimum wage still seems quite high compared to the US (at least for those aged 17 and older), also keep in mind that consumer prices are 39% lower in the US, rent prices are 48% lower, and groceries are 36% lower.[612]

To further hammer across the point that Australia is able to sustain such a higher minimum wage only for reasons pertaining to the cost of living, we can look at Norway. Norway has no minimum wage, yet their McDonald's workers earn on average the equivalent of $16-24 USD per hour (though like Australia, depending on age).[613] This isn't because your typical McDonald's manager is so chivalrous across the sea, but rather because the consumer price index in Norway is more than twice that in the US.[614]

Doing nothing would be a more palatable way of decreasing the minimum wage, as it would be done through inflation instead of the political process. Any decreases in real

---

[611] Crampton, Eric. "It's Complicated: Oz Minimum Wage Edition." 15 Feb. 2013. <http://offsettingbehaviour.blogspot.com/2013/02/its-complicated-oz-minimum-wage-edition.html>.

[612] "Cost of Living Comparison Between Australia and United States." *Numbeo*, <http://www.numbeo.com/cost-of living/compare_countries_result.jsp?country1=Australia&country2=United+States>. Updated March 2013.

[613] "McDonald's som-arbeidsgiver." <http://www.mcdonalds.no/no/jobb_og_karriere/McDonalds_som_arbeidsgiver.html>. I found the article through Reddit.com/TodayILearned, whereas the original poster did the Kroner to USD conversions (which check out).

[614] Someone posting on the thread mentioned above brought this point up. A link to CPI comparisons can be found at: "Cost of Living Index for Country for 2013." <http://www.numbeo.com/cost-of-living/rankings_by_country.jsp>.

wages from this could ideally be offset by increasing in the Earned Income Tax Credit.[615]

The Gender Wage Gap

The fact that men make more than women is hailed by feminists as proof of discrimination in the workforce. The "official" statistic tossed around where woman make "X amount of cents" for every dollar that a man makes is a poorly calculated number. To calculate this statistic, the average income of women is divided by the average income of men, and discrepancy between incomes is assumed as the result of discrimination.

The seldom-heard good news is that as of 2010, the gap has been at its lowest point on record, women earning 82.8 cents for every dollar of income men make.[616] But this number is still understated, as many variables are responsible for the gap in male and female pay, such as the amount of hours spent working, career choices, dangerousness of work, and others.

The amount of hours worked by men and women is one of the greatest sources of our gap. Even if men and women earned the same hourly wage for the same exact work, there would still be a wage gap. Men on average work 2,147 hours a year, compared to 1,851 for women.[617] Even if men and women made identical wages, say $10 an hour, men would earn $21,470 a year in this scenario, compared to $18,510 for women. Thus, even in a discrimination free world with identical wages, there

---

[615] To demonstrate the effects of the EITC, the *Heartland Institute* notes that it "already raises the effective minimum wage for a mom with two kids from $7.25 to $10.44 an hour." See: Glans, Matthew. "Research & Commentary: Earned Income Tax Credit vs. Minimum Wage Laws." *The Heartland Institute*, 19 June 2012. <http://heartland.org/policy-documents/research-commentary-earned-income-tax-credit-vs-minimum-wage-laws>.

[616] Cauchon, Dennis. "Gender Pay Gap Is Smallest on Record." *USA Today*, 14 Sept. 2010. <http://www.usatoday.com/money/workplace/2010-09-13-wage-gaps_N.htm>.

[617] "Hours Worked by Sex." *StatCrunch*, Apr. 2009. <http://www.statcrunch.com/5.0/viewreport.php?reportid=7996>.

would still be a 14-percentage point gap between the wages of men and women.

Even if we were to try to calculate the wage gap by only looking at men and women who work full time, this still wouldn't be a perfect comparison. Men who work full time work an average 8.14 hours on a workday, while a woman working full time work 7.75 hours.[618] That time difference alone explains a quarter of the wage gap when the gap is instead measured on men and women working full time.[619]

The second source of our gap is due to gender roles. It should be no surprise that women work less than men, since men don't go through the process of giving child birth, and it's generally the woman who takes off from work to raise the child. Although more women are entering the workforce, the duty of taking care of children is still done predominantly by women. Women also take time off of their careers for maternity leave. The old saying for athletes is to 'use it or lose it," and the same law applies to other careers. When people take time off, they lose skills that they would've otherwise built up during that time. As the former feminist Warren Farrell calculated, "women who have never been married and are without children earn 117% as much as their male counterparts."[620]

The majority of women are not unmarried and without children for their entire lives however. A decade after graduating from college, 39% of women are out of the workforce, while only 3% of men are. A reverse effect occurs when men and women get married. While married men work more than unmarried men, and married men with children work even longer because they have

---

[618] Lukas, Carrie. "It's Time That We End the Equal Pay Myth." *Forbes*, 16 Apr. 2012. <http://www.forbes.com/sites/realspin/2012/04/16/its-time-that-we-end-the-equal-pay-myth/>.
[619] Ibid.
[620] Farrell, Warren. "How the AAUW Pay Equity Study Undermines Women." *Glenn Sacks*, 19 Apr. 2007. <http://glennsacks.com/blog/?p=621>.

more people to take care of, married women work less than unmarried women.[621]

The third source of the income gap comes from variables within an occupation that would alter income. Dangerous jobs pay far more than the average job does, and the top ten most dangerous jobs are dominated by males. The worker fatality rate for men is 5.5 deaths per 100,000, and only 0.6 for women.[622] The leading cause of death for women in the workforce isn't a result of dangerous working conditions however – its homicide (which, as unfortunate as it is, isn't a wage increasing variable).[623]

A larger portion of men than women are employed in higher-paying fields. Only seven percent of women are employed in high paying computer and engineering fields, while thirty-eight percent of male professionals are.[624] Some may object that men are predominant in these fields because women were discriminated against, but someone has yet to claim that men are discriminated against for being underrepresented in low paying fields such as elementary education. The basic fact that men and women have different career interests best explains this divergence. Computer Science classes in high school "International Baccalaureate" programs are dominated by men, while English classes have a female majority.

---

[621] Sowell, Thomas. "Compassion versus Guilt, and Other Essays." (New York: Morrow, 1987), p. 93.

[622] Greenhouse, Steven. "The Most Dangerous Jobs in America." *The New York Times*, 20 Aug. 2010. <http://economix.blogs.nytimes.com/2010/08/20/the-most-dangerous-jobs-in-america/>.

[623] "FACT SHEET: Violence in the Workplace." *Violence Prevention Coalition of Greater Los Angeles*, June 2007. <http://www.ph.ucla.edu/sciprc/pdf/WORKPLACE_VIOLENCE.pdf>.

[624] "WOMEN IN AMERICA Indicators of Social and Economic Well-Being." *U. S. Department of Commerce Economics and Statistics Administration and Executive Office of the President Office of Management and Budget*, Mar. 2011. <http://www.whitehouse.gov/sites/default/files/rss_viewer/Women_in_America.pdf>.

Regardless, one of the best ways to test for discrimination is to compare the kinds of majors men and women chose, and how it would help them get into one of these high paying fields.

Table 4.1: Most Common Bachelor's Degrees for Men and Women 2008-2009

Top Men Majors	**# of Degrees in Major**	**Median Mid-Career Salary**	**Top Female Majors**	**# of Degrees in Major**	**Median Mid-Career Salary**
Business Administration and Management	66,190	$72,100	Psychology**	68,808	$60,400
Finance	22,931	$88,300	Business Administration and Management	64,122	$72,100
Biology	21,906	$64,800	Nursing	61,405	$67,000
Political Science	20,947	$78,200	Elementary Education and Teaching	36,358	$52,000
Accounting	20,446	$77,100	Biology	33,950	$64,800
Psychology**	20,432	$60,400	English Literature	28,945	$64,700
History	20,088	$71,000	Accounting	24,068	$77,100
Economics	17,756	$98,600	Communication Studies	22,000	$70,000
Mechanical Engineering*	15,424	$93,600	Sociology	20,064	$58,200
Marketing	14,613	$79,600	Liberal Arts	19,396	$63,200
Average Median Salary:[625]		**$71,304**			**$64,601**

Sources: National Center for Education Statistics, The Wall Street Journal, and others.[626] * = One of the Top Ten Highest Paying Majors. ** = Top 10 Lowest.[627]

---

[625] Note: Figures are adjusted for volume.

[626] Postsecondary Institutions and Price of Attendance in the United States: Fall 2009, Degrees and Other Awards Conferred: 2008–09, and 12-Month Enrollment: 2008–09." *National Center for Education Statistics*. <http://nces.ed.gov/pubs2010/2010161.pdf>;

When only the starting median salary is viewed, it's 39,923 for men, and 39,478 for women – no real gap. When mid-career salary is looked at, there's a $6,703 gap because majors that men chose have larger income growth over time. Even if career choice was the only factor in the wage gap, this accounts for 9.5% percentage points in the gap of men and women with college degrees. Of course, this data is raw, so mid-career salaries may be overestimated for women due to the variables causing the wage gap discussed (hours worked, child birth, etc.). For example – while the average business major makes $72,100 mid-career, women are less likely to accept high level business positions for personal reasons such as raising children, or having more free time, not because of discrimination.

There are other gaps that cannot logically be explained away by discrimination. Women owned businesses tend to make significantly less money than male run businesses. Unless a female employer is discriminating against herself, other factors have to be explored. Among the results from a Rochester Institute of Technology study were that money motives 76% of men, but only 29% of women. Women employers also tend to have shorter workweeks, and require more flexibility. Since most women owned small business owners don't fit the "never married and never had children" category, this should be expected. One study on women run small businesses in Australia even found that "flexibility and the ability to balance work with their

---

"Salary Increase by Major." *The Wall Street Journal*. <http://online.wsj.com/public/resources/documents/info-Degrees_that_Pay_you_Back-sort.html> and others. Salary data not included on the Wall Street Journal article was sourced from: <http://www.payscale.com/best-colleges/degrees.asp/>.

[627] Webley, Kayla. "The 20 Best- and Worst-Paid College Majors." *TIME*, 24 May 2011. <http://www.time.com/time/specials/packages/article/0,28804,2073703_2073653_2073690,00.html>.

relationships and family" was a motivating factor for starting a business.[628]

Ironically, while the male-female wage gap is used as a liberal talking point to justify legislation correcting it, the apparent gap has shrunk faster under Republican administrations. The annual wage growth of women relative to that of men's during the presidencies of Reagan and both Bush's greatly outpaced that of both Clinton and Carter. Reagan averaged 1.6% growth, while Clinton averaged 0.21%.[629]

Falling Real Wages

One myth about the economy is that while productivity has soared over the years, real wages have remained flat since the 1970's. Former Clinton Secretary of Labor economist Robert Reich has even produced a now-viral video for MoveOn.org making this point. I have already explained in chapter three that "real wage" calculations don't factor in benefits, but there are more in depth rebuttals to this myth. At face value, after adjusting for inflation using the CPI, the conclusion that real wages have remained flat appears justified. But the CPI isn't a perfect estimate. If we were to adjust wages according to the CPI, wages haven't changed since the Bureau of Labor began collecting data on them in 1964.[630] There are however, multiple ways of calculating inflation, each producing different results.

As George Mason University economics professor Don Boudreaux shows, simply measuring inflation by other standards such as the GDP Deflator shows an increase in the average wage of 18% from 1976 to 2006, while the CPI actually shows a 4%

---

[628] Still, L. & Timms, W. Women's Business: The Flexible Alternative Workstyle for Women." *Women in Management Review*, 2000. Pp. 272–283.
[629] Mattera, Jason. "Obama Zombies: How the Liberal Machine Brainwashed My Generation." (New York: Threshold Editions, 2010), p. 136.
[630] Boudreaux, Donald, and Mark Perry. "The Myth of a Stagnant Middle Class." *The Wall Street Journal*, 23 Jan. 2013. <http://online.wsj.com/article/SB10001424127887323468604578249723138161566.html?mod=rss_opinion_main>.

decline in wages during that period. Adding this newly calculated wage increase to the increase in benefits would yield a 26% increase in wages over the same period.[631]

Other studies making the same argument as Reich suffer from similar flaws. One study by economists Thomas Piketty and Emmanuel Saez claims to find that median incomes have risen only 3.2% from 1979 to 2007 after adjusting for inflation.[632] A conflicting study by Cornell economists challenges this, and finds many flaws in Piketty and Saez's analysis. The Cornell study, titled "A Second Opinion on the Economic Health of the American Middle Class" shows that when measured properly, median household income actually rose by 36.7%.[633]

The enormous gap in wage increases between the studies comes from how each study measured income gains. Pikkety and Saez focused their study on the income gains of "tax units" rather than households, which would ignore couples who live together, those who move back in with their parents after college, and senior citizens who live with their children. Piketty and Saez also don't factor in government transfers such as welfare, Social Security, health-care benefits, and tax returns into their equation.[634] Moreover, this study actually found that income inequality has shrunk slightly since 1989, with the Gini index falling from 0.372 to 0.362 in 2007.[635]

---

[631] Boudreaux, Don. "The Real "Truth About the Economy:" Have Wages Stagnated?" *Learn Liberty*, 31 Jan. 2012. <http://www.learnliberty.org/videos/real-truth-about-economy-have-wages-stagnated>.
[632] Saez, Emmanuel. "Striking It Richer: The Evolution of Top Incomes in the United States." *Berkeley*, 2 Mar. 2012. <http://elsa.berkeley.edu/~saez/saez-UStopincomes-2010.pdf>.
[633] Hall, Randy. "Study Undermines Liberal Media's 'Inequality' Meme." *Newsbusters*, 18 Apr. 2012. <http://newsbusters.org/blogs/randy-hall/2012/04/18/study-undermines-liberal-medias-inequality-meme>.
[634] Ibid.
[635] Pethokoukis, James. "Obama's Inequality Argument Just Utterly Collapsed." *American Enterprise Institute*, 11 Apr. 2012.

Even the rebuttals to Reich, Piketty, and Saez overlook another variable: household size. There were on average 3.14 people to a household in 1970, but only 2.63 in 2009.[636] All this proves is that all the incomes in median household income were increasing despite there being fewer people per household to provide income as this trend occurred. Real median income per household member was $13,938 in 1970[637] and $19,223 in 2009.[638]

Low skilled immigrants who earn low wages can make the statistical average wage appear lower than it is for the typical American. Rates of immigration remained low during the 1930s and 1940s due to the Great Depression. From 1930 to 1950, the amount of foreign born citizens dropped from 11.6% to 6.9% of the population, and bottomed out to 4.7% in 1970. The percentage of population being foreign born then began to tick upward to 6.3% in 1980, 7.9% in 1990,[639] and 16% in 2009.[640]

Purchasing Power

Everyone has heard from their Grandparents about how cheap everything else was "back then." Maybe some people actually believe that things were must cheaper in the past, except both inflation, and wage increases have to be accounted for. Charted below are the prices of household appliances, and the

---

<http://blog.american.com/2012/04/obamas-inequality-argument-just-utterly-collapsed/>.

[636] El Nasser, Haya, and Paul Overberg. "After 50 Years of Decline, Household Size Is Growing." *USA Today*, 5 May 2011. <http://www.usatoday.com/news/nation/census/2011-05-04-Census-Households-Demographics_n.htm>.

[637] $43,766 % 3.14. Sourced from US Census Bureau <http://www.census.gov/prod/2011pubs/p60-239.pdf>.

[638] $50,599 % 2.63.

[639] Thompson, Mark. "Income Inequality Explained For Robert Reich." *Florida Political Press*, 12 Sept. 2011. <http://www.floridapoliticalpress.com/2011/09/12/income-inequality-explained-for-robert-reich/>.

[640] Roberts, Sam. "Census Finds Rise in Foreign Workers." *The New York Times*, 7 Dec. 2009. <http://www.nytimes.com/2009/12/08/us/08census.html?_r=1&>.

amount of hours required to work for them at the average wage rate during those times.

Table 4.2: Wage Adjusted Cost of Household Appliances 1973 vs. 2009

Household Appliances	Retail Price 1973	Hours of Work @ $4.12	Retail Price 2009	Hours of Work @ $18.72	% Change 1973 to 2009
Washing Machine	$285	69.2	$400	21.4	**-69.1**
Clothes Dryer	$185	44.9	$400	21.4	**-52.4**
Dishwasher	$310	75.2	$570	30.4	**-59.5**
Refrigerator	$370	89.8	$425	22.7	**-74.7**
Freezer	$240	58.3	$265	14.2	**-75.7**
Stove	$290	70.4	$650	34.7	**-50.7**
Color TV	$400	97.1	$300	16.0	**-83.5**
Coffee Pot	$37	9.0	$30	1.6	**-82.2**
Blender	$40	9.7	$32	1.7	**-82.4**
Toaster	$25	6.1	$30	1.6	**-73.6**
Vacuum Cleaner	$90	21.8	$100	5.3	**-75.5**
				Average	**-70.8**

Source: Mark Perry.[641]

There do appear to be exceptions to the chart above, but other factors can account for this. Though the amount of hours of work it takes to purchase a car has remained constant over the years, the car itself has not. The price tag remains the same, but the car of 50 years ago is not the same car today. Not only are

[641] Perry, Mark J. "The Rich Are Getting Richer and the Poor Are Getting Richer; The Good Old Days Are Now." 28 Nov. 2009. <http://mjperry.blogspot.com/2009/11/rich-are-getting-richer-and-poor-are.html>.

safety features and appliances in the car greatly improved, cars last twice as long. In this case, it may appear that the price has remained constant, but the data would show that cars technically cost less than half of what they once did.

Other Objections

A more intelligent variation of the "wage stagnation" myth argues that while wages haven't been completely flat since 1970, they haven't increased relative to productivity (while they did consistently prior to 1970). Billionaire Nick Hanauer for instance argued in a speech presented as a TED Talk that had median household income "kept pace with the economy since 1970, it would now be nearly $92,000, not $50,000." Hanauer does not specify what he means by "kept pace with the economy," and neither does the *Mother Jones* article that he cited the statistic from, but I am assuming that he means productivity. Hanauer is indeed correct that there has been a growing gap between wages and productivity, and he's also correct in starting his measurement in 1970, since this is around when the gap began. This does however contradict the premise of his speech, that low taxes and inequality are responsible for this gap.

Hanauer has another version of the argument in his book *The Gardens of Democracy*, The book provides a similar argument, writing that "if the income distribution for all Americans had remained constant since 1980, the average American family would be earning $64,395 today."[642]

Regarding the first argument, we've already seen that wages are only stagnant if we me measure them using the CPI. The second argument also discounts the role that benefits plays in a person's income. To kill two birds with one stone – total employee compensation (wages + benefits) was 66% of national

[642] Liu, Eric, and Nick Hanauer. "The Gardens of Democracy: A New American Story of Citizenship, the Economy, and the Role of Government." (Seattle, WA: Sasquatch, 2011), p. 101.

income in 1970, and 64% in 2006.[643] If productivity doubled since 1970 and total employee compensation remained stagnant, we should've seen a much more drastic decline since 1970 and 2006. As productivity was increasing at an annual rate of 1.9% since 1970, real compensation rose by 1.7%.[644] That is a gap – but not stagnation.

The Shrinking Middle Class

The fact that the middle class has shrunken in recent years could be more accurately defined as a half-truth, since the implications deducted from the apparent fact are what is often politicized. The facts are undisputed, as the non-partisan Pew Research Center reports, Only 51% of adults were included in the middle class in 2011, a full 10 percentage decline from decades prior, at 61% in 1971.[645] The implication commonly drawn from this incomplete picture is simple: we're all getting poorer as a small majority gets richer.

When we categorize earners into three categories; lower income, middle income, and upper income, we get a much clearer picture. As the data also shows, in 1971, 25% were in the lower category, 61% middle, and 14% upper. By 2011, 29% were lower, 51% middle, and 20% upper. As finance blogger Mark J. Perry put it, "150 American's moved up for every 100 who moved down" during this period. Another way to look at the data would be to acknowledge that a smaller percentage were lower or middle income in 2011 (80%) than in 1971 (86%).

One fallacy in determining the size of the middle class lies in defining a fixed category of income as "middle class." As

---

643 Lester, Picker. "Total Compensation Reflects Growth in Productivity." *National Bureau of Economic Research*, Apr. 2008<http://www.nber.org/digest/oct08/w13953.html>.
644 Ibid.
645 "The Lost Decade of the Middle Class." *Pew Research Center*, 22 Aug. 2012. <http://www.pewsocialtrends.org/2012/08/22/the-lost-decade-of-the-middle-class/>.

more middle class individuals become richer, we then see the middle class "shrink." In 2007, 50.3% of American households earned $50,000 or more, but in 1970 only 33.7% of households earned that much (when adjusting for changes in purchasing power).[646]

The Unionization Correlation

At least some attempt has been made to correlate an apparent decline in the middle class with a historic decline in union membership. [647]

There's no question that unionized workers make more money – but they also produce less.[648] Like the case is with the minimum wage, the artificially high union wage prices many out of a job. Unions also impose other costs on workers (the threat of strikes, for instance) which is why some employers actually pay their workers above the prevailing union wage to incentivize them to not join a union.[649]

The simultaneous decline in both union membership and middle class income share may more be strongly correlated with declines in manufacturing, which is a heavily unionized industry. Manufacturing fell from 24.3% of GDP in 1970 to 12.8% in 2010.[650] Ironically, we could probably see the decline in union

---

[646] Sowell, "Economic Facts and Fallacies," pp. 157-159.
[647] Jilani, Zaid. "REPORT: The American Middle Class Was Built By Unions And It Will Decline Without Them." *Think Progress*, 5 Sept. 2011. <http://thinkprogress.org/economy/2011/09/05/311831/american-middle-class-organized-labor/>.
[648] Sherk, James. "What Unions Do: How Labor Unions Affect Jobs and the Economy." *The Heritage Foundation*, 21 May 2009. <http://www.heritage.org/research/reports/2009/05/what-unions-do-how-labor-unions-affect-jobs-and-the-economy>.
[649] Sowell, Thomas. "Killing the Goose." *Townhall*, 20 Nov. 2012. <http://townhall.com/columnists/thomassowell/2012/11/20/creators_oped/page/full/>.
[650] Perry, Mark J. "Manufacturing's Declining Share of GDP Is a Global Phenomenon, and It's Something to Celebrate." *Forum for Innovation*, 22 Mar. 2012. <http://forum.uschamber.com/blog/2012/03/manufacturing%E2%80%99s-declining-share-gdp>.

membership without the corresponding decline in manufacturing jobs had unionization not killed off so many manufacturing jobs. There were 11.8 million non-unionized manufacturing workers in 1975 – and 11.8 million non-unionized manufacturing workers in 2010.[651] By contrast, unionized manufacturing jobs tanked 79% from 6.7 million in 1975 to 1.4 million in 2010.[652]

When middle class income is measured in real dollars, not as a percentage of all income, this argument also appears to be much less convincing. On her MSNBC show, Melissa Harris-Perry provided the statistics that: 1) 11.8% of the US workforce was unionized in 2011, compared to 20.1% in 1983, 2) that there has been a 40% increase in income inequality in the private sector from 1983-2007, and 3) that an analysis from the Center for American Progress claiming that a 1% increase in union membership translates to an extra $153 in middle class household income.[653] Even assuming that the study from CAP is correct, middle class income in 2011 would only be $1,270 higher had unionization remained at levels that it was at in 1983. This would be a nice boost, but it's quite a stretch to attribute both the demise of the middle class and a 40% rise in income inequality to it.

Most studies show that the effect of unions in the rise of inequality is minimal, at best. One paper estimates around 10-20% of the rise in inequality to the decline in unions.[654]

But then again, unionization may only be declining in name only, since there are other forms of organized labor. One form of worker protection is licensing laws, which obviously do

---

[651] Von Spakovsky, Hans S., and James Sherk. "National Labor Relations Board Overreach Against Boeing Imperils Jobs and Investment." *The Heritage Foundation*, 11 May 2011. <http://www.heritage.org/research/reports/2011/05/national-labor-relations-board-overreach-against-boeing-imperils-jobs-and-investment>.
[652] Ibid.
[653] Melissa Harris-Perry, MSNBC, Aired February 18th 2012.
[654] Mankiw, Greg. "On Inequality and Unions." 23 Aug. 2006. <http://gregmankiw.blogspot.com/2006/08/on-inequality-and-unions.html>.

much to keep away competition, therefore boosting wages and reducing the risk of unemployment for those who hold such licenses. People employed in professions requiring an occupational license increased from 5% in 1950 to 29% in 2006.[655] This is hardly an apples to oranges comparison of forms of worker protection, since licensing laws and unionization both boost wages by the same amount.[656]

Then I suppose another flaw with this alleged correlation is that it shows a decline in middle class income share as prior middle class individuals are getting richer – as demonstrated earlier in the statistic showing the rise in households making over $50,000 a year since 1970.

Right to Work vs. Non-Right to Work

To further the point that increased unionization wouldn't boost middle class income, right to work states and non-right to work states give us a simple model to examine.

A point made by those opposed to unions is that while unions can boost the wages of their employees, they do so by increasing business costs that have to be passed onto consumers.[657] According to this argument, more unionization would lead to higher costs of living. Therefore, an accurate measure between right to work and non-right to work states in terms of income, is measuring income relative to the cost of living in those states. The averate cost of living in non-right to

---

[655] Worstall, Tim. "Declining Union Membership Does Not Mean Declining Wages." *Forbes*, 5 Sept. 2012. <http://www.forbes.com/sites/timworstall/2012/09/05/declining-union-membership-does-not-mean-declining-wages/>.

[656] Ibid.

[657] To give just one example of the extent to which unions increase the cost of doing business, the labor costs of UPS are double that of FedEx. UPS is heavily unionized since a large amount of their employees are truckers, and the National Labor Relations Act makes it easier for them to unionize. FedEx delivers a large share by flight, which exempts them from this pro-union law. See: Gillespie, Nick. "Reason.tv: UPS vs. FEDEX—Ultimate Whiteboard Remix." *Reason*, 10 Nov. 2009. <http://reason.com/blog/2009/11/10/ups-vs-fedex-whiteboard>.

work states comes out to 104% of the national average, compared to 93% in right to work states.[658]

After adjusting for the cost of living, the National Institute for Labor Relations calculates that the average weekly salary of someone in a RTW state is $638, compared to $632 in a non-RTW.[659] Though this is something of a low estimate, as a study conducted by George Mason University's Economics Department found a $2,300 yearly income advantage in RTW states, and a study at the University of Colorado found a $4,300 advantage (both after adjusting for purchasing power).[660]

Also relevant is the fact that over the past three decades RTW states have passed both the national average and average of non-RTW states in total employment growth, and growth in per capita income.[661] The unemployment rate is also higher in non-RTW states.[662] Some critics will point to higher poverty rates in RTW work states, but the official poverty statistics don't factor in the cost of living. To give one example: there is more poverty in Texas than California according to statistics provided by the Census – but more poverty in California than Texas when we adjust for the cost of living.[663]

Right to work states also fare better in other areas. In 2011 CNBC released a report on America's Top States for

---

658 "Real Earnings Higher In Right to Work States." *National Institute for Labor Relations Research*, 1 Jan. 2001. <http://nilrr.org/2001/01/01/real-earnings-higher-right-work-states/>.
659 Ibid.
660 Bannister, Craig. "Right To Work States Have Lower Unemployment, Higher Income and Healthcare Coverage, NRTW President Says." *CNS News*, 12 Dec. 2012. <http://cnsnews.com/node/618195>.
661 "Do Right-to-work or Forced Union States Create More High-paying Jobs?" *Wintery Knight*, 5 July 2011. <https://winteryknight.wordpress.com/2011/07/05/do-right-to-work-or-forced-union-states-create-more-high-paying-jobs/>.
662 Craig, "Right to Work States Have Lower Unemployment, Higher Income and Healthcare Coverage."
663 Stossel, FOX Business, Aired January 17th 2012. The title of the episode was "Texas Vs. California.

Business that year. Among the criteria used for ranking were the cost of business, workforce, economy, quality of life, transportation and infrastructure, technology and innovation, education, business friendliness, access to capital, and cost of living. There only exist 22 RTW states, yet every single one of them made it into the top 25 states for having the best workforces.[664]

The Clinton Surplus

"Clinton raised taxes, had record economic growth, and balanced the budget" goes the argument. None of this information is false. The economic growth rate in 1998 of 4.1% was the highest economic growth since 1984,[665] but it was in 1993 that Clinton raised taxes, and later ended up cutting them after adopting a Republican congress. Much more happened during the Clinton years than simply "taxes, revenue, and growth increasing."

The Clinton tax increases in 1993 created two new top income brackets of 36% and 39.6%, increased the corporate tax rate to 35%, made the 2.9% Medicare payroll tax apply to all levels of income, and added 4.3 cents in tax per gallon in gas.[666] The goal of these tax cuts was to boost revenues 0.36% of GDP the first year, and eventually up to 0.83% by 1997. The results during the 1993-1996 period were solid, but still outperformed by Reagan. Clinton averaged a 19.3% increase in tax revenues, but Reagan averaged 24.1%.[667] The Clinton growth rate during that period was 2.7%, while Reagan's average growth rate was 3.2%,

---

[664] This observation was originally made at: "Best Workforces Are In Right-To-Work States, Survey Finds." *Red State*, 30 June 2012. <http://www.redstate.com/laborunionreport/2011/06/30/best-workforces-are-in-right-to-work-states-survey-finds/>.

[665] Barro, Robert J. "Reagan vs. Clinton: Who's the Economic Champ?" *Business Week*, 22 Feb. 1999. <http://www.economics.harvard.edu/faculty/barro/files/bw99_02_22.pdf>.

[666] U.S. Department of the Treasury, Office of Tax Analysis, "Revenue Effects of Major Tax Bills," September 2006.

[667] Historical Tables, Budget of the United States Government, 1997.

and even averaged 3.8% during the 1983-89 expansion periods.[668] The increases in the rate of productivity under Reagan were 5 times higher than under Clinton (1.5% vs. 0.3%).[669] The only place where Clinton outperformed Reagan was in job creation, as he was aided by the tech-boom.

Then came 1997 when the Republican controlled congress took over and proposed a new plan. This new plan proposed deficit reduction through lowered taxes and lowered spending. As a result, the capital gains tax rate was lowered back down to 20%, a $500 child tax credit was created, estate tax exemption were increased from $600,000 to $1 million, Roth IRAs were created, income limits for deductible IRA's were increased, and education IRAs were created. The only taxes that rose were air transportation excise taxes and sin taxes (cigarettes taxed an additional 15 centers per pack).[670]

The cuts didn't outweigh the prior increases, but were estimated to reduce taxes by 0.22% of GDP by their fourth year in effect. The tax increases of 1993 amounted to an additional $114 billion in tax burden; these cuts removed $30 billion of that burden. Despite not outweighing the 1993 increases, the results were at least consistent with supply side theory, since the 1997-2000 period outperformed the previous period. The only category where both periods (1993-96 vs. 1997-2000) were virtually equal was in job creation- the first period gained 100,000 more jobs than the second. Real wage growth increased nearly tenfold, rising from 5 cents/hour during the first period to 49 cents/hour during the second. The latter period also performed better in

---

[668] Cato Analysis 261.

[669] "Economic Report of the President." Feb. 1996. <http://www.gpoaccess.gov/usbudget/fy97/pdf/erp.pdf>.

[670] Foster, J.D. "Tax Cuts, Not the Clinton Tax Hike, Produced the 1990s Boom." *The Heritage Foundation*, 4 Mar. 2008. <http://www.heritage.org/research/reports/2008/03/tax-cuts-not-the-clinton-tax-hike-produced-the-1990s-boom>.

terms of GDP growth, beating out the former period by an entire percentage by averaging 4.2% annual GDP growth.[671]

Two years after the Clinton tax hikes from 1993, the Congressional Budget Office released data predicting the budget deficit for the next few years, all of which were around $200 billion. Since Clinton's surpluses were in the years after cutting taxes, one can hardly argue that an increase of taxes balanced the budget. The Clinton deficit predictions compared to what actually happened are charted below.

Table 4.3: Deficit Predictions vs. Realized Deficits, 1994-1999

	Prediction	Actual	Difference
1994	$203	$203	0
1995	175	164	11
1996	205	107	98
1997	210	22	188
1998	210	+69 (surplus)	279
1999	200	+126 (surplus)	326
Total	1,203	301	902

Source: "The End of Prosperity," p. 129, based off data from Congressional Budget Office forecast, April 1995.

The surpluses then continued into 2000 and 2001, but weren't charted in the original source.

Perhaps the most important fact to take into account is that he was not being rhetorical when he said that the "age of big government is over." On net balance, federal spending as a percentage of GDP declined from 36.31% in 1993 to 33.33% in 2001. Some of the credit for this also goes to PAYGO, a law which required new spending to be offset by either tax increases or spending decreases elsewhere.

However, this still isn't enough of a reduction to take credit for balancing the budget, and spending still exceeded

[671] Ibid.

revenues. Neither Bill Clinton nor his Republican congress can take credit for the surplus then, but accounting gimmicks can. To make up the difference, Clinton borrowed liberally from Social Security and other governmental trust funds which made it appear that the budget was balanced. Of the $236 billion surplus in 2000, $248 billion was taken from trust funds to not only cover up the deficit but provide a surplus.[672]

The Republican Welfare State

During the 2012 presidential race, Mitt Romney sparked a great deal of phony outrage for his comments that 47% of our population will vote for Obama solely because they're "dependent upon government" and "believe that they are victims, [and] who believe the government has a responsibility to take care of them." Romney was mistakenly citing the number of Americans who pay no income tax, not the amount who receive government benefits (which is 49% - a similar number).

Some liberal bloggers then began posting that it's actually Republican states that have the largest percentages of people paying no income tax. *The Atlantic* reports that of the top 10 states with the largest percentage of non-payers, eight of them are red states.[673] It's also been pointed out previously by *Mother Jones* that most Republican states receive more in federal funds than they pay in through taxes.[674] Paul Krugman blogs that "Aaron Carroll of Indiana University tells us that in 2010,

---

[672] Steiner, Craig. "The Clinton Surplus Myth." *Townhall*, 22 Aug. 2011. <http://finance.townhall.com/columnists/craigsteiner/2011/08/22/the_clinton_surplus_myth/page/full/>.

[673] Graham, David A. "Where Are the 47% of Americans Who Pay No Income Taxes?" *The Atlantic*, 17 Sept. 2012. <http://www.theatlantic.com/politics/archive/2012/09/where-are-the-47-of-americans-who-pay-no-income-taxes/262499/>.

[674] Gilson, Dave. "Most Red States Take More Money From Washington Than They Put In." *Mother Jones*, 16 Feb. 2012. <http://www.motherjones.com/politics/2011/11/states-federal-taxes-spending-charts-maps>.

residents of the 10 states Gallup ranks as "most conservative" received 21.2 percent of their income in government transfers, while the number for the 10 most liberal states was only 17.1 percent."[675] Apparently these bloggers don't realize that there's a difference between states and individuals. How do we know that it isn't liberals in red states that are receiving all the benefits that skew the statistics?

The Maxwell Poll has data compiled on the voting patterns of those who receive government benefits from 2004-2007. Their voting patterns are, for the most part, overwhelmingly liberal.

Table 4.4: Welfare Benefits and Voting Data

Type of Benefit Received	Percent Voting Democrat	Percent Voting Republican
Public Housing	81%	12%
Medicaid	74%	16%
Food Stamps	67%	20%
Unemployment Compensation	66%	21%
Disability (from Govt.)	64%	25%
Welfare/Public Assistance	63%	22%

Source: Maxwell Poll.[676]

In regards to Romney's "47%" comment about the voting habits of those paying no income tax, what he said technically turned out to be true. Based on exit poll data, 63% of those making under $30,000 and 57% of those making between $30,000-49,999 a year voted for Obama. Nearly 80% of those who pay no

[675] Krugman, Paul. "Moochers Against Welfare." *The New York Times*, 16 Feb. 2012. <http://www.nytimes.com/2012/02/17/opinion/krugman-moochers-against-welfare.html?_r=3&>.
[676] Sanandaji, Tino. "Are Welfare Recipients Mostly Republican?" 22 Feb. 2012. <http://super-economy.blogspot.com/2012/02/do-welfare-recipients-mostly-vote.html>.

income tax were those earning under $30,000 a year.[677] Every single income category $50,000 an above voted for Romney by some margin. Now obviously the 47% figure is a misleading, since all of these people are paying payroll taxes, sales taxes, and other local taxes. Around 10% of those in the "47%" are the elderly, who are fortunate to not have to pay taxes on their Social Security benefits.[678]

Republicans and the Stock Market

I once heard an apocryphal quote attributed to the late humorist Will Rogers where when asked why he is purchasing stocks, he replies "the Republicans are in office aren't they all supposed to go up?"[679] This seems like a common attitude, but some research suggests that one area that Republican presidents appear to be denominated by Democrats is in the performance of the stock market during their tenure. British magazine *The Guardian* reports that since 1900, average monthly returns are 0.73% under Democrats, and 0.38% under Republicans.[680] At face value, this indicates that Democrats are twice as good for the stock market then Republicans are.

Greg Mankiw called this correlation "meaningless" based off the fact that the stock market isn't a perfect measurement of economic well-being, that a president is only one small variable in what effects the stock market, and that market timing is imperfect. By market timing, Mankiw elaborates that "you would expect the entire impact of a candidate's election on the market to

---

[677] "Who Doesn't Pay Federal Taxes?" *The New York Times*, 18 Sept. 2012. <http://www.nytimes.com/interactive/2012/09/19/us/politics/who-doesnt-pay-federal-taxes.html>.

[678] Ibid.

[679] It's unlikely that Rogers ever said this, mainly due to the fact that he was registered as a Democrat throughout his life. He did however support the administration of Calvin Coolidge.

[680] Elliott, Larry. "Democrats Better for Wall Street than Republicans." *The Guardian*, 29 Aug. 2012. <http://www.guardian.co.uk/business/economics-blog/2012/aug/29/democrats-better-wall-street-republicans>.

occur on election day, or maybe even during the days leading up to the election." For example, if an incumbent President is defeated, and because of that the stock market surges in value for the next few months, that growth will be attributed to the defeated incumbent. Mankiw continues that "by the time the new President takes office, the news has been fully priced in, and it will not show up in returns during his term."[681]

Some other general problems with the statistic are that it doesn't account for what party controls the House and Senate. If the market growth is driven by a bubble, it'll show artificially high gains for one president, then disastrous losses for the next president, even though the next president played no role in propping up the bubble. One of the greatest flaws however is that is doesn't account for inherited problems. As one article on *FOX Business* reported, "every Republican president since Warren Harding (1921–1923) has experienced a recession within the first two years of office, perhaps due to the excesses of the prior administration."[682]

According to Jason Zweig at the *Wall Street Journal*, What the stock markets trends do seem to correlate most strongly with are interest rates.[683] Since 1965 at least, "large stocks have returned in annual average of nearly 12 percentage points more when the Fed was cutting rates than when it was raising them."[684] In other words, the Federal Reserve, which is an autonomous organization, effects the market more than the political affiliation of those in office. Other issues Zweig takes with the "Democrats dominate the market" statistic is the small sample size to base

---

681 Mankiw, Greg. "Republicans, Democrats, and Stock Returns." 14 Oct. 2008. <http://gregmankiw.blogspot.com/2008/10/republicans-democrats-and-stock-market.html>.

682 Egan, Matt. "History Shows Stocks, GDP Outperform Under Democrats." *FOX Business*, 4 Sept. 2012. <http://www.foxbusiness.com/investing/2012/09/04/history-shows-markets-gdp-outperform-under-democrats/>.

683 Zweig, Jason. "The Winner for Investors Is…" *The Wall Street Journal*, Saturday/Sunday October 21st-22nd. P. B1.

684 Ibid., p. B2.

this observation off of, as we've only had twenty presidents since 1900.[685]

Part 2: Big Government Myths

Depression Era Myths

Three myths arise from the traditional narrative commonly believed about the Great Depression. These myths are that capitalism caused the Great Depression, that Herbert Hoover was a do-nothing president and this attitude worsened the depression, and finally that Keynesian New-Deal programs (or in another variation, the enormous spending from WWII) got us out of the Great Depression.

Was Capitalism the Cause?

Although it's rarely argued that capitalism was the sole cause of the Great Depression, there is a consensus that at least some form of capitalism played a role. Due to the enormous tax cuts enacted in the 1920's, some have argued that this was a period where the rich got rich and the poor poorer. As a result, the average person's purchasing power declined and thus under consumption became a variable in the economy's eventual downturn. The problem with this approach is quite simply that although it could explain some other kind of depression, it can't explain the American Great Depression. The 1920's were not called the "roaring twenties" because people got poorer.

---

[685] Ibid., p. B1. Zweig is basing his data off the period 1926 onward, so in the article he makes the argument about sample size based off the fact that we've only "had 15 presidents and nine elections in which control of the White House passed from one party to the other."

The top five percent's share of total income increased from 25.47% to 26.09% during the 1921-1929 period, while corporate profits averaged 8.2% during that same period.[686] This was only a 0.2% increase in corporate profits relative to the 8% average profit rate during the 1900-1920 period. As a matter of fact, workers enjoyed a larger share of corporate dollars during the 20's than prior, increasing their share from 55% to 60% of corporate income. Since the 20's were a period where consumption increased from 68% of GNP in 1920 to 75% right before the crash in the 1927-29 years, under consumption should be the last possible cause we should consider.[687]

The Myth of a Non-Interventionist Hoover

In step two of the traditional narrative, disaster strikes in wake of the 1929 stock market crash, and Hoover sits idly by. When his economic record is examined, Hoover had a lot more in common with FDR than he did with Adam Smith. Although he's commonly believed to be laissez-faire, in practice Hoover took the recommended action the Keynesian narrative tells us he failed to do.

The evidence has literally been in the face of those who purport the Hoover myth without them even noticing. Rachel Maddow, who has repeated the myth on her TV show[688] also appears in an advertisement for MSNBC where she stands in front of the Hoover Dam in praise of it. The Hoover dam did serve as a stimulus project, and this was hardly the only thing Hoover spent money on. Maddow isn't alone in advancing this myth; her colleagues and fellow liberals Chris Matthews,[689] Ed

---

[686] Folsom, Burton W. "New Deal or Raw Deal?: How FDR's Economic Legacy Has Damaged America." (New York: Threshold Editions, 2009), pp. 34-35.
[687] Ibid., p. 35.
[688] The Rachel Maddow Show, MSNBC, Aired August 3rd 2011.
[689] Hardball with Chris Matthews, MSNBC, Aired April 22nd 2011.

Schultz,[690] and Paul Krugman[691] have all peddled this myth at one time or another.

Hoover's belief in interventionism didn't originate with the onset of the Great Depression. Hoover directed many conferences on labor management in the early twenties, where he advocated government intervention on multiple occasions. Hoover, along with economists and labor leaders called for abolishing child labor, fewer work hours, national insurance for the elderly, and wider collective bargaining rights. Hoover described the "extreme right" as being opposed to his proposals.[692] Likewise, during the 1921 recession Hoover advocated using government to generate "cooperation" among businesses as opposed to competition.[693]

Hoover's anti-laissez faire principles even became a talking point in the presidential election – for FDR of all people. The Democratic Party's platform for the 1932 election was a 25% reduction in federal spending, a balanced budget, preservation of the gold standard, removal of government from areas that could be better operated by the private sector, and an end to Hoover's farm programs.[694] Meanwhile, Hoover criticized FDR as a capitalist president. Hoover warned that FDR would make the depression worse by decreasing taxes, reducing government intervention, promoting free trade, and cutting government at the federal, state, and local levels.

---

[690] Schultz, Ed. "Killer Politics: How Big Money and Bad Politics Are Destroying the Great American Middle Class." (New York: Hyperion, 2010), p. 25.

[691] Krugman, Paul. "Fifty Herbert Hoovers." *The New York Times*, 28 Dec. 2008. <http://www.nytimes.com/2008/12/29/opinion/29krugman.html>.

[692] Rothbard, Murray Newton. "America's Great Depression." (United States: CreateSpace, 2011), p. 108 and 117 (footnote).

[693] Horwitz, Steven. "Herbert Hoover: Father of the New Deal." *The Cato Institute*. September 29, 2011. <http://www.cato.org/pub_display.php?pub_id=13719>.

[694] Reed, Lawrence W. "Great Myths of the Great Depression." *The Freeman*, Aug. 1998. <http://www.thefreemanonline.org/features/great-myths-of-the-great-depression/>.

The Crash – Hoover's Non-Interventionism in Practice

The market crash of 1929 gave Hoover a perfect opportunity for intervention – but he did so down the road. One only has to observe how the state of the country got worse after Hoover intervened to see this. No one could question that the situation was bad post-market crash, but on the bright side unemployment never exceeded 10% the year following the crash. A more modern example of a similar occurrence was the stock market crash to 1987, which was similar to the crash of 1929. In that case, Reagan did not intervene at all, and clearly there were no consequences for inaction.[695]

However in the former crash, then came along Hoover. In an effort to save American jobs by reducing imports (and thus reduce competition), the largest tariff in our history, the Smoot-Hawley tariff, was passed in June of 1930 despite the public opposition of over 1000 economists and many others. Thomas Lamont, a chief executive at J.P. Morgan at the time said that he "almost went down on my knees to beg Herbert Hoover to veto the asinine Hawley-Smoot Tariff."

Resulting was a tariff was placed on 3,218 new items, 887 of them being excessive rises.[696] All legislation has its unintended consequences; Anti-American rhetoric swept through Europe, and before we knew it, our exports had been cut from $7 billion in 1929 to $2.5 billion by 1932.[697] Quite the opposite effect had been done when it came to employment, what was a 6.3% rate of unemployment the time the tariff was passed increased to 15% the next year, and 25.8% the year after that.[698] Hoover thus began his role in making the Great Depression great.

---

[695] Sowell, Thomas. "The Housing Boom and Bust. (New York: Basic Books, 2009), p.133.
[696] Folsom, "New Deal or Raw Deal," p. 31.
[697] Ibid.
[698] Sowell, Thomas. "Intellectuals and Society," p. 72. I do not believe that Smoot-Hawley is the sole cause of this increase in unemployment, but rather one factor in

Throughout 1931, what St. Lawrence University economics professor Steve Horowitz calls the "Hoover New Deal" began to unravel. Among the many programs advocated by Hoover were:

- Increased aid to Federal Land Banks
- Creation of the Public Works Administration
- Enforcement of anti-trust laws and support for work-sharing programs
- The Reconciliation Finance Corporation which lent tax dollars to banks, firms, and other institutions.
- Legalization of Hoover's executive order that blocked immigration.
- Grant loans of $300 million to states for relief. [699]

Then Hoover had to tackle the budget. From the year of the crash to the year he left office, spending grew from 11.27% of GDP to 21.19% of GDP. Measuring spending as a percent of GDP isn't perfect in this scenario, since a decline in GDP would cause the number to go up even if spending remained constant. However in real dollars, the budget more than doubled during his presidency from 3.1 billion in 1929 to over 6 billion in 1933. Since this was actually a period of deflation, the real growth is larger than appears. Then-candidate FDR seems to have been onto something when he accused "the present Administration of being the greatest spending Administration in peacetime in all our history."[700]

---

many. As Vox Day notes on page 192 of his book "The Return of the Great Depression" (Washington D.C.:WND Books, 2009), the decline in exports from 1929-33 was slightly smaller than a decline in exports that occurred from 1920-22.

[699] Horwitz, "Hoover: Father of the New Deal."

[700] "Franklin D. Roosevelt Address Sioux City, Iowa (September 29, 1932)." *Pepperdine University School of Public Policy*, <http://publicpolicy.pepperdine.edu/faculty-research/new-deal/roosevelt-speeches/fr092932.htm>.

Hoover worked diligently in achieving his goals, the *New York Times* reporting in 1932 that Hoover would commonly work over ten hours a day, sometimes working up to fifteen hours.[701] By contrast, his predecessor Calvin Coolidge spent eleven hours of his day sleeping, and would joke by asking, "is the country still here" to his aide as he woke.

There is also a wide held belief that Hoover insisted on balanced budgets. It has generally implied that this meant Hoover withheld from increasing spending, but that has Hoover's priorities completely backwards. Hoover knew that it would be impossible to increase government expenditures and cut taxes, so he opted for increasing taxes. The Revenue Act of 1932 raised the top income bracket from 25% to 63%, while the lower brackets showed increases as well. The corporate tax was also raised to 13.75% from 12%, the estate tax was doubled, and many other taxes other rose. This amounted to the largest tax increase in peacetime during the history of the United States.

Hoover was well aware of what he was doing, and certainly did not consider himself to be laissez-faire. Hoover announced his 1931 stimulus plan through radio, noting that prior action was already "providing a livelihood for nearly 700,000 families." He also mentions that he stopped all immigration, and that "measures have been adopted which will assure normal credits that thus stimulate employment in industry, in commerce, and in agriculture."[702]

Hoover also advertised his policies to his own party. At the Republican National Convention in 1932 Hoover explained:

---

[701] Speers, L.C. "PRESIDENT HOOVER'S DAY IS A DAY OF WORK; Early at His Desk, He Is Late to Leave, and His Recreation Time Is Limited (March 6th, 1932)." *The New York Times*.

[702] Hoover, Herbert H. "Radio Address to the Nation on Unemployment Relief (October 18 1931)." <
http://www.presidency.ucsb.edu/ws/?pid=22855#axzz1wcDOCsEQ>.

> We might have done nothing. That would have been utter ruin. Instead, we met the situation with proposals to private business and the Congress of the most gigantic program of economic defense and counter attack ever evolved in the history of the Republic.[703]

In an opposing quotation from his "Challenge to Liberty" speech in 1936, Hoover claimed that have "vetoed the idea of recovery through stupendous spending to prime the pump" which was "born of a British professor (Keynes),"[704] but clearly his actual record shows otherwise.

Was Keynesianism the Cure?

In the traditional mythology, our criminal laissez-faire Hoover is superseded by his philosophical opposite, Franklin Delano Roosevelt. As we have seen from Hoover's actual record, he was laissez-faire in the same way that Adam Smith was a communist. On the contrary, the American people didn't reject laissez-faire thinking after Hoover, which is why it became a crucial part of FDR's campaign platform. FDR railed against the Smoot Hawley tariff,[705] and promised that he would balance the federal budget while minimizing government intervention.[706] FDR also claimed to be opposed to public sector unions a few years into his presidency in 1937.

The New Deal could only be called new since Hoover hadn't already coined the term. Far from being anything new in reality, the so-called New Deal was an extrapolation of many of

---

[703] Hoover, Herbert H. "Presidential Nomination Address (August 11 1932)." <http://publicpolicy.pepperdine.edu/faculty-research/new-deal/hoover-speeches/hh081132.htm>.

[704] Hoover, Herbert H. "The Challenge to Liberty (October 30 1936)." <http://newdeal.feri.org/court/hoover02.htm> .

[705] Folsom, "New Deal or Raw Deal?," p. 39

[706] Raico, Ralph. "FDR - The Man, the Leader, the Legacy, Part 8." *The Future of Freedom Foundation*, Nov. 1999. <http://www.fff.org/freedom/1199f.asp>.

Hoover's programs. Rex Tugwell, a member of FDR's brain trust reflected upon the New Deal that:

> When it was all over, I once made a list of New Deal ventures begun during Hoover's years as secretary of commerce and then as president.... The New Deal owed much to what he had begun.[707]

Walter Lippmann, a progressive newspaper columnist at the time made a similar observation in 1935 that "the Roosevelt measures are a continuous evolution of the Hoover measures."[708]

While the goal of the New Deal was to increase employment, two authors writing for the *Wall Street Journal* show explain how hours works per worker actually declined:

> ...there was even less work on average during the New Deal than before FDR took office. Total hours worked per adult, including government employees, were 18% below their 1929 level between 1930-32, but were 23% lower on average during the New Deal (1933-39). Private hours worked were even lower after FDR took office, averaging 27% below their 1929 level, compared to 18% lower between in 1930-32.[709]

Both Hoover and FDR believed that falling prices caused depressions (but as Thomas Woods notes, this is a consequence of a depression, not a cause).[710] Due to this belief, many of FDR's policies aimed to artificially boost prices and wages. One of these wage-boosting policies that still exists today is the

---

[707] This isn't to say that Tugwell disapproved of FDR's New Deal at all. In 1939, he wrote attempting to expose the "myths of laissez-faire"
[708] Sowell, "Housing Boom and Bust," p. 132.
[709] Cole, Harold L., and Lee E. Ohanian. "How Government Prolonged the Depression." *The Wall Street Journal*, 2 Feb. 2009. <http://online.wsj.com/article/SB123353276749137485.html>.
[710] Woods, Thomas E. "Meltdown: A Free-market Look at Why the Stock Market Collapsed, the Economy Tanked, and Government Bailouts Will Make Things Worse." (Washington, DC: Regnery, 2009), p. 100.

minimum wage, which has been shown to have many consequences.

Two UCLA researchers published a now well-known study showing that FDR's New Deal prolonged the Great Depression by around 7 years. [711] The study explains the role of artificially heightened wages in doing so. Using data from before and during the depression, they were able to view wages, productivity, and unemployment during the depression, and able to use the prior trend to calculate what they would have been without the New Deal. They found that three years following New Deal policies, wages averaged 25% higher than they would have been in various key industries, and unemployment was also 25% higher than it should have been when accounting for increases in productivity.[712]

As common sense would tell, when people can afford less, making goods more expensive is disastrous. As the UCLA study also showed, pries in 19 industries were, on average, 23% higher than what they would have been without New Deal intervention.[713] Considering how FDR's policies worked, this should come to no surprise. The Agricultural Adjustment Act paid farmers to destroy their crops, thereby limiting the amount of goods in the market and increasing the prices. This boosted farmers' incomes, but at the expense of everyone else. This was similar to a policy of Hoover's. Hoover saw the agricultural sector as being too large, and created the Federal Farm Board in attempt to reduce it.

---

[711] Sullivan, Meg. "FDR's Policies Prolonged Depression by 7 Years, UCLA Economists Calculate." *UCLA Newsroom*, 10 Aug. 2004. <http://newsroom.ucla.edu/portal/ucla/FDR-s-Policies-Prolonged-Depression-5409.aspx>. This study was also cited in Thomas Woods' book "Meltdown", but I was familiar with it before reading Woods' book.

[712] Ibid.

[713] Ibid.

Lastly, while some conservatives like to cite FDR's opposition to public sector unions, he only "opposed" them was after passing pro-union legislation. Numerous acts signed by FDR strengthened the right to collective bargaining, among them being the National Industrial Recovery Act of 1933, and Tennessee Valley Authority Act (1933), and the National Labor Relations Act of 1935. FDR had also spoke favorably of collective bargaining in 1936 – a year before his opposition to them, and in 1930 – 3 years after voicing his opposition.[714]

How World War II Ended the Depression

Keynesians and anti-Keynesians mean two different things when claiming that World War II ended the Great Depression. Keynesians credit the heightened levels of spending during the war as ending the Great Depression. Anti-Keynesians will credit WW2 with ending the Great Depression due to the fact that it finally led to an end of the New Deal, and that once the war was over the economy could finally begin to repair itself.

A Keynesian interpretation of WW2 shows the effects of war spending being realized immediately. During the so-called "wartime prosperity" the nation's unemployment rate shrunk to nearly zero, and GDP finally began to grow. The extremely low unemployment rate is not due to an increase in private sector jobs, but because men were being removed from the labor force to fight in the war, and were therefore removed from the employment statistics. The rise in GDP wasn't due to the production of goods to raise living standards domestically, but was the result of all the bombs, tanks, airplanes, and other military supplies that were being built for the war. The portion of GDP produced by the private sector actually decreased during

---

[714] Famighetti, Karen. "Glenn Beck Needs To Look Up FDR's Record Of Supporting Collective Bargaining." *Media Matters for America*, 2 Mar. 2011. <http://mediamatters.org/research/2011/03/02/glenn-beck-needs-to-look-up-fdrs-record-of-supp/177073>.

WW2.[715] GDP as produced by the private sector was lower in 1943 and 1944 than in 1933, when the depression hit its peak.[716]

Since it was government spending that was propping up GDP, Keynesians at the time warned that the end to war spending would lead us back into depression (as if we were really out of it in the first place).[717] And there are still Keynesians today who do maintain that the end of WW2 spending caused disaster, but this comes from a misunderstanding of GDP statistics. As one Keynesian blogger argues, if we define a depression as a reduction in GDP of 10% of more, then the 10.9% decline in GDP in 1946 from the year before shows that the economy did fall back into depression.[718] But all this proves is that GDP isn't a perfect measurement of economic prosperity. This 10.9% decline reflects a decline in military expenditures, not in the private economy which nearly doubled from 1945-46.[719] Government expenditures also tend to add more to GDP than private sector expenditures, even if the same amount of net wealth was produced. As Thomas Woods explains regarding this phenomenon, "if the government spends $100 on a $20 item, that increases the GDP by $100."[720]

Obama's Stimulus

Thomas Sowell's 1995 book *The Vision of the Anointed* brilliantly lays out a patterned way of political thinking

[715] Murphy, Robert P. "The Myth of Wartime Prosperity." *The American Conservative*, 12 July 2012. <http://www.theamericanconservative.com/articles/the-myth-of-wartime-prosperity/>.
[716] Ibid.
[717] Woods, Thomas E. "Keynesian Predictions Vs. American History." Presented at Mises Circle in Houston Texas on January 23rd 2010. Available online at <http://www.tomwoods.com/blog/keynesian-predictions-vs-american-history/>.
[718] "Thomas E. Woods on Keynesian Predictions vs. American History: A Critique." 29 May 2012. <http://socialdemocracy21stcentury.blogspot.com/2012/05/thomas-e-woods-on-keynesian-predictions.html>.
[719] Murphy, "Myth of Wartime Prosperity."
[720] Day, Vox. "Interview with Thomas Woods." *Vox Popoli*, 2 Mar. 2009. <http://voxday.blogspot.com/2009/03/interview-with-thomas-woods_02.html>.

throughout history, explaining how policies are justified in the face of a crisis, and then later justified after they fail. The more recent stimulus measures under the Obama administration fulfill this pattern quite perfectly.[721] Sowell's "Patterns of Failure" is as follows:

Stage 1: The Crisis- A crisis either exists, or data is twisted to show that an apparent crisis exists. This is the problem that the anointed are bent on solving

Stage 2: The Solution – Politicians make claims over what will happen if the crisis is allowed to continue, and propose a certain solution, generally involving more government intervention.

Stage 3: The Results – The government intervenes, but the problem gets worse.

Stage 4: The Response – Even though the problem got worse, the burden of proof is shifted on the critics. Supporters of government involvement will claim that things would have been even worse without intervention.[722]

In Sowell's book, this pattern is applied to the War on Poverty, sex education, and criminal justice. Applying this pattern to the stimulus goes as follows:

Stage 1: The Crisis – The stock market had tanked under then president Bush, and unemployment was on the rise. Obama predicted that without the stimulus, unemployment would go up to 8.7%, but with the stimulus, unemployment would never pass 8% and instead peak at 7.9%. On the jobs front, Obama predicted that the stimulus would "save or create" 3.5 million jobs. Unemployment was predicted to fall down to 7% by December

---

[721] I had typed this entire section typed, then ended up discovering that a writer for the Ludwig Von Mises Institute also had a similar idea of using Sowell's book to criticize the stimulus. His article can be found at: Virgo, Charlie. "How the Stimulus Racket Works." *Ludwig Von Mises Institute*, 11 Aug. 2011. <http://mises.org/daily/5539>.

[722] Sowell, Thomas. "The Vision of the Anointed: Self-congratulation as a Basis for Social Policy." (New York: Basic Books, 1995), p. 8.

2010 with the stimulus enacted. Nancy Pelosi made the absurd claim that for each month the stimulus isn't passed, 500 million jobs would be lost, a figure that exceeds the entire population of the US.[723]

Stage 2: The Solution – Government intervention in the form of stimulus spending is proposed as the solution. In one November 2008 column, Paul Krugman worried that future stimulus spending wouldn't go far enough, and advocated that the stimulus be at least $600 billion.[724] Then in January 2009 after a $775 billion plan was offered, Krugman simply stated that it "wasn't enough," but didn't provide an actual estimate on how much this number should be.[725] Nonetheless, three days later Krugman calculated that the stimulus would at least "reduce average unemployment over the next two years from 8.7% to 7.6%; over the next three years, it reduces average unemployment from 8.4% to 7.3%."[726] The next month, in an interview with Harvard Business, Krugman stated that ideally the stimulus ought to be around $1.3-1.4 trillion.[727] Krugman was likely covering his bases in case the stimulus failed so he could claim that enough wasn't spent, but let's not forget his original $600 billion estimate.

On February 17th 2009, the American Recovery and Reinvestment Act was passed.

---

723 Allahpundit. "Pelosi: 500 Million Jobs Lost Every Month." *HotAir*, 4 Feb. 2009. <http://hotair.com/archives/2009/02/04/pelosi-500-million-jobs-lost-every-month/>.
724 Krugman, Paul. "Stimulus Math (wonkish)." *The New York Times*, 10 Nov. 2008. <http://krugman.blogs.nytimes.com/2008/11/10/stimulus-math-wonkish/>.
725 Krugman, Paul. "The Obama Gap." *The New York Times*, 8 Jan. 2009. <http://www.nytimes.com/2009/01/09/opinion/09krugman.html>.
726 Krugman, Paul. "More on Romer/Bernstein." *The New York Times*, 11 Jan. 2009. <http://krugman.blogs.nytimes.com/2009/01/11/more-on-romerbernstein/>.
727 Cliffe, Sarah. "Video: Paul Krugman on the Economy." *Harvard Business*, 10 Feb. 2009. <http://blogs.hbr.org/hbr/hbreditors/2009/02/video_paul_krugman_on_the_econ.html>.

Stage 3: The Results – Unemployment continued to increase, peaking at 10.1% in October 2009. Even though the initial goal of the stimulus was to contain unemployment below 8%, unemployment had never even gone below 9% until November 2011. In December 2010, the month when unemployment was predicted to be down to 7%, unemployment stood at 9.4%. At the same time, the size of the labor force was decreasing at a heightened rate, which makes the abysmal unemployment rate statistics lower than they would otherwise be.[728]

GDP Growth did appear positive but this isn't an exact science when government money is involved, as noted earlier in the example that Thomas Woods gave (that when government purchases something, it increases GDP by however much it spends on a particular item regardless of its market value). Either way, positive GDP growth doesn't mean healthy GDP growth. GDP growth averaged 0.6% during Obama's first term, which means that his average GDP growth could've doubled and it still would've been the worst growth in sixty years.[729]

Stage 4: The Response – The response to the failure of the stimulus received the same defense that any failed government policy receives: "things would've been worse had we done nothing." But some can deny the failure, as the Obama administration has gone in releasing the masterpiece in deception pictured below:

---

[728] McNeal, Greg. "Data Shows Clear Decline in Labor Force Participation Under President Obama." *Forbes*, 13 Oct. 2012. <http://www.forbes.com/sites/gregorymcneal/2012/10/13/labor-force-participation-under-obama/>.

[729] Anderson, Jeffrey H. "Obama's Economic Growth Record Is The Worst In 60 Years." *Investors Business Daily*, 12 Feb. 2013. <http://news.investors.com/ibd-editorials-viewpoint/021213-644194-obama-growth-record-is-worst-in-60-years.htm?p=full>.

One blogger used this chart as part of his guide on "making numbers say anything you want." Even by December 2009, only 10% of the stimulus was spent, so it is hard to attribute the apparent upswing in job losses to it.[730]

The lack of context given by the chart is only the first problem. The next problem is that although it gives the appearance of an increase in employment during the timeframe pictured, it doesn't measure *cumulative* job losses. The way the bikini chart is graphed makes any job loss that's less than the amount of losses in the previous month look positive.

[730] "Debunking the Obama Stimulus Chart or 'How to Make Numbers Say Anything You Want.'" *Political Math Blog*, 12 Mar. 2010. <http://www.politicalmathblog.com/?p=394>.

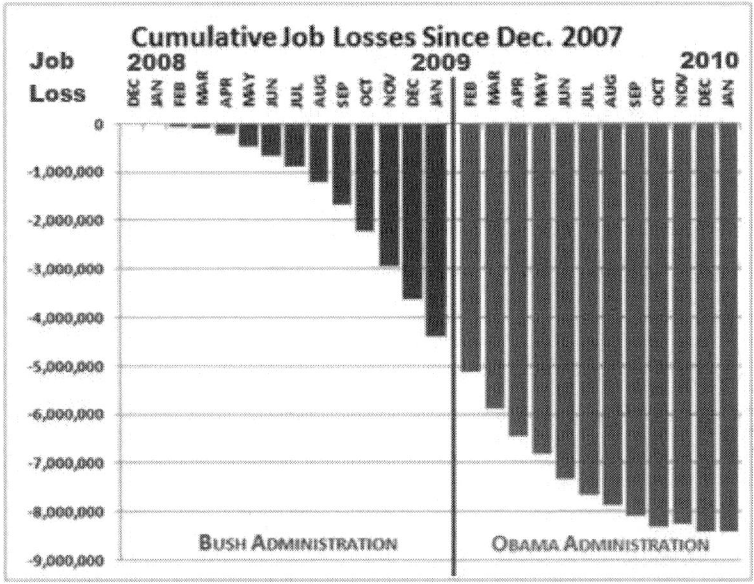

Source: Creekside Chat.[731]

Lastly, even if we were to pretend that the alleged upward slope was the result of stimulus spending (that didn't get occur), it still fails miserably compared to the predictions of the stimulus, where every single line from February 2009 onward should've represented a job gain.[732]

For the jobs that the stimulus did actually create, the cost of employment has to be examined. When Jeffrey Anderson of the *Weekly Standard* released a report arguing that the stimulus cost $278,000 per job created,[733] the White House quickly came to their own defense, arguing that the stimulus created far more jobs than Anderson's estimates. Even dividing the cost among the

[731] "Obama Job Admin Chart." 27 Feb. 2010, <http://www.editgrid.com/user/soquel_by_the_creek/Obama_Admin_Job_Chart>.
[732] For a more visual example, see: "President Obama, I Fixed Your Chart for You." *Political Math Blog*, 18 Feb. 2010. <http://www.politicalmathblog.com/?p=364>.
[733] Anderson, Jeffrey H. "Obama's Economists: 'Stimulus' Has Cost $278,000 per Job." *Weekly Standard*, 3 July 2011. <http://www.weeklystandard.com/blogs/obama-s-economists-stimulus-has-cost-278000-job_576014.html>.

amount of jobs the White House retorted with, the stimulus would still come out to $185,000 per job.[734]

Even early estimates were far from optimistic regarding the cost. Writing in January of 2009, Paul Krugman responded to estimates of the per job cost of the stimulus by arguing that since stimulus spending has a multiplier effect which will in turn create jobs for many years in the future, it's unfair to measure the cost of the stimulus based on its performance for the first two years. Even so, Krugman still states that the cost per job will exceed $100,000.[735]

Regardless, and sort of "recovery" hardly benefited the common person. During the post-recession period of the years of 2009 and 2010, the top 1% of income earners received 93% of income gains,[736] which amounts to a larger increase in income inequality than during the Bush years (more specifically, during the boom of 2002-07).[737]

Can a Different Kind of Stimulus Work?

There are two common reasons given for the failure of Obama's stimulus. They are that a) while stimulus spending can work, this money was not spent correctly, and b) the stimulus wasn't big enough.

---

[734] Geraghty, Jim. "White House: Nuh-Uh! Stimulus Jobs Only Cost $185K Each!" *National Review Online*, 5 July 2011. <http://www.nationalreview.com/campaign-spot/271107/white-house-nuh-uh-stimulus-jobs-only-cost-185k-each>.

[735] Krugman, Paul. "Bad Faith Economics." *The New York Times*, 25 Jan. 2009. <http://www.nytimes.com/2009/01/26/opinion/26krugman.html>.

[736] Eichler, Alexander. "Richest 1 Percent Account For Nearly All Of U.S. Recovery's Gains: Report." *The Huffington Post*, 5 Mar. 2012. <http://www.huffingtonpost.com/2012/03/05/1-percent-income-inequality_n_1321008.html>.

[737] Stoller, Matt. "Growth of Income Inequality Is Worse Under Obama than Bush." *Naked Capitalism*, 11 Apr. 2012. <http://www.nakedcapitalism.com/2012/04/growth-of-income-inequality-is-worse-under-obama-than-bush.html>.

Some more consistent Keynesians have maintained that the '09 stimulus was poorly created, which explains its failure. Paul Krugman's articulate counterpart Joseph Stigliz explained that the stimulus increased federal funding while state budgets were contracting – "we're firing teachers to hire construction workers" as he put it. While there is no disagreement on my part that the stimulus was poorly designed, this doesn't necessitate another stimulus of larger size or different style.

The best writing on the economic fallacies of stimulus spending comes from economist Henry Hazlitt's classic post-depression era book *Economics in One Lesson*. Hazlitt's criticism was of the public works programs of FDR's New Deal, but the same logic is applicable by any form of "priming the pump." While Hazlitt maintained that government spending was essential for certain public works, such as streets, roads, bridges, tunnels, police, and fire departments, it was creating public works programs solely for the sake of providing employment that Hazlitt had an issue with. While an increase in crime will result in an increase in police, and increase in fires an increase in fire fighters, and crumbling roads result in updated roads, but this is all changed when stimulus funds are involved.

As Hazlitt puts it, "when providing unemployment becomes the end, need becomes a subordinate consideration. "projects have to be invented."[738] One example Hazlitt cites is bridge building, noting that when stimulus funds are involved, people will come up with excuses of why a bridge should connect two places, the project soon becoming "absolutely essential." This is an interesting example considering the "bridge to nowhere" that we have today.

Every dollar spent on a public works program has to be taken out of the private sector. "If the bridge costs $1,000,000 the taxpayers will lose $1,000,000." Hazlitt concludes "therefore for

[738] Hazlitt, Henry. "Economics in One Lesson." (Auburn, Ala.: Ludwig Von Mises Institute, 2008), p. 18.

every public job created by the bridge project a private job has been destroyed somewhere else."[739] The '09 stimulus wasn't even well enough designed to appeal to infrastructure spending to necessitate its existence, as only 3% of the stimulus went towards infrastructure,[740] and 900,000 jobs in the construction industry were lost two and a half years after the stimulus.[741] Deficit spending is one way to get around Hazlitt's logic here, since the million dollar bridge would be built, but not paid for immediately. But even so, the bridge will have to be paid for in the future, and with interest. Other consequences of a stimulus would be the crowding out effect, whereas deficits negatively impact the private sector by various means, such as using up resources that would be used more efficiently in private hands, and by competing with private entrepreneurs for loans, therefore increasing the price of borrowing.[742]

Hazlitt makes a powerful case against stimulus spending in theory but even more convincing is that the data does show negative effects on the economy as a result of stimulus spending. Antony Davies, an economics professor at Duquesne University has compiled all cases of stimulus spending from 1954 to 2011, then showed the effects on the economy in the immediate short run, after 1 year, and after 2 years based on how they affect real GDP per capita. He also looks at the effects of cumulative stimulus spending during the same years. The results showed no effects in the short run, or after one or two years, and negative

---

[739] Ibid., p. 10

[740] De Rugy, Veronique. "The Facts About Stimulus Spending." *Reason*, 8 July 2011. <http://reason.com/archives/2011/07/08/the-facts-about-stimulus-spend>.

[741] Epstein, Jim. "Why Obama's Stimulus Failed: A Case Study of Silver Spring, Maryland." *Reason*, 8 Dec. 2011. <http://reason.com/blog/2011/12/08/why-obamas-stimulus-failed-a-case-study>.

[742] See: Mitchell, Matthew, and Jakina R. Debnam. "In the Long Run, We're All Crowded Out." *Mercatus Center*, 22 Sept. 2010. <http://mercatus.org/publication/long-run-we-re-all-crowded-out>.

real per-capita GDP growth when the spending is cumulative over four and over eight quarters respectively.[743]

Austerity Horrors

Fear of austerity is bipartisan for the public and politicians alike.[744] Austerity's remedy for excessive debt is hawked as a combination of spending cuts and tax increases. No person wants their services cut, nor their taxes increased, so pressure is usually against this sort of policy. But tax increases can always be advertised as being for "the rich," so it's much easier for politicians to weigh more of their austerity plans on tax increases rather than spending cuts – especially when foreign countries don't have their own Grover Norquists.

The way austerity is reporting on also fuels negative perceptions of it. The Left had a field day in citing the UK's reversion back into a recession in 2012 as proof of austerity's failures. Among the headlines were:

> Austerity Pushes The UK Back Into Recession — Will American Conservatives Learn The Lesson? – *Think Progress* (Pat Garafalo, April 25th).[745]
>
> David Miliband: austerity measures put UK and Germany on the back foot – *The Guardian* (Nicholas Watt, April 30th).[746]
>
> Eurozone finally admitting that austerity measures are not working – *The New York Times* (Paul Krugman, April 30th).[747]

---

[743] Davies, Antony. "Can the Government Spend Us out of Recession." *Duquesne University*, <http://www.antolin-davies.com/conventionalwisdom/spend.pdf>.
[744] For example, in an interview with Stanford University's Hoover Institution, Paul Ryan hawked his budget proposal for reforming entitlements as a way to avoid austerity.
[745] http://thinkprogress.org/economy/2012/04/25/470781/uk-recession/
[746] http://www.guardian.co.uk/politics/2012/apr/30/david-miliband-austerity-uk-germany

Austerity in Britain: Not Working, Not About to End – *Slate* (David Weigel, April 25th).[748]

Austerity Britain: Lesson for the U.S.? – *The New Yorker* (John Cassidy, March 23rd).[749]

The Consequences of Austerity in One Chart? – *The Washington Post* (Ezra Klein, April 26th).[750]

TV's talking heads didn't let it pass by either. On March 30th, Martin Bashir compared the budget plans of Mitt Romney and Paul Ryan "almost exactly, word for word" to those in the UK.[751] MSNBC's Chris Hayes and Rachel Maddow reported on the awful results of British austerity as well.[752] Over at CNN, Fareed Zakaria picked up on the story to point out that the US economy practiced stimulus measures while the UK practiced austerity, and the US is now better off.[753]

And so the evidence seemed to suggest, if you want to help a failing economy, don't cut spending by any means. Good thing that isn't what actually happened.

Austerity is an umbrella term which doesn't specify the ratio of tax increases to spending cuts. Apparently these liberal

---

[747] http://economictimes.indiatimes.com/features/investors-guide/eurozone-finally-admitting-that-austerity-measures-are-not-working/articleshow/12916130.cms

[748] http://www.slate.com/blogs/weigel/2012/04/25/austerity_in_britain_not_working_not_about_to_end.html

[749] http://www.newyorker.com/online/blogs/johncassidy/2011/03/austerity-britain-lesson-for-the-us.html

[750] http://www.washingtonpost.com/blogs/ezra-klein/post/the-consequences-of-austerity-in-one-chart/2012/04/26/gIQAi24EjT_blog.html

[751] Sheppard, Noel. "Bashir Falsely Claims British and Spanish Recessions Are 'Romney-Ryan Budget in Action' - Omits They Raised Taxes" *NewsBusters*, 30 Apr. 2012. <http://newsbusters.org/blogs/noel-sheppard/2012/04/30/bashir-falsely-claims-british-and-spanish-recessions-romney-ryan-budg>.

[752] Up With Chris Hayes, MSNBC, Aired April 29th 2012, and The Rachel Maddow Show

[753] GPS with Fareed Zakaria, CNN, Aired May 30th 2012

commentators listened that politicians in the UK claimed that they were going to pursue an austerity agenda, but never actually bothered to look at what happened to spending. Spending in the UK declined a mere 1.2% of GDP from 2010-2012, from 45.31% of GDP to 44.11% of GDP. But on net basis during the first decade of the 21st century, spending began at 34.63% of GDP in 2000, and then consistently inched upward from there.[754] Spending isn't even being cut in real dollars; the pace at what it increases is just being slowed.

The UK also implemented a series of takes hikes. In 2010, the capital gains rate was increased from 18% to 28% for higher earners, and there was speculation that the rate could increase to as high at 50%.[755] The same year, the top marginal tax rate was raised to 50% for high earners, which ended up totaling 52% after the extension of National Insurance payments. This new rate was high enough to act as a disincentive, and ended up losing revenue,[756] so it later had to be slashed down to 45% in March of 2012. In 2010, The VAT tax was increased to 20% in 2010, previously at 17.5%.[757]

If austerity is being practiced, the indication of such a policy still has yet to be seen in the UK's debt figures. Debt in 2012 was nearly double what it was in 2008 (increasing from 36.25% of GDP to 65.26%).[758] Debt to GDP isn't even projected

---

[754] "Total Spending Fiscal Years 2000 to 2012." <http://www.ukpublicspending.co.uk/spending_chart_2000_2012UKp_12c1li011mcn_F0t>.

[755] Teather, David. "Capital Gains Tax Rises to 28% for Higher Earners." *The Guardian*, 22 June 2010. <http://www.guardian.co.uk/business/2010/jun/22/budget-capital-gains-tax-rises>.

[756] Morrissey, Ed. "Surtax on Wealthy in UK Results in Lower Revenue." *HotAir*, 22 Feb. 2012. <http://hotair.com/archives/2012/02/22/surtax-on-wealthy-in-uk-results-in-lower-revenue/>.

[757] "Increase in the Standard Rate of VAT to 20 per Cent." *HM Revenue & Customs*. <http://www.hmrc.gov.uk/vat/forms-rates/rates/rate-increase.htm>.

[758] Data available from: http://www.ukpublicspending.co.uk/.

to drop until 2015, where debt will drop by 0.37% of GDP from the year before from 69.93% to 69.56%.[759]

While the UK remains the poster boy for austerity's failures among bloggers on the left, it's a big stretch to say that any austerity is actually taking place. These individuals are also pushing nonsense when blaming poor economic conditions on austerity. Austerity measures are put in place as a response to unsustainable burdens of debt, which would have their own series of consequences if left unattended.

What we do know is that spending cuts do not necessarily led to a contraction in the real GDP. Cuba's private sector workforce grew 23% in 2012 as their private sector workforce declined by 5.7%.[760] The success of Canadian austerity measures in the 1990s could also be pointed too.[761] Alternatively, if anyone wants to argue that Canadian austerity only worked because Canada wasn't in a recession as they were implemented, the US's response to the depression of 1920 can be cited in affirmation of austerity.[762]

Making Austerity Work

Clearly, different types of austerity exist. For Krugman and other Keynesians, merely cutting spending qualifies as austerity. In Canada during the 1990's, they balanced their budgets through a combination of budget cuts and tax increases (cuts far outweighing tax increases), while the UK's austerity

---

[759] Ibid.

[760] Frank, Marc. "Cuba Cuts State Payroll, Private Sector Jobs Grow 23 Pct in 2012." *Reuters*, 27 Dec. 2012. <http://www.reuters.com/article/2012/12/27/cuba-economy-reform-idUSL1E8NQ23A20121227>.

[761] Stossel, John. "U.S. Could Learn a Valuable Financial Lesson from Canada." *FOX Business*, 15 June 2011. <http://www.foxnews.com/opinion/2011/06/15/us-could-learn-valuable-financial-lesson-from-canada/>.

[762] Murphy, Robert P. "The Depression You've Never Heard Of: 1920-1921." *The Freeman*, 18 Nov. 2009. <http://www.fee.org/the_freeman/detail/the-depression-youve-never-heard-of-1920-1921/#axzz2JcIf12fr>.

package functions in the opposite way, relying mainly on tax increases.

The real question is over what kind of austerity measures work by examining what kind of balance between spending cuts and tax increases is necessary. Summarizing the findings of the book *Chipping Away at Our Debt*, which examines the results of 66 different kinds of fiscal adjustments in the US, Canada, France, Japan, Germany, and Italy, Veronique de Rugy reports that:

> -Successful fiscal adjustments were grounded in structural reforms. Such reforms include welfare reforms as well as comprehensive expenditure review in the context of repositioning the role of the state (think Canada and Germany).
> -Plans that avoided structural reforms failed to meet their targets.
> -Successful plans were often grounded in real budget cuts.
> -Expenditure cuts didn't materialize to the extent initially envisioned.
> -Revenue-based plans without well-specified tax-policy measures — a majority of the revenue-based cases — failed.[763]

In other words, austerity can work, but only when you do the opposite of what the UK did.

Estonia

The case of Estonia is worth singling out for the sole fact of its president's own interaction with Krugman. It all began with a short blog post (66 words to be exact) on Krugman's part

[763] Everything listed is directly quoted. See: De Rugy, Veronique. "What Successful Fiscal Adjustments Look Like." *National Review Online*, 26 Oct. 2011. <http://www.nationalreview.com/corner/280773/what-successful-fiscal-adjustments-look-veronique-de-rugy>.

mocking Estonia's economic situation.[764] Estonia's president Toomas Hendrik didn't take kindly to the comments. Firing back on Twitter, he linked to Krugman's article, adding his own commentary: "Let's write about something we know nothing about & be smug, overbearing & patronizing: after all, they're just wogs:" Three more tweets afterward were directed at Krugman.[765] Krugman replied the next day (hilariously, in my opinion) that he is "hearing from various sources that my rather mild-mannered post on Estonia has generated a vitriolic response from the nation's president. I'm not going to try to track the thing down."[766]

For the record, Estonia cut government spending by lowering the salaries of government workers, raising ages for their pension system, and even lowered taxes in the face of a 18% decline in output in 2008. Estonia's economy grew 7.6% in 2012, and was the only country in the Euro-zone to have a balanced budget that same year.[767] You would be correct to assume that these facts were excluded from Krugman's initial blog post.

Debt and Growth Revisited

The most influential contemporary research into government debt and growth comes from Carmen Reinhart and Kenneth Rogoff's study "Growth in a Time of Debt."[768] One of the key statistics cited from the study is that once government

---

[764] Krugman, Paul. "Estonian Rhapsody." The *New York Times*, 6 June 2012. <http://krugman.blogs.nytimes.com/2012/06/06/estonian-rhapsdoy/>.

[765] Keating, Joshua. "President of Estonia Goes Ballistic on Paul Krugman." *Foreign Policy*, 6 June 2012. <http://blog.foreignpolicy.com/posts/2012/06/06/president_of_estonia_goes_ballistic_on_paul_krugman>.

[766] Krugman, Paul. "Ballistic in the Baltics." *The New York Times*, 7 June 2012. <http://krugman.blogs.nytimes.com/2012/06/07/ballistic-in-the-baltics/>.

[767] Stossel, John. "The Austerity Myth." *FOX Business*, 8 June 2012. <http://www.foxbusiness.com/on-air/stossel/blog/2012/06/08/austerity-myth>.

[768] Reinhart, Carmen M., and Kenneth Rogoff. "Growth in a Time of Debt." *Harvard University*, 2010. <http://scholar.harvard.edu/files/rogoff/files/growth_in_time_debt_aer.pdf>.

debt tops 90% of GDP, economic growth takes a nosedive. Some flaws were later uncovered with their research, but not enough to fully discredit the "high debt leads to less growth" claim. Some of the problems Reinhart and Rogoff's research came mainly from human error. For instance, there were errors in the excel spreadsheet that leave countries such as Denmark, Canada, Belgium, Austria, and Australia out of their calculations. A critique of the Reinhart and Rogoff research published at the University of Massachusetts at Amherst calculates that the real GDP growth of countries with debt to GDP ratios over 90% is really 2.2%, not -0.1% like originally calculated.[769]

This was certainly a flaw in the research of Reinhart and Rogoff, but hardly proves that high debt has no effect on long term economic growth. Even if we use the data from UMass, the average economic growth for an economy with a debt to GDP ratio between 0% and 30% is 4.2%, the figures for ratios of 30-60% are 3.1%, 3.2% for ratios of 60-90%, and 2.2% for ratios above 90%.[770] While many websites reporting on the study seem to be reporting it as a deathblow to austerity's main study, they apparently didn't even bother to compare the findings against the study it was criticizing.

As was cited in Chapter 3, we've seem among advanced countries the tendency for "small government" countries to grow at a much faster pace than their "big government" counterparts, though this measured government spending and taxes, not debt. The evidence is clear the less debt is better in the long run, even if austerity does cause some turbulence on the path to prosperity.

---

[769] Herndon, Thomas, Michael Ash, and Robert Pollin. "Does High Public Debt Consistently Stifle Economic Growth? A Critique of Reinhart and Rogoff." *University of Massachusetts Amherst*, 15 Apr. 2013. <http://www.peri.umass.edu/fileadmin/pdf/working_papers/working_papers_301-350/WP322.pdf>.

[770] Reinhart, Carmen M., and Kenneth Rogoff. "Reinhart-Rogoff Response to Critique." *The Wall Street Journal*, 16 Apr. 2013. <http://blogs.wsj.com/economics/2013/04/16/reinhart-rogoff-response-to-critique/>.

Obama the Fiscal Conservative

Debt

A chart released by Nancy Pelosi in 2011 makes the following claims: Ronald Reagan increased the national debt by 189%, Bush Sr. by 55%, Clinton by 37%, and George W. Bush by 115%. But Barack Obama? Only 16%, according to this chart.[771]

Despite all these numbers, they tell us absolutely nothing about the amount of debt each president actually added. Using hypothetical data, let's say Reagan increased the national debt from $1 million to $2 million – a 100% increase. Then let's say Bush Sr. comes along and increases the national debt from $2 million to $3 million – only a 33% increase. Clearly both presidents added the same amount of debt in this scenario, yet measuring debt using percentages clouds this fact.

There are two serious ways to measure debt accumulated by president, the first being the obvious of looking at real dollars added by president, and the second by measuring increases in debt as a percentage of GDP.

To measure debt increases in dollars by each president, Reagan increased the debt by $1.77 trillion, Bush Sr. by 1.49 trillion, Clinton by 1.54 trillion, George W. Bush by 4.9 trillion, and Obama by about 5.8 trillion during his first term.[772] If we

---

[771] "Nancy Pelosi Posts Questionable Chart on Debt Accumulation by Barack Obama, Predecessors." *PolitiFact*, <http://www.politifact.com/truth-o-meter/statements/2011/may/19/nancy-pelosi/nancy-pelosi-posts-questionable-chart-debt-accumul/>.

[772] Most of this data comes from: "Dueling Debt Deceptions." *FactCheck.org*, 2 Feb. 2012. <http://factcheck.org/2012/02/dueling-debt-deceptions/>. The statistic about debt accumulation under Obama's first term is from: Jeffrey, Terence P. "First Term: Obama Increased Debt $50,521 Per Household; More Than First 42 Presidents in 53 Terms Combined." *CNS News*, 19 Jan. 2013. <http://cnsnews.com/news/article/first-term-obama-increased-debt-50521-household-more-first-42-presidents-53-terms>.

measure how much each president increased the national debt by as a percentage of GDP, we find a 14.8% increase under Reagan, a 8.7% increase under George H.W. Bush, a 16.8% decline under Clinton, a 21% increase under Bush, and a 23.5% under Obama for only his first term.[773]

If we use percentages like Pelosi does, we can "prove" that Democrat controlled congresses rack up an immense amount of debt compared to their Republican counterparts. During their majority from 1981-95, and 2007-11, Democrats increased the debt 471%, compared to 105% for the Republicans from 1995-2007, and 2011-13.[774] Granted this is an equally poor argument, because Democrats have been the majority party for longer and thus had more time to rack up debt, and because I'm using percentages instead of real dollars, but the point is to show that twisting the data can go both ways in this case.

Spending

An article that soon went viral after being published on finance website *MarketWatch* recycled many of the same methods in hiding Obama's fiscal record as did Pelosi with the release of her bogus chart. The article titled "Obama's Spending Binge Never Happened" by columnist Rex Nutting once again makes his case by measuring percentages instead of real numbers.

Using Nutting's data, spending has only risen by 1.4% from 2010 to 2013. This is, according to Nutting, the slowest increase in spending since Eisenhower at the end of the Korean War. Nutting at least doesn't buy into a previously debunked

---

[773] Goff, Emily. "In Pictures: Debt by President? Obama Leads the Pack." *The Heritage Foundation*, 5 Oct. 2011. <http://blog.heritage.org/2011/10/05/in-pictures-debt-by-president-obama-leads-the-pack/>.

[774] Anderson, Daniel. "Who REALLY Increased the Debt?" *FreedomWorks*, 31 Jan. 2012. <http://www.freedomworks.org/blog/daniel-anderson/who-really-increased-the-debt>.

myth when he writes that "even hapless Herbert Hoover managed to increase spending more than Obama has."[775]

It should be obvious from the period Nutting measures that he doesn't even get his time frame correct, since his measurements begin in 2010. He also only attributes $140 in stimulus spending to Obama. To justify his starting point in 2010, Nutting writes that "what people forget (or never knew) is that the first year of every presidential term starts with a budget approved by the previous administration and Congress." What Nutting forgers (or never knew), is that the 2009 budget proposed by Bush spent $3.107 trillion, while the actual 2009 budget passed by the Democrat run congress and signed by Obama actually spent $3.518 trillion – which creates quite a large discrepancy between the two.[776] While it is true that the predecessor usually signs the budget into office for the next president's first year, one columnist at *The Washington Examiner* notes that:

> In most cases, that would be fair, because presidents typically sign the next year's spending bills in the calendar year before they leave office. But not in 2009. The Democratic Congress, confident Obama was going to win in 2008, passed only three of fiscal 2009′s 12 appropriations bills (Defense; Military Construction and Veterans Affairs; and Homeland Security). The Democrat Congress passed the rest of them, and Obama signed them.[777]

---

[775] Nutting, Rex. "Obama's Spending Binge Never Happened." *MarketWatch*, 22 May 2012. <http://articles.marketwatch.com/2012-05-22/commentary/31802270_1_spending-federal-budget-drunken-sailor>.

[776] "MarketWatch Rebuttal Infographic: How to Make Obama's Spending Look Small." *HotAir*, 24 May 2012. <http://hotair.com/archives/2012/05/24/how-to-make-obamas-spending-look-small-marketwatch-rebuttal-infographic/>.

[777] "Examiner Editorial: Big-spending Obama Frames Himself as Scrooge." *The Washington Examiner*, 24 May 2012. <http://washingtonexaminer.com/article/650536#.UCsa3J1lRD0>.

This is part of why we see a nearly $400 billion discrepancy between what Bush proposed to spend and what was actually spent that year. Factcheck.org estimates that Obama is responsible for a maximum of $203 billion in additional spending in 2009 – or 38% of the $535 billion increase in that year since 2008.[778]

Now, Nutting's article was published in May of 2012, but predicts what Obama would spend in 2013 by following the CBO baseline (a projection of what spending will be). When Nutting appeared on a Pittsburgh talk show shortly after his article took off, one caller pointed out that Nutting was using baseline budgeting. Nutting's response was "what is that?" The caller was eventually cut off after he pointed out that spending for ObamaCare is put off until 2014 and therefore not included in Nutting's "proof."[779]

The 2012 budget would've likely been slightly higher than it was, but the Budget Control Act of 2011 which was passed during the debt ceiling "panic" of 2011 constrained spending. While the Act does not actually cut spending, it does slow the rate of spending by $917 billion over one decade, $22 billion of which is applied to the 2012 budget.[780] Also, since TARP spending in 2009 accounted for $154 billion that year (which was passed by Bush, but Obama voted in favor of it as a Senator), but did decrease federal spending by $108 billion in 2010, and $39 billion in 2011 which made the 2010 and 2011 budgets decrease artificially.[781] I write this sentence literally two hours before the sequester is scheduled to go into effect on March

---

[778] Jackson, Brooks. "Obama's Spending: 'Inferno' or Not?" *FactCheck.org*, 4 June 2012. <http://factcheck.org/2012/06/obamas-spending-inferno-or-not/>.

[779] The caller appeared on the Rush Limbaugh Show on May 24th 2012 to discuss what happened. A transcript can be found at: <http://www.rushlimbaugh.com/daily/2012/05/24/the_pelosi_chart_that_inspired_rex_nutting>.

[780] "The Budget Control Act of 2011." *House Budget Committee*, 27 July 2011. <http://budget.house.gov/budgetcontrolact2011/>.

[781] Jackson, "Obama's Spending: 'Inferno' or Not?"

1st 2013 which would gut $85 billion from the budget – which Obama opposes. These are all spending cuts that were either opposed by or are unrelated to Obama's alleged fiscal conservatism.

It is also important to remember that Obama has not received all the spending that he is desired. Had congress taken Obama's advice regarding the 2011 American Jobs Act and "passed this bill," another $447 billion in stimulus spending would have occurred. However, it's not only the Republicans holding Obama back. In particular, Obama's 2013 budget were rejected by Democrats and Republicans alike. Senator Jeff Sessions (R-Ala.) submitted a budget nearly identical to that of Obama's 2013 resolution. The resolution in question would have created $6.4 trillion in new deficits by 2022. This reality didn't go over to well, which resulted in the budget being shot down 99-0 in the Senate and 414-0 in the House.[782]

Aside from these problems, the data is at least out there to answer the question of if Obama is a big spender. With the exception of the years 1942-46 during World War II, US government spending has never been over 23.5%. During Obama's first year in office, spending soared to 25.2% of GDP, partially thanks to TARP, but also to the stimulus. This amounts to a 21.2% increase in spending from the year before, when spending is measured against GDP. To better show the extent of Obama's spending binge, from 2001 to 2008, federal spending rose from $1.8 trillion to $2.9 trillion, but shot up to $3.5 trillion in 2009.[783] Now from 2010 onward, Obama basically sustained his level of spending after the spike, which is what Nutting measured. If Nutting measured spending as a percentage of GDP,

[782] Dinan, Stephen. "Obama Budget Defeated 99-0 in Senate." *The Washington Times*, 16 May 2012. <http://www.washingtontimes.com/blog/inside-politics/2012/may/16/obama-budget-defeated-99-0-senate/>.
[783] Suderman, Peter. "The Obama Spending Binge." *Reason*, 23 May 2012. <http://reason.com/blog/2012/05/23/the-obama-spending-binge>.

he could actually have "proved" that Obama shrunk spending slightly, but his article would've been much less believable had he opted to do so.

Ask yourself this, who's the bigger spender in the following scenario: a man who spends $1 one year, and $2 the next year, or another man who spends $1 million one year and $999,999 the next year? According to Rex Nutting, the first man is the bigger spender because he doubled spending. As for the second man, while he increased spending by an enormous amount relative to the prior man, we can ignore this because spending stagnated the next year.

Spending vs. Debt

Defenders of Nutting's article have pointed to an analysis by PolitiFact which rated the claims of Nutting as "mostly true." However, all PolitiFact "proved" was that spending has increased at a slow rate using inflation adjusted dollars under the same false criterion Nutting uses. Spending increases as a percentage of GDP are not even mentioned, nor are comparisons of Obama's level of spending relative to other presidents.[784]

In what would appear to be a contradiction, an older post on PolitiFact which examined Pelosi's bogus debt figures that was previously debunked, it was concluded, "Obama is the undisputed debt king of the last five presidents."[785] While PolitiFact's defense of Nutting's article is deeply flawed, they do note that even if Obama has increased spending slowly, he's still racked up an unsustainable amount of spending.

---

[784] "Viral Facebook Post Says Barack Obama Has Lowest Spending Record of Any Recent President." *PolitiFact*, 23 May 2012. <http://www.politifact.com/truth-o-meter/statements/2012/may/23/facebook-posts/viral-facebook-post-says-barack-obama-has-lowest-s/>.

[785] "Nancy Pelosi Posts Questionable Chart on Debt Accumulation by Barack Obama, Predecessors." *PolitiFact*, 19 May 2011. <http://www.politifact.com/truth-o-meter/statements/2011/may/19/nancy-pelosi/nancy-pelosi-posts-questionable-chart-debt-accumul/>.

After receiving criticism over this, PolitiFact actually organized some of it and posted it up on their website on a blog post that featured criticism from the Heritage Foundation, Reason, and the Cato Institute.[786]

[786] Jacobson, Louis. "Lots of Heat (and Some Light) on Obama's Spending." *PolitiFact*, 25 May 2012. <http://www.politifact.com/truth-o-meter/article/2012/may/25/lots-heat-and-some-light-obamas-spending/>.

Chapter 5

Intellectuals and Capitalism

Some ideas are so absurd that only intellectuals could believe them.

– Anonymous (often misattributed to George Orwell)

Two books have influenced me to write this chapter: *Intellectuals and Society* by Thomas Sowell, and *Intellectual Morons* by Daniel Flynn. Sowell's book is a more serious look at the influence of intellectuals throughout world history, and how wrong they often were. Flynn's book takes a more comical approach to the issue, focusing on intellectuals who have held to hilariously idiotic views. My goal with this chapter is to correct various criticisms of capitalism from today's living intellectuals by exposing the shoddy research behind their claims.

Naomi Klein

Like many of the intellectuals that will be discussed in this chapter, Klein falls into the category of the criminally under qualified. Klein first gained fame with the publication of *No Logo*, an anti-globalization book that one reviewer described as "the bible for anti-corporate militancy." One company attacked in the book, Nike, saw fit to respond with their own defense of themselves after the book gained traction.[787] Another bestseller of Klein, *The Shock Doctrine*, is written as a story detailing the horrors of what she calls "disaster capitalism," with Milton Friedman as the stories chief villain. The book received favorable reviews from both Nobel Prize winning economist Joseph Stiglitz and the late Howard Zinn.

The *Shock Doctrine* creates the impression that its author has at least some sort of economics background, as the author description on the first page points out that Klein is a "former Milband Fellow at the London School of Economics," who holds an honorary Doctor of Civil Laws degree from the University of King's College. This is misleading, since Klein's highest level of education is a bachelor's degree in English and philosophy from

---

[787] "Nike's Response to No Logo (by Naomi Klein)." *Nike*, 8 Mar. 2000. <http://web.archive.org/web/20010618162615/http://nikebiz.com/labor/nologo_let.shtml>.

the University of Toronto.[788] As for the fact that she has an honorary doctorate, so does Chuck Norris (though no offence to Chuck Norris is implied here).

This critique of Klein's work relies heavily on the scholarship of Johan Norberg's paper "The Klein Doctrine: The Rise of Disaster Politics." Norberg created a series called Free or Equal for Milton Friedman's Free To Choose Network. That series largely expands upon Friedman's TV series for the book Free to Choose in the 1990's. Norberg also stared in his own mini-documentary titled "Globalization is good." As such, Norberg has an immense amount of expertise on both the effects of globalization, and the character of Milton Friedman.

The Case of Milton Friedman

Naomi Klein's *Shock Doctrine* aims to provide an historical overview and critique of free market economics. The first chapters lay out the analogy of the title, which is referencing shock therapy. Just as shock therapy can transform a patients mind into a "blank slate," the "disaster capitalists" use disasters as their blank slate to build a new economy from. Klein hypothesizes that while people would naturally have a reluctance to many free market policies, destruction serves as a catalyst for acceptance towards these views.

Klein linked Milton Friedman to many global misdeeds worldwide stemming from "disaster capitalism." The core focus of Klein's criticism of Friedman is to the activity of him and other Chicago school economists (known as the Chicago Boys) in Chile. When not explicitly criticizing Friedman, she allows the mind of the reader to fill in the blanks. Since the metaphor of "shock" is a theme of the book, it comes to no surprise that Klein tries to make it almost seem like Friedman supports actual shock therapy to some extent.

---

788 Viner, Katharine. "Hand-To-Brand-Combat: A Profile Of Naomi Klein." *Common Dreams*, 23 Sept. 2000. <http://www.commondreams.org/views/092300-103.htm>.

To show Friedman's support for a form of "blank slate" style change, she quotes from what she calls "one of his most influential essays,"[789] where he writes that "only a crisis – real or perceived – produces real change." This quotation isn't form Friedman's most influential essay, but from the introduction to his book "Capitalism and Freedom." Considering that Klein cited her source correctly in her footnotes,[790] one can only wonder how she got the idea that this qualified as an influential essay. What Klein wants the reader to get from this quotation is more visible from her documentary based off the book, where she displays that quotation over video footage of people being tortured.

Friedman's quotation isn't even sinister regardless, and is instead pointing to a very basic truth that people are more accepting of change in a time of crisis. For example, people were much more accepting of the New Deal in a time of depression than they would've otherwise been (and no, I'm not pointing this out in one of my most influential essays).

Friedman in Chile

Most disparaging of Friedman's character in Klein's book isn't his allegedly failed policies, but his alleged support of Chilean dictator Augusto Pinochet. This isn't a new claim either. In a 1991 question and answer session following a speech by Friedman, one of the questions suggested that Friedman supported Pinochet, so which Friedman briefly replied "I never advised Pinochet, I never supported Pinochet."[791]

Klein also claims that Friedman worked as an advisor to Pinochet, but this happened nowhere other than in Klein's imagination. His only direct correspondence with Pinochet is a

---

[789] Klein, Naomi. "The Shock Doctrine: The Rise of Disaster Capitalism." (New York: Picador, 2008), p. 7.
[790] Ibid., p. 592.
[791] Friedman, Milton. "On Liberty and Drugs." November 16th 1991 at America's Drug Forum, sponsored by The Drug Policy Foundation.

brief one-hour meeting with him, followed by a letter in which he offered solutions to the economic problems Chile faced.[792] Many of Pinochet's advisers were versed in Chicago School economics, but because the University of Chicago had a partnership with the Catholic University of Chile in which Chileans would be given scholarships to study in America.[793]

Friedman never received any monetary compensation from the Chilean government, and even turned down two honorary degrees from the Chilean government because he didn't want to be seen as supporting the Chilean regime.[794] Commenting on the combination of free market policies and dictatorship of Pinochet, Friedman observed in an interview in 2000 that "the really extraordinary thing about the Chilean case was that a military government followed the opposite of military policies."[795]

Regarding a speech that he gave at the Catholic University of Chile, Friedman said that "the essence of the talk was that freedom was a very fragile thing and that what destroyed it more than anything else was central control; that in order to maintain freedom you had to have free markets, and that free markets would work best if you had political freedom."[796] He continues that "it was essentially an anti-totalitarian talk." This prompted the interviewer to ask "so you envisaged, therefore, that the free markets ultimately would undermine Pinochet?" to which Friedman replied "oh absolutely."[797]

But aside from the question of whether or not Friedman endorsed the dictatorship (which he clearly did not), the question

---

[792] Doherty, Brian. "The Economist and the Dictator." *Reason*, 15 Dec. 2006. <http://reason.com/archives/2006/12/15/the-economist-and-the-dictator>.
[793] Ibid.
[794] Norberg, Johan. "The Klein Doctrine: The Rise of Disaster Politics." *The Cato Institute*, 14 May 2008. <http://www.cato.org/sites/cato.org/files/pubs/pdf/bp102.pdf>.
[795] Friedman, Milton. "The Indispensable Milton Friedman: Essays on Politics and Economics." Ed. Alan O. Ebenstein. (Washington, DC: Regnery, 2012), p. 249
[796] Ibid., p. 250.
[797] Ibid.

of whether or not the free-market policies Friedman and the Chicago-boys prescribed still remains.

Klein is good at tossing out statistics which would suggest otherwise. Trying to explain that the Chicago Boys' policies failed, Klein writes that "in 1974, inflation reached 375 percent – the highest rate in the world and almost twice the top level under Allende."[798] There is one problem with this statement – Friedman didn't go to Chile to offer his solutions on hyperinflation until 1975.[799]

She also neglected to mention that the inflation rate was 508% *before* the Chicago Boys saw their policies implemented.[800] Measuring a policy by its effect after only one year is a terrible way of conducting analysis anyway, as inflation was cut to 30% in 1979, and went as "low" as 9% in 1981.[801]

Disaster Capitalism That Wasn't

Many of Klein's examples of "disaster capitalism" are in countries which showed little or no increase in economic freedom even after their economies were supposedly 'made new'. As Johan Norburg shows using data from the Fraser Institute's index of economic freedom, economic freedom is fairly easy to track. Klein's example of the Argentinian dictatorship, which lasted between 1976-1983, is a prime example. On a scale of 1 (the least economically free) to 10 (most free), Argentina's economic freedom barely increased from 3.25 in 1975 to 3.86 in 1985.[802] To put this in perspective, this is a lower economic freedom

---

[798] Klein, "The Shock Doctrine," p. 97.
[799] Norberg, "The Klein Doctrine."
[800] Historic Inflation Chile - CPI Inflation." *Worldwide Inflation Data.* <http://www.inflation.eu/inflation-rates/chile/historic-inflation/cpi-inflation-chile.aspx>.
[801] Ibid.
[802] Norberg, "The Klein Doctrine."

index than all Eastern European communist-bloc countries that Frasier tracked at the time.[803]

The Other Shock-Therapists

Milton Friedman is far from being the only person to prescribe economic shock therapy. In a profile of Polish economist Leszek Balcerowicz, the *Wall Street Journal* described his economic philosophy as "shock therapy to slay hyperinflation and build a free market." His "Balcerowicz Plan" was known as a form of economic "shock therapy" as it was being promoted in 1989 as a way to shift Poland from a Communist economy to a Capitalist one.

The *Wall Street Journal* reported that in regards to the Balcerowicz Plan "Overnight, prices were freed, subsidies were slashed and the zloty currency was made convertible. It was harsh medicine, but the Polish economy recovered faster than more gradual reformers in the old Soviet bloc." Considering that Poland hasn't experienced a recession since 1989 (and is the only European country to pull off such a feat),[804] Poland's economy indeed shows some strength.

That isn't to say that Poland doesn't have problems, but the problems Klein attributes to economic shock therapy are non-existent. According to Klein, these reforms "caused a full-blown depression: a 30 percent reduction in industrial production in the two years after the first round of reforms."[805] The more contemporary problems she lists are a 20% unemployment rate (in 2006), and an increase of the impoverished from 15% of the population in 1989 to 59% in 2003.[806] She claims to have sourced these figures from The World Bank.[807] Apparently, there are two

---

[803] Ibid.
[804] Cienski, Jan. "A Market for the Newly Wealthy." *Financial Times*, 28 May 2012. <http://www.ft.com/intl/cms/s/0/9fd24a46-a0e2-11e1-851f-00144feabdc0.html>.
[805] Klein, "Shock Doctrine," p. 241.
[806] Ibid., pp. 241-2.
[807] Ibid., p. 241.

World Banks, one which provides economic statistics about countries around the globe, and one that Naomi Klein cites when creating statistics out of thin air.

In some circles, a depression is defined as a 10% or larger reduction in GDP. Poland did indeed experience a decline in GDP during their transition stage, and it was a 22% decline in GDP from 1989-1990. The economy rebounded quickly, and GDP in 1991 was higher than in 1989. In fact, GDP growth was almost flat before reforms were enacted. The World Banks's actual statistics for Poland's GDP begin in 1985:

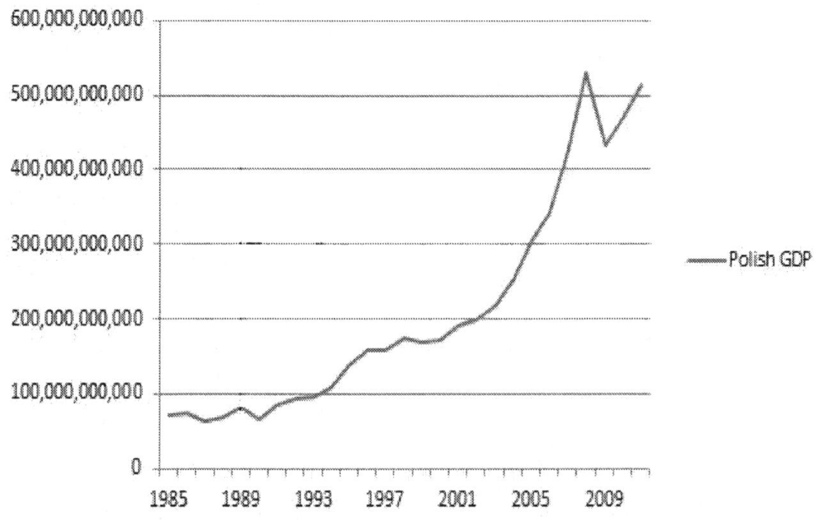

Source: The World Bank.[808]

In a 1994 report on poverty in Poland, the World Bank reported that "Throughout the 1980s, the poverty rate…oscillated between 5 and 10 percent of the population. In 1990, the first year of the stabilization, it jumped to 15 percent where it has stayed since.

[808] "GDP (current US$)" *The World Bank*, <http://data.worldbank.org/indicator/NY.GDP.MKTP.CD>.

However…the poverty rate in 1993 seems to be edging downwards."[809] And indeed, it continued to edge downward. The World Bank's statistics show that the poverty rate in Poland was 10.6 in 2008,[810] which is quite a stretch from Klein's mythical "59%" figure for the year 2003. It also has to be remembered that while Poland's poverty rate hasn't changed much, those impoverished are defined as such in a now much richer country.

Real GDP per capita began to take off in 1992, after some small declines during the transition. Real GDP per capita increased a measly $1,912 under a centrally planned Poland from 1980 to 1989, but by $4,467 from 1990-2000. Real GDP almost doubled from 2000-2010, increasing from $10,310 to $18,981.[811]

Friedman vs. Neo-Conservatives

Further misunderstanding the philosophy of Friedman, Klein brands him as a "neo-conservative," a term used to brand him as one favoring a heavy military presence in foreign nations. Capitalism, Corporatism, and Neo-Conservativism are three terms used interchangeably throughout *The Shock Doctrine*, which misleads readers into thinking that there's no difference between the terms. Of course, the difference is that one term refers to an economic system, the second is a sociological term, and the third refers to foreign policy.

After being criticized by Johan Norburg of the Cato Institute for this gross mischaracterization,[812] Klein backtracked and wrote that she "never said Milton Friedman was a "neo-

---

[809] "Poverty in Poland." *The World Bank*, Sept. 1994. <http://web.worldbank.org/WBSITE/EXTERNAL/TOPICS/EXTPOVERTY/EXTPA/0,,contentMDK:20205276~menuPK:435735~pagePK:148956~piPK:216618~theSitePK:430367,00.html>.

[810] "Poverty Headcount Ratio at National Poverty Line (% of Population)." *The World Bank*, <http://data.worldbank.org/indicator/SI.POV.NAHC/countries/PL?display=graph>.

[811] "Poland GDP (purchasing Power Parity)." *Index Mundi*, <http://www.indexmundi.com/poland/gdp_(purchasing_power_parity).html>.

[812] Norberg, "The Klein Doctrine."

conservative" – all while claiming that Milton Friedman supported the Iraq war.[813]

It's hard not to reply to all of the minor inconsistencies in Klein's work. Even if she didn't explicitly claim that Friedman was a neo-conservative, she did an impressive job providing the reader with that impression. Klein mentions that George W. Bush's speechwriter (David Frum) was neo-conservative, and wanted "shock therapy style economic revolution in the U.S.,"[814] which she believes Friedman wanted abroad. Early in the book, she mentions that although Friedman's beliefs would be characterized as conservative in the US, they would be known as neo-liberal in most of the world.[815] Three hundred pages later, Klein describes the Chicago School of Economics (of which Friedman belonged) as neo-liberal, noting that it would be called neoconservative in the US.[816] In Klein's view, think tanks that she considers neoconservative include the American Enterprise Institute, Heritage Foundation, and Cato Institute, which she also describes as being Friedmanite to their core.[817]

Throughout all this, Klein seems ignorant of one of Milton Friedman's revolutionary ideas: a volunteer military. While serving as an advisor in the Nixon administration, Friedman would "return to our heritage, get rid of the compulsion in our military service, and return to a voluntary system."[818] Nixon held a commission to debate ending the draft, and appointed Friedman to speak. Friedman debated General Westmoreland at this commission, to whom he posed the

---

[813] Klein, Naomi. "One Year After the Publication of The Shock Doctrine, A Response to the Attacks." 2 Sept. 2008. <http://www.naomiklein.org/articles/2008/09/response-attacks>.

[814] Klein, "Shock Doctrine," p. 13.

[815] Ibid., 17.

[816] Ibid., 319.

[817] Ibid., 407.

[818] See the documentary: "The Commanding Heights, the Battle for the World Economy." PBS, 2002.

question "would you rather command a slave force?" Westmoreland "didn't like to hear his drafted soldiers referred to as slaves," and Friedman "didn't like to hear my patriotic volunteers referred to as mercenaries." Alan Greenspan, who also was appointed to speak at the commission described Friedman as "taking apart his [Westmoreland's] arguments piece of piece, never raising his voice. The general got redder and redder, and at the end of this set of dissections, the mercenary argument was thoroughly demolished." Additionally, Martin Anderson, another advisor of Nixon who wrote a policy paper advocating the abolition of the draft claimed to have "borrowed liberally from Milton's paper."[819]

As an interesting side note, the 6,300 word Wikipedia entry on the term "Neoconservatism" mentions Milton Friedman a total of zero times.[820]

Elizabeth Warren

Warren and Economics

Co-authored along with her daughter, Warren's book *The Two Income Trap* documents how since 1970, the rise of the two-worker household has led to unpredicted results. These results include that fact that the dual-income household not only has less discretionary income than the one-income household did decades prior, but that bankruptcy is also on the rise among middle class households.

Warren also gave a talk at UC Berkeley titled "The Coming Collapse of the Middle Class" which is based on her book. One of Warren's observations about a certain problem facing the economy is spot on: personal savings is declining. Figuring out why savings are declining is what she aims to determine. As she discovers, people are spending less as a

[819] See: Ibid.
[820] < http://en.wikipedia.org/wiki/Neoconservatism>. Accessed on February 15th 2012.

proportion of their total income on clothes, food, appliances, and cars today than a generation ago. She's economically literate enough to know that the causes of this are many, including lower cost imported clothes, big box stores for food and appliances, and declines in repair costs for cars. Warren has an epiphany when she discovers one area where spending increased massively: housing. From 1970 to 2004, spending on housing increased 76%.[821] There is no problem with any of the data that Warren has presented to us so far, but she's at a loss as to why people have been spending more on housing.

In her UC Berkeley talk, Warren emphasizes that the increase in housing costs isn't due to an increase in the size of houses, since the median home only grew slightly in size, from 5.8 rooms to 6.1 rooms. This sounds like a minor increase, except that during Warren's timeframe (1970-2004) the average home's size increased from 1,400 square feet to 2,330 square feet.[822] In her book Warren actually acknowledges that the average home size as measured in square feet has increased, but claims that the "overwhelming majority of middle-income families don't live in one of those spacious new homes."[823]

She bases her statement on the fact that there has been a 50% rise in people living in older homes over the past generation. This is probably due to the fact that as time progresses, homes tend to get older. The 50% measurement here isn't specific enough from which to base a conclusion. If 1 in 10 people lived in old homes in previous generations, compared to 1.5 in 10 people for the current generation, she arrives at her 50% figure, but this doesn't prove that most people are downgrading.

---

[821] Warren, Elizabeth. "The Coming Collapse of the Middle Class. Presented at UC Berkeley on June 11th 2007.

[822] "Downsize Your Home To Downsize Expenses." *Investopedia*, 25 Feb. 2009. <http://www.investopedia.com/articles/pf/07/downsize.asp#axzz2AjPG8WqW>.

[823] Warren, Elizabeth, and Amelia Warren Tyagi. "The Two-income Trap: Why Middle-class Parents Are Going Broke." (New York, NY: Basic, 2004), p. 21.

In addition to the increasing size of homes, another reason we have seen an incredible 76% increase in spending on housing is because Warren's measurement ends right before the peak of the housing bubble. With home size and inflation adjusted for, there was a 40% increase in real housing price per square foot from 1970-2004.[824] But if we go back to 2000, there was only a 19% increase in the price of housing per square foot since 1970.[825] If we look at 1996 prices, we see only a 3.7% increase in the price of housing per square foot since 1970.[826] Once again, this isn't to say that a home in 1996 only cost 3.7% more than a home in 1970, but that a home cost only 3.7% more in 1996 after you adjust for increases in inflation and home size.

Her theory behind the rising costs is that it is the fault of the education system. She concludes that suburban areas with good school districts attract more families, which lead to a bidding war on housing. It's undeniable that good nearby schools increase housing values, especially since this sort of environment is also accompanied by high income earners and a low crime area. But the extent to which this is occurring is certainly overstated since the housing bubble was primarily responsible for the cost increases that we saw. The positive side to Warren's talk is that her solution to this problem is school vouchers,[827] the same approach that I outlined in Chapter 3.

According to Warren's calculations, other big increases in expenditures facing the middle class are taxes (+25%) and health insurance (+74%).[828] The reason for the increase in taxes is that the added income from a second worker pushes a family's total income into a higher tax bracket. Todd Zywicki, a blogger for

[824] A spreadsheet sourcing inflation adjusted home prices from 1970- 2011 is available at:
<http://www.jparsons.net/housingbubble/>. After adjusting for inflation and household size, real home prices averaged $145,983 in 1970, and $242,975 in 2004.
[825] 145,983 % 179,208
[826] 145,983 % 151,513
[827] Warren, "Two Income Trap," pp. 34-35.
[828] Warren at UC Berkeley.

The Volokh Conspiracy showed that Warren underestimated the increase in taxes – the real increase is actually 140%.[829]

When measured as a percentage of total family income, taxes and child care are to blame for the decline in discretionary income since 1970. The typical single-worker household in the early 1970s spent 3% of its income on health insurance,[830] 14% on the mortgage, and 13% on automobile expenses. The two-worker household of the early 2000s spent 2% on health insurance, 13% on the mortgage, and 12% on cars. But the difference between the early 1970s and early 2000s households is that taxes increased dramatically, from 24% of income to 34% of income, and child care became a new expense which now consumes 14% of income.[831]

The Shrinking Safety Net

Another theme to Warren's book is that the safety net is shrinking.[832] When most people talk about a shrinking safety net they're referring to government welfare spending, but most of this type of talk is just hype. Welfare spending as a percentage of GDP was 2.15% in 1970 when Warren's measurements began, and 3.44% when they ended.[833] Not once during the 1970-2004 period did welfare spending fall below what it was in 1970.

But the safety net Warren is talking about isn't government-based, it's the safety net provided by a non-working

---

[829] Zywicki, Todd. "Christopher Caldwell Falls for the Two-Income Trap." *The Volokh Conspiracy*, 28 July 2011. <http://www.volokh.com/2011/07/28/christopher-caldwell-falls-for-the-two-income-trap/>.
[830] Health insurance remained so low as a percentage of income despite soaring costs because healthcare is received in the form of benefits for most people, instead of being paid for directly in cash.
[831] Zywicki, Todd. "Evaluating The Two-Income Trap Hypothesis." *The Volokh Conspiracy*, 6 Aug. 2007. <http://www.volokh.com/posts/1185883980.shtml>.
[832] Warren, "Two Income Trap," pp. 55-70.
[833] "Welfare Spending Chart" *UsGovernmentSpending*, <http://www.usgovernmentspending.com/spending_chart_1970_2017USp_13s1li111mcn_40t_40_Welfare_Spending_Chart>.

mother who can care for her children and find a job if her husband loses his. The stay at home mom also negates the expense of child care, and incurs less of the of the other expenses associated with a job (gas, food/lunches outside the home, etc.).

There is a tradeoff that occurs when a second parent enters the workforce, and there seems to be no real way around it. Warren looks into the possibility of government-funded day care, but explains that "every dollar spent to subsidize the price of day care frees up a dollar for the two-income family to spend in the bidding wars for housing, tuition, and everything else that families are competing for".[834] Even if Warren's bidding hypothesis is faulty, the government already subsidizes day care for low income earners (which, by the way, doesn't aid the middle class two-earner household). In 1997, the Cato Institute estimated that around 40% of day care costs were funded by government at the local, state, and federal levels.[835]

Tackling the problem of child care costs is better solved by altering tax incentives than by expanding the role of government in the matter. Expanding the Child and Dependent Care Credit would be the simplest way to do this. The maximum tax credit that most families can receive is $1,050 for one child, or $2,100 for two, but the credit phases out as one goes up the income ladder. For example, a household with $50,000 a year in earnings is only eligible for a credit of $600.[836]

The Rise in Bankruptcy

I have criticized Warren criticized in Chapter Two when I showed that a study she took part in on the topic of medical

---

[834] Warren, "Two Income Trap," pp. 39-40.
[835] Olsen, Darcy. "The Advancing Nanny State: Why the Government Should Stay Out of Child Care." *The Cato Institute*, 23 Oct. 2007. <http://www.cato.org/pubs/pas/pa-285.html>.
[836] Faulhaber, Lilian V. "How the I.R.S. Hurts Mothers." *The New York Times*, 3 Apr. 2013. <http://www.nytimes.com/2013/04/04/opinion/lean-in-what-about-child-care.html?_r=1&>.

bankruptcy was poorly constructed. The data presented in *The Two Income Trap* is an attempt to explain the rise in bankruptcy filings, but as a professor of bankruptcy law, Warren ought to know better. If anything, filings for bankruptcy correlate most heavily with how appealing the law is to potential filers. When bankruptcy law was altered in 1978 in ways that made it more appealing, there was a marked increase in bankruptcy filings the next two years before leveling off.[837] Bankruptcies then shot up following additional modifications to the Bankruptcy Code, which lasted until 2005.[838] By 2005, there were 7.2 times as many bankruptcies as in 1978.[839] When bankruptcy law was modified in 2005 to make filing for bankruptcy more difficult, bankruptcies began to decline.[840] Obviously, it seems unlikely that there was such a striking increase in bankruptcies due to any economic problems in the 80s and 90s, since this was a period of major economic growth.[841]

Nick Hanauer

Nick Hanauer plays the perfect role as a leftist activist – he's both a self-made billionaire and supports raising taxes on the rich. When liberal bloggers and pundits cite him, he isn't "Nick Hanauer," he's "billionaire Nick Hanauer." Even more ideal is the fact that Hanauer made his breakthrough to leftist advocacy posing as a victim.

It all started with a talk that Hanauer gave at a TED conference, where speakers present new ideas concerning technology, education, politics, science, and other fields. Hanauer's talk dealt with the issue of income inequality. Controversy followed soon after, not due to the content of the talk itself, but because TED failed to upload the talk onto their

---

[837] Murray, "Coming Apart," pp. 197.
[838] Ibid.
[839] Ibid.
[840] Ibid., p. 196.
[841] Ibid.

website. It then spread like wildfire through the blogosphere that Hanauer's talk was "too hot for TED" and "deemed too controversial" to be posted.

The problem with this entire narrative is that it only exists because Hanauer paid a PR firm to create it. TED only posts one talk per day to their YouTube channel – from a pool of around 250 talks recorded at their conferences, and over 10,000 from their worldwide "TEDx" conferences. In the past, TED posted a lengthy talk titled "How Income Inequality Harms Societies," clearly contradicting the narrative the TED is somehow against posting talks related to income inequality. In fact, TED's curator posted on his blog about the controversy, noting in regards to Hanauer that "[his] talk tapped into a really important and timely issue. But he framed the issue in a way that was explicitly partisan." He continues with "The audience at TED who heard it live (and who are often accused of being overly enthusiastic about left-leaning ideas) gave it, on average, mediocre ratings - some enthusiastic, others critical."[842]

Numerous blogs commenting on the issue seemed never to cease bringing up the fact that the talk received a standing ovation, but after viewing other TED talks it seems rare for any talk not to receive a standing ovation.

The great "revelation" of the speech is in Hanauer's explanation of why the rich are not job creators. How could they be job creators after all, when they wouldn't be able to sell their products without middle class consumers purchasing them? From this premise, Hanauer concludes that the rich aren't job creators, middle class consumers are. He is right to a point - all rich people aren't job creators. Some inherit wealth, some gain it by gambling, and others from equity investing – but it seems absurd to conclude from this that the average small business owner isn't a job creator because it's his customers' money that pays his bills.

---

[842] Anderson, Chris. "TED and Inequality: The Real Story." *TEDChris*, 17 May 2012. <http://tedchris.posterous.com/131417405>.

If business truly worked the way Hanauer thought it does, we should start pointing a finger at the middle class every time a small business fails.

Granted, if you have a bunch of entrepreneurs set up shop without any customers they won't get very far, but if you have a bunch of middle class consumers running around with no entrepreneurs or producers to make products for them to purchase, many jobs aren't going to be created either. This form of argument almost the age-old question of whether the chicken or the egg came first. In this case, the answer is neither.

The rest of the talk gives a careless history on how America became such an unequal society and the consequences of this inequality. These types of arguments have been debunked earlier in the book in the earlier sections titled "Income Inequality and Economic Freedom" and "Declining Real Wages" in this book. All that is left to debunk is a bogus chart which Hanaeur created himself, and is presented on the following page.

Job Creators

Millionaires' Effective Tax Rate vs. Unemployment

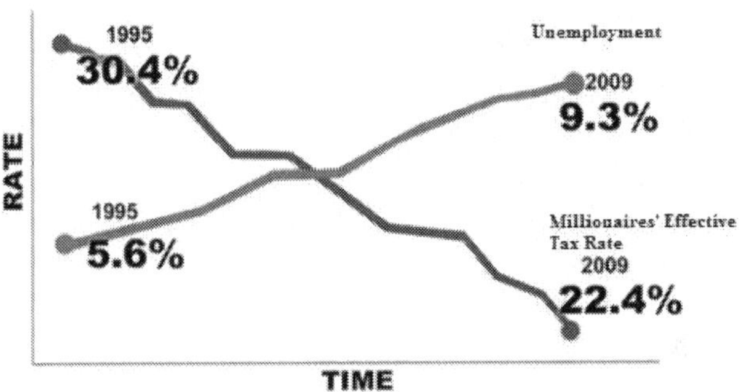

[843]

Here, Hanauer charts the unemployment rate as increasing from 5.6% to 9.3% between 1995 and 2009, while the effective tax rate on millionaires declined from 30.4% to 22.4%. While a chart so poorly constructed should have received widespread criticism, the only source I could find criticizing it was an article written by Bruce Upbin in *Forbes* magazine. In the article, Bruce writes that this is "leading us to parse how a 22.4% tax rate can fall below a 9.3% unemployment rate."[844] When you actually look at unemployment data for the period, the steady uptick in unemployment that Hanauer presents does not exist (until the recession of 08, obviously).

[843] The chart has been edited slightly to make it compatible with this book's black and white coloring. I removed Hanauer's "key" and replaced it with the labeling next to the 9.3% and 22.4% figures on the chart.

[844] Upbin, Bruce. "The Real Reason That TED Talk Was 'Censored'? It's Shoddy And Dumb." *Forbes*, 17 May 2012. <http://www.forbes.com/sites/bruceupbin/2012/05/17/the-real-reason-that-ted-talk-was-censored-its-shoddy-and-dumb/>.

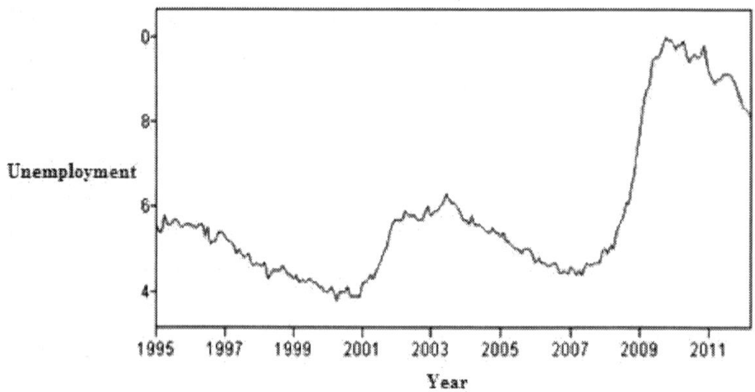

Source: Forbes.[845]

Commenting further on the chart, Upbin notes that "Unemployment didn't keep going up. It FELL **twice** (once from 1995-2001 and again from 2003-2007)." When Upbin had his data analyst look at the chart, he commented that "it looks like Hanaeur just took the unemployment rate from 1995 and the unemployment rate in 2009 and drew a random squiggly line between them."

Hanauer and Corporate Profits

Hanauer seems so impressed by his own jokes that he feels a need to repeat and apply them to as many things as possible. Appearing on Thom Hartmann's television show on Russia Today, he made the claim that "rich people taking credit for creating jobs are like squirrels taking credit for evolution."[846] He seemed so proud of that analogy that he repeated it in his TED Talk. He also made sure that Fareed Zakaria included the comment in an introduction to a segment which including him and former Bain Capital executive Ed Connard.[847]

---

[845] Ibid.
[846] The Big Picture, Russia Today, Aired December 6th 2011.
[847] Fareed Zakaria Global Public Square, July 8th 2012.

In his TED talk, he mentioned that "had it been true that lower taxes on the rich and more wealth for the wealthy led to job creation we would be drowning in jobs today." Speaking about corporate profits, he writes that "corporate profits are at a 50-year high while unemployment is also at a 50-year high. If it was true that the rich and business were the job creators, we'd be drowning in jobs today." On his personal twitter account, he tweeted months after both statements that "if high corporate profits led to growth and jobs, today we would be drowning in jobs."[848] This is a large amount of attention to bring to a statement that isn't witty in any way, let alone insightful.

The "50-year high" statement is true but misleading. Corporate profits were also at "50-year highs" in the mid-2000s before the tech-bubble crash – then they rebounded after bottoming out.[849] I don't understand what Hanauer is trying to prove here, as he seems to be assuming that if you believe that entrepreneurs create jobs you must also believe that corporate profits should translate to more jobs. Unemployment is high, but hardly at 50-year highs considering that he made the statement in February of 2012, a time when the unemployment rate was at 8.3% and falling. The only recent time when unemployment had topped 8% was during the recession of the early 1980s, which was thirty years ago, not fifty.

Another variant of this argument is that as corporate profits reach all-time highs, wages reach all-time lows as a percentage of GDP. Part of this seems logical: if something is profitable, it is only because it was not given out in the form of wages. However, benefits aren't included in this measurement of wages, and a sizeable portion of calculating GDP is classified as "depreciation," which makes GDP an imperfect measure to

---

[848] Hanauer, Nick. Twitter, 3 Oct 2010 at 10:47pm. Viewable at <https://twitter.com/NickHanauer/status/253733044370948096>.

[849] Eby, Eli. "Debunking Nick Hanauer, Profits, and Unemployment." *Daily Eli*, 4 July 2012. <http://dailyeli.blogspot.com/2012/07/debunking-nick-hanauer-profits-and.html>.

compare profits and wages against. To cite one misuse of this measurement, it was pointed out by the Center on Budget and Policy Priorities that the percentage of GDP going to wages decreased from 49.5% to 45.4% from 2001-2004, while corporate profits increased from 7.8% to 10.1% during that same time period.[850]

However, when 2004's $1.5 trillion in depreciation is taken out of the equation and we look at "national income," we would find that total employee compensation as a percentage of national income remained virtually unchanged, showing a much smaller decline from 66.2% in 2001 to 64.8% in 2004. Regardless, we could also show no decline at all, depending on what three-year time frame we cherry-pick. For instance, wages and benefits were 65.7% of GDP in 2000, and 65.7% in 2003. Ironically, my source for this is a separate report by the very same Center on Budget and Policy Priorities.[851]

The Green Energy Charade

The failure of Solyndra and a handful of other investments that the government made into green energy are now well known. But maybe we should look at other countries to see if we did something wrong with these investments. Hanauer notes that as he's writing, "the Chinese government is making massive, determined, strategic investments in their renewable energy industry."[852] He's referring to a five year plan that China made in 2010 to give state support to solar and wind power, and electric automobiles.

---

[850] Reynolds, Alan. "Mythology Of Wages Vs Profits." *The Cato Institute*, 11 Nov. 2004. <http://www.cato.org/publications/commentary/mythology-wages-vs-profits>.
[851] Aron-Dine, Aviva, and Isaac Shapiro. "Share of National Income Going To Wages and Salaries at Record Low in 2006 Share of Income Going to Corporate Profits at Record High." *Center on Budget and Policy Priorities*, 29 Mar. 2007. <http://www.cbpp.org/cms/?fa=view&id=634>.
[852] Hanauer, "Gardens of Democracy," p. 86.

Two years into China's massive investments, we can measure the results.

Two years is an unusually small time to do any kind of economic measurement on a policy's success or failure, but not when a policy's intent crashes and burns. As the *Wall Street Journal* reported, "State subsidies have spawned dozens of Chinese Solyndras that are now on the verge of collapse." LDK Solar, the second largest polysilicon solar water producer in the world defaulted on $95 million. The company also lost $589 million in the fourth quarter of 2011, and $185 million in the first quarter of 2012, which cost around 10,000 jobs. China's top wind manufacturers saw their earnings disappear as well. Goldwind saw their earnings tank 83%, while Sinovel's dropped 96%.[853]

Intellectuals and the Crisis

A proper understanding the financial crisis of 2007 seems to be a challenge to many of today's intellectuals. The various analyses are as plentiful as they are wrong. The Occupy Wall Street movement placed their blame on one group: the top 1% of income earners. Paul Krugman has attributed income inequality to the financial crisis to one degree or another in a 2010 talk he gave to the Luxembourg Income Study. [854] But as is common to Krugman's style, two years later he blogged that the rise of the 1% "probably contributed," though didn't identify it as a sole factor.[855] As has been documented regarding Krugman's commentary on the stimulus, he is being as purposely vague as he can be on any issue so that he can backtrack later when criticized.

[853] Chovanec, Patrick. "China's Solyndra Economy." *The Wall Street Journal*, September 11th, 2012, p. A16.
[854] Krugman, Paul. "Inequality and Crisis." *The New York Times*, 28 June 2010. <http://krugman.blogs.nytimes.com/2010/06/28/inequality-and-crises/>.
[855] Krugman, Paul. "Plutocracy, Paralysis, Perplexity." *The New York Times*, 3 May 2012. <http://www.nytimes.com/2012/05/04/opinion/krugman-plutocracy-paralysis-perplexity.html>.

There are some other odd culprits given for the recession as well. Columbia University economics professor Joeseph Stiglitz (also a Nobel Laureate) blamed the Iraq War for causing the great recession by increasing the cost of oil – which lead the federal reserve to lower interest rates and lighten up banking regulations.[856] Stiglitz's explanation is even more far-fetched, but bank deregulation as a cause of the meltdown is a popular explanation.

In the 2008 presidential debates, then Senator Obama blamed the crisis on deregulation. The meme continued in the next presidential election, where at the DNC Bill Clinton described Obama's opposition as the type of people who want to "to get rid of those pesky financial regulations designed to prevent another crash and prohibit future bailouts."[857]

So when in doubt, the liberals blame deregulation. It's a shame that no one can ever name any specific regulations that were removed that contributed to the crisis, and I imagine this is due to the lack of any actual deregulation. In the past three decades there have only been three major actions of deregulation in the financial sector.[858] These three acts of deregulation were the Depository Institutions Deregulation and Monetary Control Act of 1980, the Garn-St. Germain Depository Institutions Act of 1982, and the repeal of Glass Stegall in 1999.[859]

The first Act removed regulations that limited the amount of interest that users could earn from both their savings and checking accounts. The second Act allowed banks to begin

---

[856] Stiglitz, Joe. "War and the Economy: The True Cost of Conflict." Affordable World Security Conference 2012. Available online at <http://fora.tv/2012/03/27/War_and_the_Economy_The_True_Cost_of_ Conflict>.

[857] Transcript available at: <http://www.nydailynews.com/news/politics/bill-clinton-dnc-speech-full-transcript-article-1.1153058>.

[858] Randazzo, Anthony. "The Myth of Financial Deregulation." *Reason*, 19 June 2009. <http://reason.com/archives/2009/06/19/the-myth-of-financial-deregula>.

[859] Ibid.

offering money market accounts with no limits on the interest rates offered and also allowed banks to provide adjustable-rate mortgage loans. Some do attribute the 1982 Act to the savings and loan crisis in the late 1980s, though Anthony Randazzo at *Reason* argues that the real cause was the combination of bad regulation and the perceived issue of "too big to fail."[860]

The repeal of Glass-Stegall was arguably the most controversial. Glass-Stegall had "kept deposit-bearing banks and investment banks from competing for over six decades."[861] The repeal did allow banks to grow until they became "too big to fail," but bad regulation was also at fault. Again quoting Randazzo, "had market-to-market regulations been more flexible, banks would have had more time to raise capital and sell assets."[862]

Even if there were consequences to these particular acts of deregulation, the amount of regulation on net balance has been on the rise. The amount of government spending on financial regulation nearly tripled from 1980 to 2007 in real dollars.[863] Funding of the Securities and Exchange Commission in particular increased by 76% in real dollars under George W. Bush's tenure.[864]

While the amount of actual financial deregulation has been minimal, and any negative effects thereafter can't be linked explicitly to it, financial deregulation should be ruled out as a factor. It's ironic that Clinton can blame non-existent deregulation on the part of Republicans for the crisis, when it was he who repealed Glass-Stegall.

---

[860] Randazzo, "The Myth of Financial Deregulation."
[861] Ibid.
[862] Ibid.
[863] Brook, Yaron, and Don Watkins. "Why The Glass-Steagall Myth Persists." *Forbes*, 12 Nov. 2012. <http://www.forbes.com/sites/objectivist/2012/11/12/why-the-glass-steagall-myth-persists/>.
[864] Calabria, Mark A. "Did Deregulation Cause the Financial Crisis?" *The Cato Institute*, July-Aug. 2009. <http://www.cato.org/sites/cato.org/files/serials/files/policy-report/2009/7/cpr31n4-1.pdf>.

The Role of the Community Reinvestment Act

In 1977 the government attempted to relax lending standards by passing the Community Reinvestment Act. The act's genesis was in 1976 with community activist Gale Cincotta, who noticed that banks in poor neighborhoods tended to make most of their loans to wealthier areas.[865] Hence, relaxing lending standards that had made it hard for a poor person to get a loan would help the community be "reinvested" in.

The effects of the act were minimal at first, but the act would later evolve.[866] Some of the justification for the act were well-publicized studies in the 1990s showing inequality between the rates at which whites and blacks were approved for mortgage loans.[867] The data also showed that Asian Americans were approved at a higher rate than whites, but this was conveniently left out of the reporting.[868] The real reasons for the white/black gap in loan approval has nothing to do with discrimination, but more with differences in income and net worth between whites and blacks. Over three times more blacks than whites have credit scores classifying them as subprime borrowers than whites.[869]

So when loans are being denied to someone not due to discrimination, but because they're too risky for a bank to turn a profit, it raises the question of how one can force a bank to loan to them and expect a positive outcome. Unfortunately, the politicians used the discrimination narrative. The Department of Housing and Urban Development brought legal action against banks which "declined a higher percentage of minority applicants

---

[865] Schweizer, Peter. "Architects of Ruin: How Big Government Liberals Wrecked the Global Economy--and How They Will Do It Again If No One Stops Them." (New York: HarperCollins, 2010), pp. 1-27.
[866] Sowell, Thomas. "The Housing Boom and Bust." (New York: Basic, 2009), pp. 36-37.
[867] Ibid., p. 37.
[868] Ibid., p. 97.
[869] Ibid., p. 101.

than white applicants" beginning in 1993.[870] In 1995, banks had to start proving that they made a certain amount of loans to low and moderate-income individuals.[871]

The "easy housing" policies of the 90s were furthered by George W. Bush with his goal of an ownership society. The goal of home ownership for all may seem like a noble one, but it's not a sign of a healthy society. The countries with the highest home ownership rates are Romania, Lithuania, and Croatia, while those with the lowest rates are Switzerland, Germany, and Austria.[872] Regardless, Bush's American Dream Downpayment Act of 2003 began subsidizing the down payments for those with incomes below a certain amount.[873] According to a critical evaluation by the Heritage Foundation, those qualifying could receive "cash grants of as much as $10,000 to individuals and families wanting to buy a house, but without subjecting themselves to the burden of having to save for the down payment."[874]

The Federal Reserve

Much of my analysis in identifying the Community Reinvestment Act as a main factor in the financial crisis is in apparent contradiction to what most Austrian economics see as the main factor: the Federal Reserve.[875] In fact, the Austrian theory of the business cycle cites the Federal Reserve's setting of

---

[870] Ibid., p. 40.
[871] Ibid., p. 39.
[872] Cowen, Tyler. "Is a High Home Ownership Rate a Sign of a Successful Country?" *Marginal Revolution*, 16 June 2012. <http://marginalrevolution.com/marginalrevolution/2012/06/is-a-high-home-ownership-rate-a-sign-of-a-successful-country.html>.
[873] Sowell, "Housing Boom and Bust," p. 41.
[874] Utt, Ronald D. "American Dream Downpayment Act: Fiscally Irresponsible And Redundant to Existing Homeownership Programs." *The Heritage Foundation*, 5 Dec. 2003. <http://www.heritage.org/research/reports/2003/12/american-dream-downpayment-act-fiscally-irresponsible-and-redundant-to-existing-homeownership-programs>.
[875] Thomas Woods for example, briefly criticizes Sowell's "Housing Boom and Bust" in: "Krugman Failure, Not Market Failure." *Lew Rockwell*, 19 June 2009. <http://www.lewrockwell.com/woods/woods116.html>.

interest rates as a main cause of the boom and bust cycle. To briefly state the Austrian theory, as articulated by Thomas Woods:

1) Interest rates can fall two ways – either by public savings or by the Federal Reserve lowering them artificially. If a bank needs more money, they attract new customers by offering higher interest rates. When a bank has all the capital it needs, it is due to people saving more money, which allows them to lower interest rates without fearing the loss of any capital. This is no different from how a business that needs sales will try to attract new customers by cutting prices.

2) Since borrowing money is cheaper, and consumers are saving, it encourages business expansion for two reasons. These two reasons are the fact that borrowing money is cheaper, and because people are saving money, it won't be spent until later (hopefully once these big projects are finished.)

3) If interest rates are lowered due to increasing savings, the market works naturally. If the interest rates are lowered due to intervention by the Federal Reserve, borrowers will be investing in unsustainable projects.

4) Wood's gives this analogy: "Imagine a home builder who believes he has 20% more bricks than he actually has. He will build a different kind of house than he would if he had an accurate count of his brick supply." In other words, when interest rates are lowered artificially businesses will over-expand.

5) In the real world, much of the new investment of the 2000s went into housing. The public wasn't saving as much, so there ended up not being enough buyers for the

> housing projects that existed. Eventually, the housing bubble burst.[876]

I see the Austrian theory and my prior analysis as not being in conflict, but in need of being synthesized. Peter Schiff seems to espouse a similar view, arguing that since there were no good investments to be made in the 2000s, money was instead funneled into housing.

The Special Case of Krugman

At the "Take Back the American Dream" conference, MSNBC host Chris Hayes asked Paul Krugman what could be done if he were made dictator. This question got a round of applause and some laughter out of the audience.[877] The *Washington Examiner* reported on this as a thought experiment posed by Hayes, but we already know what kind of world we would live in had we taken Krugman's advice. After all, let's see what Krugman said about the housing market in 2002 in a column titled "Dubya's Double Dip?":

> The basic point is that the recession of 2001 wasn't a typical postwar slump, brought on when an inflation-fighting Fed raises interest rates and easily ended by a snapback in housing and consumer spending when the Fed brings rates back down again. This was a prewar-style recession, a morning after brought on by irrational exuberance. To fight this recession the Fed needs more than a snapback; it needs soaring household spending to offset moribund business investment. And to do that, as Paul McCulley of Pimco put it, **Alan Greenspan needs**

---

[876] Woods, "Meltdown," pp. 74-75.

[877] Klein, Philip. "Three Cheers for Dictator Krugman." *The Washington Examiner*, 19 June 2012. <http://washingtonexaminer.com/three-cheers-for-dictator-krugman/article/2500064#.UNyOjm_76yV>.

to create a housing bubble to replace the Nasdaq bubble.[878]

Oops. As has been observed with Krugman a dozen times over, he's smart enough to know when he's wrong. This doesn't mean that he's necessarily smart enough to cover up his tracks effectively though.

When Krugman responds to his critics regarding the housing bubble comment, he defends the comments made on his "Dubya's Double Dip" piece as being a joke. He says this as if this was the one time that he advocated such a policy, but it is not.

On the Lou Dobbs show in 2001 Krugman said that "economic policy should encourage other spending to offset the temporary slump in business investment. Low interest rates, which *promote spending on housing* and other durable goods, are the main answer."[879] In 2006 he made his argument again in a blog post where he answered readers' questions. In response to a reader who thinks that Greenspan has done a disservice by creating the housing bubble, and asks if this was the right course of action, Krugman replies "As Paul McCulley of PIMCO remarked when the tech boom crashed, Greenspan needed to create a housing bubble to replace the technology bubble. So within limits he may have done the right thing." He then continues "But by late 2004 he should have seen the danger signs and warned against what was happening; such a warning could

[878] Krugman, Paul. "Dubya's Double Dip?" *The New York Times*, 2 Aug. 2002. <http://www.nytimes.com/2002/08/02/opinion/dubya-s-double-dip.html>.
[879] Lou Dobbs Moneyline, July 18, 2001. Transcript accessible online at <http://www.pkarchive.org/economy/ML071801.html>.

have taken the place of rising interest rates. He didn't, and he left a terrible mess for Ben Bernanke."[880]

That particular blog post linked to another from earlier that day where Krugman at least realized that the bubble was bursting, but this apparently wasn't much to worry about since "Merrill Lynch predict[ed] that the unemployment rate will rise from 4.6 percent now to 5.8 percent by the end of next year."[881] Krugman had advocated the housing bubble so many times that I could fill the next few pages entirely with quotes from him. The Ludwig von Mises Institute has found at least seven other examples that I haven't listed here.[882]

Thomas Frank

Thomas Frank is best known for his 2004 book *What's the Matter with Kansas?*, which looks at the causes of conservatism's popularity, focusing mostly on his home state of Kansas.

Frank's book boils down to the observation that Kansans aren't voting in their best interest by voting for conservative candidates. Frank attributes this to Kansans voting on social issues rather than economic ones.[883] Another theory to explain the trend towards conservatism is the growing perception of liberals as elites, while the average American wants to be simply viewed as an "average American". Or as Frank puts it, "above all,

---

[880] Henderson, David. "Paul Krugman's Switch on the Housing Bubble." *Library of Economics and Liberty*, 17 Aug. 2011. <http://econlog.econlib.org/archives/2011/08/paul_krugmans_s.html>.

[881] Krugman, Paul. "Bursting Bubble Blues." *The New York Times*, 30 Oct. 2006. <http://select.nytimes.com/2006/10/30/opinion/30krugman.html?hp&_r=1&>.

[882] Thornton, Mark. "Krugman Did Cause the Housing Bubble." *Ludwig Von Mises Institute*, 17 June 2009. <http://archive.mises.org/010153/>.

[883] Frank, Thomas. "What's the Matter with Kansas? How Conservatives Won the Heart of America." (New York: Owl Books, 2004), pp. 67-77.

a red-stater is a regular, down-home working stiff, whereas a blue-stater is always some sort of pretentious paper shuffler."[884]

UCLA political scientist Tim Groseclose offered the explanation that Kansan voters are perhaps voting based on economic values rather than their own personal values. He continues that "maybe they also recognize the immorality in government's taking from people what they have produced honestly by their own labor."[885] Groseclose's explanation makes sense, but I'm still unsure as to whether or not it's even necessary to explain such a phenomenon.

Voting against apparent self-interests isn't a phenomenon that is applicable solely to conservatives. A poll in 2006 showed that over 35% of Russians would vote for Joseph Stalin if he were still alive.[886] And when a billionaire like Bill Gates or Warren Buffet expresses that they want to pay more in taxes, it's unlikely that Frank is going to sit around pondering why both men are acting against their own self-interest. Of course, when a rich person wants to pay less in taxes however,, they're not acting in their own self-interest, they're simply branded as "greedy."

The story that this book tells is of an economically decaying Kansas, which coincidentally occurs as the state becomes more conservative. More specifically, the state's agriculture is hemorrhaging jobs, and "deregulated capitalism is what has allowed Wal-Mart to crush local businesses" across the state.[887] This portion of the book's thesis was taken to pieces, ironically by a left-of-center Princeton University professor, who has published a book blaming income inequality on Republican

---

[884] Ibid., p. 23.

[885] Groseclose, Timothy. "Left Turn: How Liberal Media Bias Distorts the American Mind." (New York: St. Martin's, 2011), p. 248

[886] http://www.foreignaffairs.com/articles/61367/sarah-e-mendelson-and-theodore-p-gerber/failing-the-stalin-test

[887] Frank, "What's the Matter with Kansas?" p. 62.

politicians. (In other words, publishing this critique was against his own self-interest.)

As a whole, the bottom third of our nation's income earners have become more Democrat-leaning over the past 50 years.[888] Additionally, social issues are less strongly related to party identification than economic issues. A CBS poll on the 2012 election found that only 3% of people thought abortion to be the most important issue of the election, while 5% said that illegal immigration was the most important issue.[889] That isn't to say that only 3% of American's think the issue of abortion is significant (in May 2012, the number of pro-choice Americans hit a record low[890]), but that economic issues trump abortion in terms of importance.

As for the claims that Kansas became more conservative as the economy faltered, Steven Malanga at the *Wall Street Journal* has provided good data suggesting the opposite to be true. As he writes:

> Kansas's economy has actually outpaced the nation's for years. Throughout the 1990s and the first part of this new decade, Kansas had a lower unemployment rate than the U.S. as a whole. In fact, when the country's unemployment rate dipped below 5% from 1997 to 2001, Kansas's fell under 4%--a level so low that economists basically consider it full employment. Overall, the state's economy added 256,000 new jobs during the 1990s, a 24% growth rate, compared with a 20% national gain in the same period. Even when the economic slowdown set

---

[888] Bartels, Larry M. "What's the Matter with What's the Matter with Kansas?" *Woodrow Wilson Department of Public and International Affairs: Princeton University*, Sept. 2005. <http://www.princeton.edu/~bartels/kansas.pdf>.
[889] "The Economy, the President and the General Election." 18 Jan. 2012. <http://www.cbsnews.com/htdocs/pdf/Jan_12b_Prez_Econ_Gen_Elec.pdf>.
[890] Saad, Lydia. ""Pro-Choice" Americans at Record-Low 41%." *Gallup*, 23 May 2012. <http://www.gallup.com/poll/154838/pro-choice-americans-record-low.aspx>.

> in and the recession finally hit in 2002 and 2003, Kansas lost jobs at a slower rate than the national economy did.[891]

As for that failing agricultural sector, "Kansas farm jobs shrank by about 9% in the 1990s, a result of farms becoming larger and more efficient (and producing more), but the state's total agricultural economy grew by 10%, some 30,000 jobs, as areas like food processing and agricultural wholesaling expanded."[892]

At times, I'm not even sure Frank knows whose self-interest some policies favor. Early on in the book Frank quotes a man from rural Pennsylvania who explains that his neighbors voted for Bush because they were tired of moral decay, and were "tired of everything being wonderful on Wall Street and terrible on Main Street."[893] Frank responds: "let me repeat that: they're voting *Republican* in order to *get even with Wall Street*."[894] The tone of Frank's response is in mockery, but when it actually came time to bail out the banks in 2008, 212 Democrats voted in favor, compared to 124 Republicans who did the same.[895] This can be interpreted to show that more Democrats favored the bailouts, but considering how close the numbers actually are I think it would be safer to say that someone fed up with Wall Street isn't going to find refuge in either political party.

---

891 Malanga, Steven. "What's the Matter With Kansas?" *The Wall Street Journal*, 6 Dec. 2004. <http://www.manhattan-institute.org/html/miarticle.htm?id=3064>.
892 Ibid.
893 Frank, "What's the Matter With Kansas?," pp. 23-24.
894 Ibid., p. 24.
895 Combining votes in the House and Senate. "H.R. 1424 (110th): Emergency Economic Stabilization Act of 2008 (On Passage of the Bill)." *Govtrack.us*, <http://www.govtrack.us/congress/votes/110-2008/s213> and "H.R. 1424 (110th): Emergency Economic Stabilization Act of 2008 (On the Senate Amendment)" *Govtrack.us*, <http://www.govtrack.us/congress/votes/110-2008/h681>.

Richard Wilkinson

British researcher Richard Wilkinson's book *The Spirit Level* presents an impressive array of statistical data demonstrating that countries with less income inequality are generally more healthy. He also presented a TED Talk explaining the same thesis of the book and its arguments. To briefly summarize his ideas, the higher a nation's Gini index, the poorer it does when measured on an "index of health and social problems," which includes life expectancy, math and literacy, infant mortality, homicides, imprisonment, teenage births, trust, obesity, mental illness (including alcohol and drug abuse), and social mobility.[896]

Inequality and Health

Right off the bat it's easy to tell that some of the items that make up the index are flawed. As we've seen in chapter 2, life expectancy statistics are easily skewed by murders, suicides, car accidents, and such. But even worse, the correlation between inequality and longer life expectancy only exists depending on what year you choose to do the measurement for. If you use 2004 data like Wilkinson did in his book, his argument bears out.[897] But if you use the data from 2006 or 2009, you get an opposite result, with lifespan increasing as inequality increases.[898]

Infant mortality statistics are similarly useless in cross-country comparisons since countries calculate the number differently (as we saw in Chapter 2). The correlation between inequality and infant mortality is almost negligible, with 20 of the 28 countries graphs all having between 3.9 and 5.2 deaths per 1,000 live births.[899] The US appears as a clear outlier in Wilkinson's data, which raises the question of whether or not the

[896] Wilkinson, Richard. "How Economic Inequality Harms Societies."
[897] Snowdon, Christopher. "The Spirit Level Delusion: Fact-checking the Left's New Theory of Everything." (Ripton, North Yorkshire: Little Dice, 2010), p. 27.
[898] Ibid., pp. 28-29.
[899] Ibid., p. 87.

correlation would even exist if the US were excluded. In addition to the differences in calculating infant mortality, it's also important to understand the causes of infant mortality in the US and whether or not they pertain to income, let alone income inequality. Among them are congenital abnormalities (accounting for 20% of infant mortalities), premature birth (17%), cot death (7%), maternal complications (6%), and complications with the umbilical cord (4%).[900]

The only cause of infant mortality shown to correlate with income is cot death,[901] which is also known as sudden infant death syndrome. We know that infants exposed to tobacco smoke are more likely to die of cot death, and lower income individuals are more likely to smoke,[902] so this correlation at least makes sense. But out of all causes, only 7% of infant mortalities can be attributed to income and it's unclear whether or not there's even a correlation between income inequality and cot death.

Similar to the almost non-existent trend line that the correlation between inequality and infant mortality demonstrates, obesity shows no real correlation either. One interesting thing gleaned from the data is that Japan, Korea, Singapore and Hong Kong all have the lowest obesity rates, despite Japan and Korea being some of the most equal nations and Singapore and Hong Kong being some of the most unequal.[903] This data makes perfect sense, as it is diet that dictates a person's weight, not the difference between his income and his neighbor's. Researchers at Cornell and Harvard have formulated an Asian version of the food pyramid, which has rice, noodles, breads, corn, and other grains on the bottom, followed by fruits, nuts, seeds, and

[900] Ibid., p. 94.
[901] Ibid.
[902] Murray, "Coming Apart," pp. 36 and 109.
[903] Snowdon, "The Spirit Level Delusion," p. 26.

vegetables on the next floor upward.[904] If your diet fits that model, there's a good chance you won't be obese.

A correlation between inequality and mental disorders is easily skewed by how lax the standards are for defining mental illness. As we also become better at diagnosing mental illness, the amount of people diagnosed with mental illnesses has increased, even if the total number of people with these illnesses remains constant. Let's take autism as an example, since it is defined as a mental disorder. From 1993-2003, there was a 805% increase in the diagnosis of autism.[905] That isn't to say that 805% more kids were autistic, but that the process of diagnosing them became more efficient and accurate. This would show our nation's incidence of mental illness as increasing, even though on net balance the percentage of people with a mental illness wasn't increasing.

Collecting accurate and comparable data on mental health disorders in other countries is no easy task either. More than a dozen countries in the European Union produce no statistics on the prevalence of mental disorders at all.[906]

Inequality and Criminology

A possible link between inequality and crime does sound viable. We know from psychological studies that most people would rather earn $50,000 a year in a world where everyone else earns $25,000 than earn $100,000 in a world where everyone else

---

904 Lang, Susan. "CU Scientists Help to Develop Asian Diet Pyramid." *The Cornell Chronicle*, <http://www.news.cornell.edu/chronicle/96/1.18.96/AsianDiet.html>.

905 Marlett, Christy. "The Effects of the Idea Reauthorization of 2004 and the No Child Left Behind Act on Families with Autistic Children: Allocation of Burden of Proof, Recovery of Witness Fees, and Attainment of Proven Educational Methods for Autism." 9 Feb. 2009. <http://www.law.ku.edu/sites/law.drupal.ku.edu/files/docs/law_journal/v18/marlett.pdf >.

906 Snowdon, "The Spirit Level Delusion," p. 38.

earns $250,000.[907] The implications of this phenomenon are that more inequality leads to a more envious underclass, which would cause class conflict (i.e. crime).

The data does show that more unequal societies have more arrests than equal societies.[908] Apparently neglected in citing this as "proof" that inequality breads crime is that people in jail cannot commit more crimes until they are freed. Indeed, there's an inverse correlation between income inequality and recorded crimes, thefts, and the percentage of people reporting to be a victim of a crime within the past five years.[909]

The only correlation that does exist is between inequality and homicides. But the US being the unusually violent country that it is acts as an outlier, and the correlation ceases to exist when it's excluded from the data.[910]

The Positive Side of Inequality?

The research of Christopher Snowdon (cited liberally in this section) shows that if we are going to correlate inequality with social problems, we can correlate them with social health as well. Overall, there's a positive correlation between inequality and the quality of life index, donations to charity as a percentage of GDP, and inverse correlations between inequality and suicide and divorce rates.[911] It would be obviously absurd to say that inequality is causing these positive trends, and it's no less absurd to believe that inequality is causing the negative trends that Wilkinson shows, especially considering that many of them don't actually exist.

---

[907] Shermer, Michael. "Why People Believe Weird Things About Money." Jan. 2008. <http://www.michaelshermer.com/2008/01/weird-things-about-money/>.
[908] Snowdon, "The Spirit Level Delusion," p. 72.
[909] Ibid., pp. 73-75.
[910] Ibid., pp. 80-81.
[911] Ibid., pp. 60, 68-69, 97.

Made in the USA
Middletown, DE
19 January 2017